ROCKVILLE CAMPUS LIBRARY

D1548474

SHAKESPEARE'S ROME

P E R *medios hosteis patriæ cùm ferret ab igne*
Aeneas humeris dulce parentis onus:
Parcite, dicebat: vobis sene adorea rapto
Nulla erit, erepto sed patre summa mihi.

Andrea Alciati, *Omnia Emblemata: cum Comentariis* (Antwerp, 1577), p. 628. Reprinted with permission of the Folger Shakespeare Library.

SHAKESPEARE'S ROME

ROBERT S. MIOLA
Department of English
Loyola College, Baltimore

CAMBRIDGE UNIVERSITY PRESS
Cambridge
London   New York   New Rochelle
Melbourne   Sydney

Published by the Press Syndicate of the University of Cambridge
The Pitt Building, Trumpington Street, Cambridge CB2 1RP
32 East 57th Street, New York, NY 10022, USA
296 Beaconsfield Parade, Middle Park, Melbourne 3206, Australia

© Cambridge University Press 1983

First published 1983

Printed in the United States of America

Library of Congress Cataloging in Publication Data
Miola, Robert S.
Shakespeare's Rome.
Includes index.
1. Shakespeare, William, 1564–1616 – Knowledge – Rome.
2. Shakespeare, William, 1564–1616 – Sources.   3. Rome in
literature.   I. Title.
PR3069.R6M56   1983   822.3′3   83-1777
ISBN 0 521 25307 1

To DANIEL, CHRISTINE, *and* RACHEL

CONTENTS

ACKNOWLEDGMENTS

Thanks first go to all Shakespearean scholars, past and present, whose labors have charted the terrain. I owe special debts of gratitude to many supportive and stimulating teachers, colleagues, and friends: William Dunn, Brian Duffy, James Wing, James Loughran, S.J., Joseph Marchesani, Raymond Hilliard, Joseph Summers, Cyrus Hoy, David Johnson, Leonard Artigliere, Howard Marblestone, and Donald Miller.

I happily acknowledge here my debt to Lafayette College for generously funding my research and to the superior reference staff of Skillman Library. I am deeply grateful to Alvin B. Kernan, who took time out of his busy schedule at Princeton University to share his genial humor and keen insight; to Timothy S. Healy (S.J.), who introduced Shakespeare to me and taught me that all ladders do indeed start in the foul rag-and-bone shop of the heart; to John W. Velz, who pointed the way at every turn, offered numerous suggestions and criticisms, and talked (over Franconian wine and American beer) late into the night. No teacher or friend could do more. So learned and wise a constellation of scholars, of course, cannot be held responsible for whatever is faulty or wanting here.

My greatest debts are nonacademic ones. I thank my many friends and my extended and colorful family, the Sloands, for blessings throughout the years. I thank my brother, Steven, and my parents for their great faith and love. I especially thank my mother for typing several versions of the manuscript with wondrous speed and accuracy. I thank my children, the dedicatees, for making absolutely certain that I never lingered in my bed or at my desk overlong. And, finally, I thank my wife, Beth, who in this, as in all things, kept the faith, bore the chalice, and provided shelter from the storm.

ROBERT S. MIOLA

NOTES ON SOURCES

Unless otherwise noted, I have used throughout G. Blakemore Evans, *The Riverside Shakespeare* (Boston: Houghton Mifflin, 1974) for references to Shakespeare's text (hereafter cited as Evans); *Virgil with an English Translation by H. Rushton Fairclough*, 2 vols, rev. ed., The Loeb Classical Library (1978) for references to Vergil's text and for translations (hereafter cited as Vergil); *"Metamorphoses" with an English Translation by Frank Justus Miller*, The Loeb Classical Library, 2 vols. (I: 3rd ed., 1977; II: 1916, rpt. 1976) for references to Ovid's *Metamorphoses* and translations (hereafter cited as Ovid); *Plutarch's Lives of the Noble Grecians and Romans Englished by Sir Thomas North, Anno 1579*, 6 vols., The Tudor Translations, First Series, 7–12 (1895–6; rpt. New York: AMS Press, 1967) for references to Plutarch's *Lives* (hereafter cited as Plutarch). The abbreviations for learned journals conform to the standard list supplied by MLA in its annual bibliography. For references to Renaissance texts I have used freely and extensively the microfilm series *Early English Books, 1475–1640, Selected from Pollard and Redgrave's "Short Title Catalogue"* (Ann Arbor: University Microfilms International, 1938–). To reduce the bibliographical baggage for Renaissance books, I have shortened the titles and omitted reference to the place of publication when it is London. I have also used a shortened publication format for reference to the well-known Loeb editions of classical authors and the following abbreviations for frequently cited works:

Baldwin   Baldwin, T. W. *William Shakspere's Small Latine & Lesse Greeke.* 2 vols. Urbana: University of Illinois Press, 1944.

Brower   Brower, Reuben A. *Hero & Saint: Shakespeare and the Graeco-Roman Heroic Tradition.* New York: Oxford University Press, 1971.

Bullough   Bullough, Geoffrey. *Narrative and Dramatic Sources of Shakespeare*. 8 vols. London: Routledge and Kegan Paul, 1957–75.

Cantor   Cantor, Paul A. *Shakespeare's Rome: Republic and Empire*. Ithaca, N.Y.: Cornell University Press, 1976.

Charney   Charney, Maurice. *Shakespeare's Roman Plays: The Function of Imagery in the Drama*. Cambridge, Mass.: Harvard University Press, 1961.

Knight   Knight, G. Wilson. *The Imperial Theme: Further Interpretations of Shakespeare's Tragedies Including the Roman Plays*. London: Oxford University Press, 1931.

MacCallum   MacCallum, M. W. *Shakespeare's Roman Plays and Their Background*. London: Macmillan, 1910.

Simmons   Simmons, J. L. *Shakespeare's Pagan World: The Roman Tragedies*. Charlottesville: University Press of Virginia, 1973.

Traversi   Traversi, Derek. *Shakespeare: The Roman Plays*. Stanford, Calif.: Stanford University Press, 1963.

I

THE ROADS TO ROME

Shakespeare's conception of ancient Rome has long been a focal point in the larger debate concerning his classical learning. This debate began in earnest with Jonson's notorious aphorism imputing to Shakespeare "small *Latine,* and lesse *Greeke*" (1623), but hints of it appear earlier. The first printed allusion to Shakespeare, Robert Greene's attack on the "vpstart Crow, beautified with our feathers" (1592), expressed the indignation of a university man at the pretensions of a less-educated rival.[1] And in *The Return from Parnassus, Part 2* (performed ca. 1600, pub. 1606), William Kemp humorously praised Shakespeare for outdoing those who "smell too much of that writer *Ouid,* and that writer *Metamorphosis,* and talke too much of *Proserpina* & *Iuppiter.*" The debate, ably documented elsewhere, continued throughout the centuries and attracted luminaries to both sides.[2] In 1664, for example, Margaret Cavendish, Duchess of Newcastle, admired the verisimilitude of the Roman plays, where fancy, it seemed, almost outworked nature:

> & certainly *Julius Caesar, Augustus Caesar,* and *Antonius,*
> did never Really Act their parts Better, if so Well, as he
> hath Described them, and I believe that *Antonius* and
> *Brutus* did not Speak Better to the People, than he hath
> Feign'd them; nay, one would think that he had been
> Metamorphosed from a Man to a Woman, for who could
> Describe *Cleopatra* Better than he hath done.[3]

[1] Evans, Appendix B, "Records, Documents, and Allusions," p. 1835. The quotation below appears on p. 1838.
[2] See Baldwin, Vol. I, pp. 1–74; John W. Velz, *Shakespeare and the Classical Tradition: A Critical Guide to Commentary, 1660–1960* (Minneapolis: University of Minnesota Press, 1968), pp. 3–13; and his "The Ancient World in Shakespeare: Authenticity or Anachronism? A Retrospect," *ShS,* 31 (1978), 1–12.
[3] Evans, p. 1847.

Others, including John Dennis and Richard Farmer, noted inaccuracies, collected anachronisms, and scoffed. The controversy goes on in our century. In 1952 a classicist, J. A. K. Thomson, reviewed the evidence and concluded solemnly that Shakespeare was "no scholar."[4] In 1976, however, Paul A. Cantor based his *Shakespeare's Rome: Republic and Empire* on the assumption that the Roman plays provide "an opportunity to learn something about Rome as well as about Shakespeare."[5]

Although the debate about Shakespeare's learning continues, "the ground of argument has shifted in the twentieth century," according to one chronicler, John W. Velz.[6] Since the time of M. W. MacCallum's *Shakespeare's Roman Plays and Their Background* (1910), students of Shakespeare's classicism have paid increasing attention to the Elizabethan and Jacobean context of his work. Instead of imposing modern notions of the classical world on Shakespeare, an impressive group of scholars has sought to discover contemporary ideas about the ancients. Robert Kilburn Root and Douglas Bush have traced the highways and byways behind Shakespeare's use of classical mythology. T. W. Baldwin, with daunting thoroughness, has studied Elizabethan school curricula and their possible influence on Shakespeare. Virgil K. Whitaker has explored the connections between Shakespeare's learning and his development as a dramatist. T. J. B. Spencer has illuminated contemporary attitudes toward ancient Greeks and Romans. Kenneth Muir and Geoffrey Bullough have reclaimed source study as a legitimate and potentially valuable interest and constructed a solid foundation for future scholarship. Reuben A. Brower has perceptively analyzed the commingling of classical and Christian in Shakespeare's England and in his works. And Emrys Jones has contributed stimulating studies of Shakespeare's imaginative processes and origins.[7]

[4]*Shakespeare and the Classics* (New York: Barnes & Noble Books, 1952), passim.
[5]Cantor, p. 7.
[6]"Ancient World in Shakespeare," p. 3.
[7]Root, *Classical Mythology in Shakespeare,* Yale Studies in English, No. 19 (New York: Holt, 1903); Bush, *Mythology and the Renaissance Tradition in English Poetry,* rev. ed. (New York: Norton, 1963); Whitaker, *Shakespeare's Use of Learning: An Inquiry into the Growth of His Mind and Art* (San Marino, Calif.: Huntington Library, 1953); Spencer, "'Greeks' and 'Merrygreeks': A Back-

In the intense light of these efforts it seems clear that some consideration of Elizabethan classicism should preface consideration of Shakespeare's Rome. Review of the standard sources and methods of classical learning in the period can illuminate the playwright's intentions and achievements. Surveying the substance and methods of English humanism will not, to be sure, guarantee understanding or appreciation of Shakespeare's art; it may, however, direct criticism by guarding against anachronistic misreading and by pointing out likely possibilities.

The roads to Rome in the Renaissance were many, winding, and various. Although they often ran concurrently, the major routes were well marked, and the most widely traveled one was probably that of the grammar schools. T. W. Baldwin has shown that elementary education included study of the *Disticha Moralia*, Terence, Plautus, Seneca, Cicero, Quintilian, *Ad Herennium*, Ovid, Vergil, Horace, Juvenal, Persius, and possibly Lucan and Catullus. The texts were often colored by commentary – grammatical, moral, or both – and accompanied by collections, that is, anthologies of memorable snippets and shavings culled from various sources. A schoolboy learned to parse his Latin, for example, by working with Leonhardus Culmannus's *Sententiae Pueriles* or the *Sententiae Ciceronis*. He learned to speak the mother tongue by memorizing phrases and sentences from collections of conversations (colloquia) or from florilegia. Later on, he modeled the substance and style of his prose on a Latin translation of Aphthonius, with reference to the *Adagia* of Desiderius Erasmus or the *Apothegms* of Conrad Lycosthenes. For verse he imitated the ex-

ground to *Timon of Athens* and *Troilus and Cressida*," in *Essays on Shakespeare and Elizabethan Drama in Honor of Hardin Craig,* ed. Richard Hosley (Columbia: University of Missouri Press, 1962), pp. 223–33; also his "Shakespeare and the Elizabethan Romans," *ShS,* 10(1957), 27–38; Muir, *Shakespeare's Sources I: Comedies and Tragedies* (London: Methuen, 1957), revised and reprinted as *The Sources of Shakespeare's Plays* (New Haven: Yale University Press, 1978); Jones, *Scenic Form in Shakespeare* (Oxford: Clarendon Press, 1971); also his *The Origins of Shakespeare* (Oxford: Clarendon Press, 1977).

amples of Octavian Mirandula's *Flores Poetarum* with assistance from Simon Pelegromius's *Synonymorvm Sylva* or Ravisius Textor's *Epitheta*. He probably supplemented his reading of Roman historians with a handbook on the order of Thomas Godwin's later *Romanae Historiae Anthologia* (1614); he sometimes resorted to Valerius Maximus, compiler of famous deeds and men, or to Florus, the epitomator. The study of moral philosophy, of course, was implicit in the whole enterprise, from the elementary sayings of Cato and Cicero on up, but there were numerous and hectic moral compendia available in Latin and English. William Baldwin's *A Treatise of Morall Philosophy* (1547, reprinted often with revisions and additions) was widely read, probably because it resembled neither a treatise of morals nor of philosophy.

Such a diversity of texts so variously presented could hardly have indoctrinated the student in the glories of Roman civilization or in the turpitude of the pagan ethos. Rome was much too vast and amorphous for simplistic reductions. The tendency to acquire classical learning by means of exuberantly miscellaneous collections characterized the age and worked against the development of any single political, theological, or historical perspective. *Copia*, not coherence, was the ideal that governed English humanism. And because rhetoric broadly defined, rather than history or philosophy, dominated the curricula, students learned to take a polemical approach to the classics, to watch for usable exempla, arguments, and rhetorical flourishes, and to record them in notebooks for future use. The reassessment and reconsideration of antiquity, as T. J. B. Spencer notes, was a common activity and a deeply ingrained habit of mind.[8]

The ideal of *copia* is evident in the second major source of classical learning – the growing number of English translations. Shakespeare relied on Englished classics throughout his career and in his Roman works made use of Golding's Ovid, North's Plutarch, W. B.'s Appian, possibly Heywood's *Thyestes* (for *Titus Andronicus*), Holland's Livy (for *Coriolanus*), and Underdowne's Heliodorus (for *Cymbeline*). His preference for Ovid's mythological treasury, Plutarch's moral and anecdotal history, and Appian's lively and readable chronicle mark him as a man of his time. For

[8]"Shakespeare and the Elizabethan Romans," p. 33.

Elizabethans demanded from their classics a generous supply of myth and an abundance of entertaining fact.[9] In such a climate florilegia flourished; there appeared in translation bouquets from Ovid and Terence, as well as whole gardens of classical flowers: Richard Taverner's *The Garden of Wysedome* (1538), for example; Erasmus's *Adagia* in Taverner's translation (1539); his *Apophthegmata* in Nicholas Udall's translation (1542); Timothy Kendall's *Flowers of Epigrammes* (1577). The environment was also hospitable to excerpts, abridgments, and epitomes. Polybius, Lucan, Caesar, Plutarch, and Livy all appeared in partial English versions. To be sure, there were classical scholars of great learning – men such as Thomas Drant, Henry Savile, Thomas Wilson, and the prolific Philemon Holland.[10] Yet, these men were exceptions in the age of the amateur translator, the age whose critical temper is best illustrated by William Painter's well-read *Palace of Pleasure* (1566–7). This anthology of Continental *nouvelle* and classical story satisfied in one serving the public appetite for ancient anecdote, romantic intrigue, and lurid adventure. The miscellany of sources behind Painter's forty-one classical stories reveals the gloriously slapdash character of Elizabethan classicism: "Herodotus (two stories); Aelian (three); Plutarch's *Morals* (one); Aulus Gellius (twelve); Livy (eight); Quintus Curtius (three); Xenophon (one); Pedro Mexía (two); Guevara's *Letters* (three); Bandello (six)."[11]

A third major source of classical learning, one that catered largely to the public demand for quick information, was the various reference books of the Renaissance. The popular mythographies of Giovanni Boccaccio, Lilius Giraldus, Natalis Comes, and Vincenzo Cartari[12] begot English offspring: Stephan Batman, *The Golden Booke of the Leaden Goddes* (1577); Abraham Fraunce, *The Third Part of the Countesse of Pembrokes Yuychurch* (1592); and Richard Linche, *The Fountaine of Ancient Fiction* (1599). Related to these handbooks in content and influence were the

---

[9]See Henry Burrowes Lathrop, *Translations from the Classics into English from Caxton to Chapman, 1477–1620* (1933; rpt. New York: Octagon, 1967).
[10]I rely here on Lathrop, *Translations*, especially p. 232.
[11]Bush, *Mythology*, p. 33.
[12]Boccaccio, *Genealogia Deorum Gentilium* (14th cent.); Giraldus, *De Deis Gentivm* (1548); Comes, *Mythologiae; sive, Explicationum Fabularum* (1551); Cartari, *Le Imagine, con la Spositione de i Dei degli Antichi* (1556).

dictionaries of Sir Thomas Elyot, Thomas Cooper, and the Stephani (Robert and Charles), works that apparently everyone used, including Edmund Spenser, William Shakespeare, Ben Jonson, Thomas Heywood, and John Milton.[13] The quintessential Renaissance reference book – the encyclopedia – borrowed from various traditions and gathered information into vast, sometimes accessible summaries of human learning. Such works as Pierre Charron's *Of Wisdome* (1606) and Pierre de La Primaudaye's *The French Academie* (1618) crammed classical lore, legend, fact, and fiction into essays that addressed an astonishingly diverse range of topics.

Living after the labors of Diderot in an age of computerized bibliography, many today may entertain misconceptions about the nature of Renaissance encyclopedias. Typically, such volumes gathered in one place essays on subjects as far apart as the Creation, the vices of Heliogabalus, and the unique properties of bulls' blood. Some, such as the works of Charron and La Primaudaye, were organized after a fashion and showed signs of a guiding intelligence and purpose; others were not. An instructive example of the disorganized type is Pedro Mexía's Spanish compilation, *Silva de Varia Lecion* (1542), which achieved translation and popularity on the Continent as well as in England. An abridged and Englished version of Mexía's work appeared as *The Foreste* (1571, 1576), translated by Thomas Fortescue from a French version. Much of *The Foreste,* along with much else of Mexía, reappeared in the first volume of Thomas Milles's *The Treasvrie of Avncient and Moderne Times* (1613), translated largely from French and Italian versions. This book clearly illustrates the motley abundance of Renaissance classicism as well as Elizabethan willingness to use intermediary translations. Here biographical sketches (e.g., Polybius 4:32; Tamberlaine 7:2) and stories about ancient lives and works (Plutarch 1:19; Diogenes 3:7) sit quite comfortably with unrelated chapters on history, both civil (Sparta 2:3; Athens 2:4) and ecclesiastical (Popes 1:27; Heresies 6:14). Travelogs describe such exotic lands as Persia (4:1), Fez (6:1), and Moscovia (7:34); moral essays strike closer to home, reminding the reader of his duties (Manhood 3:11; Prodigality

[13]Here I rely upon De Witt T. Starnes and Ernest William Talbert, *Classical Myth and Legend in Renaissance Dictionaries* (Chapel Hill: University of North Carolina Press, 1955).

6

8:20). Essays in the sciences – natural (Honey 3:15; Crocodiles 5:31; Gold 8:30), medical (Melancholy 5:26; Dangerous Years 4:16), and political (Monarchy 8:33; Foreign Civil Wars 9:9) – do not dilute the effects of the abounding mirabilia (Man 3:8; Marvelous Things 9:30). An allegorical description of Charon (2:23), paradoxes (4:38; 7:43; 8:38), moral tales (8:15), and romantic tragedies (7:46) round out the collection. The range of purposes and historical methods here may be illustrated by comparison of the chapter on Ancient Rome (3:1), a detailed and objective description of civil institutions running thirty folio pages, with the brief account of the legendary maiden of Poictu (6:8), who reportedly lived for three years without food or drink.

At the turn of the century the Elizabethan who studied Latin sententiae in school, who browsed through translations as they appeared, or who came upon intriguing Roman examples in the pages of reference books could easily acquire further information from numerous chronicles and biographies. Livy and Tacitus told the story of Rome in the original language and in translation; Saint Augustine and Orosius offered a Christian reading of the history and achievements of the Earthly City. Polybius, Velleius Paterculus, Pomponius Mela, Lucan, Josephus, Pliny, Aulus Gellius, Solinus, Aelianus, Eutropius, and Ammianus Marcellinus also provided occasional commentary. Holinshed's *Chronicles* contained information on Roman–British relations in antiquity, as did other histories of Britain. Some English writers were more intent on boiling Roman history down to a tasteless porridge of platitudes on the horror of rebellion, the punishment of pride, the necessity of obedience or monarchy. William Fulbecke's *An Historicall Collection of the Continvall Factions, Tvmvlts, and Massacres of the Romans and Italians* (1601) is a clear example of the type.[14] Biographical information was available in the histories

---

[14]Cf. Richard Reynoldes, *A Chronicle of All the Noble Emperours of the Romaines* (1571). J. Leeds Barroll, "Shakespeare and Roman History," *MLR*, 53 (1958), 327–43 (335–6), considers briefly other Elizabethan chronicles of Rome (I list first editions only): Thomas Lanquet, *Epitome of Cronicles* (1549); John Sleidan, *Brief Chronicle of the Foure Principall Empires*, trans. Stephen Wythers (1563); Lodowick Lloid, *The Consent of Time* (1590); John Carion, *Three Bokes of Cronicles*, trans. Walter Lynne (1550); Joseph Ben Gorion, *A Compendious and Most Marueilous Historie* (1558); the first part of Richard Grafton's *Chronicle at Large and Meere History* (1569); David Lyndsay, *The*

themselves and in the works of Plutarch and Suetonius. A popular form of pseudobiography was the collecting of wise men's sayings. This subgenre of "dictes," according to D. T. Starnes, began in England with Walter Burley's *De Vita* and William Caxton's *Dictes or Sayengis of the Philosophres* (1477) and continued (sometimes indirectly) in similar compilations by Erasmus, Sir Thomas Elyot, William Baldwin, Nicholas Ling, Robert Allott, John Bodenham, Thomas Floyd, Henry Crosse, and Francis Bacon.[15]

As every student knows, the literature of England rooted itself in classical examples and blossomed with classical allusions. Sometimes the *imitatio* is bold and blatant; sometimes it is subtle and implicit – *ut intelligi simile queat potius quam dici,* "so that the likeness can be sensed rather than defined."[16] Whatever the form, imitation of classical models is pervasive and transformative. Prose writers such as Thomas Lodge, Philip Sidney, and Robert Greene, for example, breathed new life into Greek romances; William Painter and George Pettie diluted old wine and poured it into new bottles. Every poet, it seems, from the plodding undergraduate versifier to the brilliant and courtly Edmund Spenser, busied himself with imitations of Horace, Vergil, or Ovid. And some, more strictly meditating the thankless Muse, tried to fit their native English to classical meters. No form of literature was more steeped in classical example than the drama. The use of classical subjects and conventions in the plays of Nicholas Udall, Thomas Kyd, Christopher Marlowe, George Peele, William Shakespeare,

---

Monarche (Edinburgh, 1552); Arthur Kelton, *A Chronycle with a Genealogie* (1547); *Romes Monarchie*, trans. E. L. (1596); Giovanni Botero, *Observations,* trans. B. J. B. (1602).

[15] "Sir Thomas Elyot and 'Sayings of the Philosophers,'" *Texas University Studies in English,* 13 (1933), 5–35. Starnes gives the titles and dates of first editions as follows: Erasmus, *Apophthegmes* (1531); Elyot, *The Bankett of Sapience* (1539); Baldwin, *A Treatise of Morall Philosophy* (1547); Ling (?), *Politeuphuia or Wits Commonwealth* (1597–8); Allott (?), *Wits Theater of the Little World* (1599); Bodenham, *Belvedére, or the Garden of the Muses* (1600); Floyd, *The Picture of a Perfit Commonwealth* (1600); Crosse, *Vertues Commonwealth* (1603); Bacon, *Apophthegmes New and Old* [1625].

[16] I quote from a letter of Petrarch reprinted in Thomas M. Greene's "Petrarch and the Humanist Hermeneutic," in *Italian Literature: Roots and Branches, Essays in Honor of Thomas Goddard Bergin,* ed. Giose Rimanelli and Kenneth John Atchity (New Haven: Yale University Press, 1976), p. 211.

Ben Jonson, and George Chapman is well known, but the cumulative importance of classical elements to English drama defies tabulation. Harbage and Schoenbaum's *Annals of English Drama, 975–1700* records, on the average, the appearance of at least one classical drama for every year of Shakespeare's life.[17] And according to Clifford J. Ronan, no fewer than forty-three Roman plays survive from the period 1588–1651.[18]

The ubiquity of the classical presence in Elizabethan and Jacobean literature should humble any surveyor of English humanism. The effort to chart the main courses of classical learning in the Renaissance must end by soberly acknowledging the magnitude of the source material and the incalculable variety of the conduits. The routes of classical learning were crisscrossed at every point by auxiliary roads and bypaths. Miscellaneous sources abounded, each with its own coloration and perspective. In addition to those noted above, there were medieval works by William Caxton, John Lydgate, John Gower, and Geoffrey Chaucer, as well as the *Gesta Romanorum*. Also pervasive and influential was the classical learning contained in various mirrors, emblem books, cosmographies, biblical commentaries, homilies, political treatises, theological debates, and works of art – paintings, tapestries, and statues. The figure of Hercules holding up the world at Shakespeare's Globe images the vital and supportive relationship of the classics to Elizabethan culture.

After even so brief a survey several observations seem reasonable. The prevailing attitude toward the classics in England was enthusiastically acquisitive and undiscriminating. The impulse to collect was so forceful as to overwhelm whatever reservations many had about context or accuracy. This impulse was, at bottom, utilitarian. For Elizabethans, ancient authors provided a treasury of practical information on everything from the raising of bees to the attaining of wisdom. Their advice and examples pointed the way to a better, richer, and fuller life. As a result, English classicism came to be ahistorical and eclectic in character, little

---

[17]Alfred Harbage, *Annals of English Drama, 975–1700*, rev. S. Schoenbaum (Philadelphia: University of Pennsylvania Press, 1964).
[18]"The 'Antique Roman' in Elizabethan Drama," dissertation, University of California, Berkeley, 1971.

concerned with understanding the past on its own terms. Shakespeare's anachronisms are to the point here, evidencing the age's disregard for historical accuracy, at least as we understand the concept. Also pertinent are the classical translations that directly aim at establishing instructive parallels between ancient history and contemporary politics.[19]

What is more, English humanism was undogmatic and flexible in character. Writers continually appropriated the same classical figures and incidents to point different (sometimes contradictory) morals and to adorn a wide variety of tales.[20] This flexibility bespeaks a deep fascination with classical culture and a serious (though not scholarly) engagement with it. Speaking of the Elizabethan view of ancient Rome, Emrys Jones describes succinctly the origins and nature of this engagement:

> Those who had been through a grammar-school had been saturated in the literature of classical Rome. There was an immense amount of learning by rote. Boys who had spent the best part of six long days a week for perhaps as many as ten or eleven years reading, translating, analysing, and explicating Latin literature would have memorized hundreds, perhaps thousands, of lines or scraps of lines from the poets, as well as having innumerable phrases, constructions, and rhythms from the prose writers impressed on their minds. A classical colouring would be cast over everything they read or wrote.[21]

Such early training, continued by innumerable other contacts and experiences, deserves notice and respect. It provided the material,

[19]Sir Anthony Cope, for example, translated the story of Hannibal and Scipio from Livy (1544) to embolden Henry VIII and to assist England against its enemies. Thomas Wilson's translation of Demosthenes (1570) incited readers against Philip of Spain, not Philip of Macedon.

[20]Some of the finest studies of classical backgrounds recognize this diversity: Marilyn L. Williamson, *Infinite Variety: Antony and Cleopatra in Renaissance Drama and Earlier Tradition* (Mystic, Conn.: Lawrence Verry, 1974); Bullough, Vol. V, pp. 3–57. See also Robert Kimbrough, *Shakespeare's "Troilus & Cressida" and Its Setting* (Cambridge, Mass.: Harvard University Press, 1964), pp. 27–39; and Mark Sacharoff, "The Traditions of the Troy-Story Heroes and the Problem of Satire in *Troilus and Cressida*," *ShakS*, 6 (1972 for 1970), 125–35, for discussions of various attitudes toward Troy and Trojans.

[21]*Origins of Shakespeare*, pp. 12–13.

means, and audience for Shakespeare's transmutation of diverse classical traditions into complex works of art.

In light of the above, it seems unlikely that any single and exclusive perspective could define the ubiquitous presence of Rome in Elizabethan culture. A place like Corinth might become known as a lustful, sin-filled city, and a people like the Parthians might be remembered largely for their tactic of shooting arrows behind them as they retreated. Neither Rome nor Romans, however, could be so easily fitted into categories or so summarily reduced. Conscious of the city's multifaceted diversity, Shakespeare did not insist on any exclusive, dogmatic interpretation, but drew upon various attitudes, stories, and traditions as he pleased.

Several important scenes from the Roman plays clearly illustrate the nature of Shakespeare's response to his cultural and intellectual environment. The account of the portents preceding the assassination in *Julius Caesar,* for example, probably derives from North's Plutarch, Ovid's *Metamorphoses* (XV), Lucan's *Pharsalia* in the original or in Marlowe's partial translation, Vergil's *Georgics* I and (I shall argue) the *Aeneid*.[22] Similarly, Menenius's belly fable in *Coriolanus* is a composite of passages from Livy, North's Plutarch, William Averell's *A Mervaillous Combat of Contrarieties* (1588), William Camden's *Remaines* (1605), possibly Camerarius's *Fabellae Aesopicae* (1573), and Sidney's *Apology* (1595).[23] In each instance we glimpse the playwright at work. From diverse and sometimes unrelated elements he forges speeches and scenes of striking power and resonance. The sovereign imag-

[22]See Muir, *Sources of Shakespeare's Plays*, pp. 122–5.
[23]See ibid., p. 238; Baldwin, Vol. I, p. 622; Philip Brockbank, ed., *Coriolanus,* The Arden Shakespeare (London: Methuen, 1976), pp. 29–30. A few decades ago, Kenneth Muir called attention to the working of Shakespeare's imagination on various sources. See his "Portents in 'Hamlet,'" *NQ,* 193 (1948), 54–5; "Menenius's Fable," *NQ,* 198 (1953), 240–2; "Pyramus and Thisbe: A Study in Shakespeare's Method," *SQ,* 5 (1954), 141–53; "Shakespeare Among the Commonplaces," *RES,* NS 10 (1959), 282–9.

ination invades, appropriates, combines, and transforms; the old elements become part of a new creation, something rich and strange.

Just as the examination of a cell reveals the biology of an entire organism, examination of the sources behind these speeches reveals Shakespeare's creative method in his Roman works. In a fine frenzy rolling, Shakespeare's eye ranged over a variety of classical texts, translations, and contemporary works, taking and leaving according to his fancy. In each Roman work, as in his other plays, he brought together different elements and struck a new balance. In the early works, for example, he relied on Ovid, Vergil, and Seneca; in the middle, on Plutarch; in the end, on Holinshed and possibly Heliodorus.

At this point, students of Shakespeare's Rome may naturally wonder about its unity and coherence. Yet, some of the most important studies of this century have subordinated this question to other concerns or ignored it entirely. M. W. MacCallum's seminal *Shakespeare's Roman Plays and Their Background* (1910), for example, concentrates largely on Shakespeare's presentation of character and use of Plutarch in *Julius Caesar, Antony and Cleopatra,* and *Coriolanus.* He does not seek to analyze the ties that bind the plays together. In *The Imperial Theme* (1931), G. Wilson Knight discusses the imagery of the Plutarchan plays perceptively, but offers little insight into their relations to each other. Maurice Charney follows the Wilson Knight line of imagistic criticism in *Shakespeare's Roman Plays: The Function of Imagery in the Drama* (1961), adding consideration of visual or "presentational" images on stage. He relegates to an appendix some of the arguments for regarding the Plutarchan plays as a group. At the outset of *Shakespeare: The Roman Plays* (1963), Derek Traversi declares that the Plutarchan plays combine the impersonal political process of Shakespeare's histories with the heroism of the tragedies. He devotes most of his energy thereafter to close reading and analysis, however, not to the support of this observation.

Other studies have found coherence in the Roman plays by interpreting them in the light of preexisting ideological frameworks. The tendency to read Shakespeare's Roman works in terms of Elizabethan political theory, illustrated in an extreme form by

James Emerson Phillips, Jr., *The State in Shakespeare's Greek and Roman Plays* (1940; rpt. 1972), is evident in much criticism of the individual works.[24] The tendency to view Shakespeare's Rome *sub specie aeternitatis* is also prevalent, appearing at the end of J. Leeds Barroll's learned "Shakespeare and Roman History" and throughout J. L. Simmons's *Shakespeare's Pagan World: The Roman Tragedies* (1973). According to Simmons, the Roman plays are united by their common depiction of a pagan world, one in which the characters "must perforce operate with no reference beyond the Earthly City." "The antedating of Christian revelation," Simmons contends, "is the most significant historical factor in these historical tragedies" and Saint Augustine's *De Civitate Dei* provides the appropriate light by which to read them.[25]

More recently, two critics have constructed their own politico-moral frameworks for the interpretation of Shakespeare's Rome. In *Rome and Romans According to Shakespeare* (1976), Michael Platt traces the rise and fall of the Republic through *Lucrece*, *Coriolanus*, *Julius Caesar*, and *Antony and Cleopatra*. In *Shakespeare's Rome: Republic and Empire* (1976), Paul A. Cantor distinguishes between Shakespeare's portrayal of the Republic in *Coriolanus* and the Empire in *Antony and Cleopatra*. He concludes that *thumos*, or "public spiritedness," characterizes Shakespeare's Republic and *eros*, or "desire," his Empire.[26]

[24]Phillips (1940; rpt. New York: Octagon, 1972).

[25]Simmons, pp. 7, 8.

[26]Platt, Salzburg Studies in English Literature, JDS, No. 51 (Salzburg: Institut für Englische Sprache und Literatur, 1976). There have been other studies of the Roman works. Judah Stampfer's *The Tragic Engagement: A Study of Shakespeare's Classical Tragedies* (New York: Funk & Wagnalls, 1968) superficially treats *Titus Andronicus* and the Plutarchan tragedies. Michael Payne's *Irony in Shakespeare's Roman Plays*, Salzburg Studies in English Literature, ES, No. 19 (Salzburg: Institut für Englische Sprache und Literatur, 1974) is brief and disappointing, largely because irony is defined so variously. David C. Green has written two unilluminating studies: *"Julius Caesar" and Its Source*, Salzburg Studies in English Literature, JDS, No. 86 (Salzburg: Institut für Anglistik und Amerikanistik, 1979), and *Plutarch Revisited: A Study of Shakespeare's Last Roman Tragedies and Their Source*, Salzburg Studies in English Literature, JDS, No. 78 (Salzburg: Institut für Anglistik und Amerikanistik, 1979). See also John Alvis, "The Coherence of Shakespeare's Roman Plays," MLQ, 40 (1979), 115–34, a condensed and improved version of Chapter V of his dissertation, "Shakespeare's Roman Tragedies: Self-Glorification and the Incomplete

The political and moral frameworks advanced thus far fail to define the unity and coherence of Shakespeare's Rome for three reasons. First, they do not adequately take into account the diversity of Rome in the canon and the era, the undogmatic flexibility of English humanism, and the ambivalent nature of Shakespearean drama, where political and moral issues are complex and difficult. Second, whether the plays tend to justify monarchy, according to the political interpretation, or to portray the world before Christ, according to the moral one, the reign of Augustus is made to assume a climactic importance in Shakespeare's view. The "ass unpolici'd" of Cleopatra's conception becomes the prince of peace in the critical opinion, as he does in his own. Shakespeare nowhere portrays this miraculous transformation, and the coming apotheosis must be inferred from hints and half-guesses, all removed from their qualifying dramatic context. Third, incredibly, no interpretation to date treats all the works of Shakespeare's Roman canon: *The Rape of Lucrece, Titus Andronicus, Julius Caesar, Antony and Cleopatra, Coriolanus,* and *Cymbeline.* Only Maurice Charney has offered a rationale for regarding the Plutarchan plays as a distinct group, citing three external criteria: "(1) the use of 'Roman' costume on the Elizabethan stage; (2) the Roman praise of suicide as an act of moral courage and nobility, an attitude very different from Christian belief; and (3) the common source in North's Plutarch."[27] If, for the moment, one accepts these criteria, one wonders about the exclusion of *Lucrece,* which features pagan praise of suicide, and of *Titus Andronicus,* which derives in part from North's Plutarch and which, apparently, was played in Roman costume. But these criteria are simply inadequate. The little we know about Elizabethan costuming is insufficient for such conclusions; suicide is only one thematic motif that Shakespeare con-

---

Polity," University of Dallas, 1973. The article is thoughtful, but limited by its exclusive focus on the Plutarchan plays. Another dissertation of interest is David Lord Kranz's *Shakespeare's Roman Vision,* University of California, Berkeley, 1977, which finds in *Lucrece, Titus Andronicus,* and the Plutarchan tragedies a cohesive vision of Rome. Kranz examines the city itself, Stoicism, rhetoric, and the conflict between art and nature in the works, but does not note how these motifs change in the Roman canon or how different each work is.

[27]Charney, p. 207.

sidered typically Roman; and North's Plutarch is only one source of Shakespeare's Roman vision.

Modern criticism of the Roman plays suggests an alternate approach to the problem of coherence: the organic one. In 1951 Roy Walker made a stimulating observation: "Shakespeare's idea of Rome was not built in a day, or built at all. Like other living things it was subject to growth and decay, and to trace the course of that organic development is not to impute to the poet a neat plan of construction, conscious from the outset."[28] Walker went on to trace some imagistic and thematic patterns from *Titus Andronicus* through *Cymbeline*, noting significant recurrences of idea, but also the different contexts. The inductive approach he outlined and attempted rests on the notion that the Roman works bear a family resemblance to each other and show signs of internal coherence; it allows, however, for the possibility of change, of "growth and decay." Some decades later John W. Velz called for study of Shakespeare's Rome along similar lines of approach. He suggested that future critics might discuss Shakespeare's Rome as a world apart by focusing on its *eloquentia*, national character, institutions, or topography, as each motif manifests itself in all six Roman works.[29]

The present study takes an organic approach to the problem of coherence in Shakespeare's Rome as the city appears in *The Rape of Lucrece, Titus Andronicus*, the Plutarchan tragedies, and *Cymbeline*. It attempts to identify internal similarities while recognizing differences, to reveal central themes while tracing their development or disappearance. Such an approach requires reconsideration of Shakespeare's sources, broadly defined as possible influences and analogs. This reconsideration seeks not to discover direct sources (although such discoveries are always welcome), but

---

[28] "The Northern Star: An Essay on the Roman Plays," *SQ*, 2 (1951), 287.
[29] "Ancient World in Shakespeare," pp. 9–12.

to penetrate into the deep sources lying below the surface of the text, to those various subterranean streams that give, enrich, and nourish its life.

Studying all of Shakespeare's Roman canon chronologically has clear advantages over other methods.[30] Most obviously, it can reveal that Shakespeare viewed ancient Rome as a place apart and that his vision of the city and its people evolved dynamically throughout his career. Embryos of idea and image grow to maturity and die. The Vergilian virtue of *pietas,* for example, central to Shakespeare's first four Roman works, is only marginally important to *Antony and Cleopatra,* but central again, although strangely transformed, to *Coriolanus* and *Cymbeline.* The hint of a blood ritual at the end of *Lucrece* becomes a potent symbol in *Titus Andronicus, Julius Caesar, Antony and Cleopatra,* and *Coriolanus,* only to be rejected finally in *Cymbeline,* wherein Roman *severitas* gives way to British mercy. A sequential examination, moreover, can show Shakespeare reworking dramatic situations and scenes in his Roman art. Lucrece's suicide, for example, is replayed variously by Brutus, Antony, Cleopatra, and Imogen, who, of course, stops at the crucial moment. The rape of Lavinia provides a model for Iachimo's unlawful invasion of Imogen's bedchamber. Brutus's death scene supplies important details for Antony's and Coriolanus's. Caesar's triumphant procession sweeps on, although to different effects and ends, in *Antony and Cleopatra* and *Coriolanus.* The poem and the plays are connected by an intricate, yet largely unnoticed and unexplored, network of images, ideas, gestures, and scenes. Although the elements of this network appear elsewhere sporadically, here in the Roman canon, transfigured so together, they grow to something of great constancy, howsoever strange and admirable. Viewed in their entirety, they testify compellingly to the coherence of Shakespeare's Roman vision.

At the center of this vision stands the city of Rome. This "city," of course, Shakespeare defines variously: Rome is an extension of

---

[30]Obviously, one must rely on a general conception of sequence rather than on precise dating. Whether *Titus Andronicus* properly follows or precedes *Lucrece,* whether *Antony and Cleopatra* or *Coriolanus* is Shakespeare's last Roman tragedy, or whether some works were written simultaneously, the conclusions of this study remain the same.

Collatine's household in *Lucrece,* a wilderness settlement in *Titus Andronicus,* a political arena in *Julius Caesar,* an Empire in *Antony and Cleopatra,* a sharply drawn *urbs* in *Coriolanus,* and a vaguely localized anomaly, part ancient, part modern, in *Cymbeline.* It is sometimes metaphor, sometimes myth, sometimes both, sometimes neither. Despite its metamorphoses, Rome maintains a distinct identity. Constructed of forums, walls, and Capitol, opposed to outlying battlefields, wild, primitive landscapes, and enemy cities, Rome is a palpable though ever-changing presence. The city serves not only as a setting for action, but also as central protagonist. Embodying the heroic traditions of the past, Rome shapes its inhabitants, who often live and die according to its dictates for the approval of its future generations. These Romans, capable of high courage and nobility, struggle with a city that demands them to be both more and less than human. Shakespeare tells their stories by combining various sources, by reworking the political motifs of invasion and rebellion, and by exploring the thematic implications of three Roman ideals: constancy, honor, and *pietas* (the loving respect owed to family, country, and gods). He makes continual reference to Troy, the city that gave birth to Rome and that, in many ways, foretells Rome's later tragedies. Increasingly critical of Rome, Shakespeare finally writes *Cymbeline,* a valediction to the Eternal City that so long and so deeply engaged his intelligence and imagination.

II

THE RAPE OF LUCRECE
ROME AND ROMANS

Shakespeare's *The Rape of Lucrece* has been judged an interesting but ungainly child. Most readers, impatient with Tarquin's revolting will and with Lucrece's stylized complaints to Night, Opportunity, and Time, agree that such rhetorical exercise impedes movement and stifles dramatic potential. As a result, *The Rape of Lucrece* has gained reputation as the homely younger sister of *Venus and Adonis,* as an awkward Ovidian exercise, further encumbered by the conventions of the popular complaint.[1] Efforts to reevaluate the poem have not vindicated its lumbering movement, its disproportionate parts, and its excessive rhetoric;[2] some of the

[1]See the summary of criticism in Hyder Edward Rollins's New Variorum edition, *The Poems* (Philadelphia: Lippincott, 1938), pp. 476–523; and J. W. Lever's retrospect in "Twentieth-Century Studies in Shakespeare's Songs, Sonnets, and Poems," *ShS*, 15 (1962), 1–30 (22–5). See also the appraisals of T. W. Baldwin, *On the Literary Genetics of Shakspere's Poems & Sonnets* (Urbana: University of Illinois Press, 1950), p. 153; C. S. Lewis, *English Literature in the Sixteenth Century Excluding Drama* (Oxford: Clarendon Press, 1954), pp. 499–502; F. T. Prince, ed., *The Poems*, The Arden Shakespeare (1960; rpt. London: Methuen, 1968), pp. xxxiii–xxxviii; Douglas Bush, *Mythology and the Renaissance Tradition in English Poetry*, rev. ed. (New York: Norton, 1963), pp. 148–55; and J. C. Maxwell, ed., *The Poems* (Cambridge: Cambridge University Press, 1966), pp. xx–xxvi. The poem is sometimes referred to as an epyllion, or "minor epic," as well.

[2]Among those who make modest but more positive claims for *Lucrece* are Hallett Smith, *Elizabethan Poetry: A Study in Conventions, Meaning, and Expression* (1952; rpt. Cambridge, Mass.: Harvard University Press, 1966), pp. 113–17, who attempts to clarify its nature and purpose; Robert J. Griffin, "'These Contraries Such Unity Do Hold': Patterned Imagery in Shakespeare's Narrative Poems," *SEL*, 4 (1964), 43–55; and Robert L. Montgomery, Jr., "Shakespeare's Gaudy: The Method of *The Rape of Lucrece*," in *Studies in Honor of De Witt T. Starnes*, ed. Thomas P. Harrison et al. (Austin: University of Texas Press, 1967),

more interesting, however, have called attention to the poem's importance in Shakespeare's artistic development, a topic of critical interest, J. W. Lever points out, at least since the days of Walter Whiter and Edmond Malone.[3]

Recent commentary on *Lucrece* in Shakespeare's development has led almost exclusively to discussion of the great tragedies, particularly *Hamlet* and *Macbeth*. The poem presents, however, an early and full depiction of Shakespeare's Rome.[4] It displays many of the distinctively Roman features that appear in *Titus Andronicus, Julius Caesar, Antony and Cleopatra, Coriolanus,* and *Cymbeline.* Central to its imagery is the Roman city under siege, complete with walls, outlying battlefields, a private house, and an invader. Here also is a lightly sketched portrayal of the Roman family, its values, and its significance to the city. The image of Troy rises up here, as it will later, to enrich character and clarify theme. The poem depicts a Roman struggling with Rome, the city that demands almost inhuman constancy and heroic self-sacrifice for the rewards of honor and fame. As do the other works (perhaps excepting *Cymbeline*), *The Rape of Lucrece* balances itself between tragedy and history as it progresses through disorder, loss, and sorrow to the costly expiation of evil and the chastened emergence of new order. Audible here, though sometimes

---

pp. 25–36, who discuss the rhetoric; Jerome A. Kramer and Judith Kaminsky, " 'These Contraries Such Unity Do Hold': Structure in *The Rape of Lucrece,*" *Mosaic,* 10 (1977), 143–55, who examine the relation between idea and structure.

[3]Lever, "Twentieth-Century Studies," p. 24; see M. C. Bradbrook, *Shakespeare and Elizabethan Poetry* (London: Chatto & Windus, 1951), pp. 110–16; Bullough, Vol. I, pp. 182–3; Franklin M. Dickey, *Not Wisely But Too Well: Shakespeare's Love Tragedies* (San Marino, Calif.: Huntington Library, 1957), pp. 53–62; Sam Hynes, "The Rape of Tarquin," *SQ,* 10 (1959), 451–3; Harold R. Walley, "*The Rape of Lucrece* and Shakespearean Tragedy," *PMLA,* 76 (1961), 480–7; Robert Bernard DiGiovanni, "Shakespeare's *Lucrece:* A Topical Evaluation of and Supplement to the Scholarship and Criticism Since 1936," dissertation, University of Michigan, 1971; Reno Thomas Simone, *Shakespeare and "Lucrece": A Study of the Poem and Its Relation to the Plays,* Salzburg Studies in English Literature, ERS, No. 38 (Salzburg: Institut für Englische Sprache und Literatur, 1974).

[4]The exact date of composition is uncertain. Most scholars believe it earlier than *Titus Andronicus.* See, for example, Baldwin, *Genetics of Shakspere's Poems,* pp. 131–2.

faint and incomplete, are the same melodies that resound later in the grand music of the Roman plays.

꘏꘏꘏꘏

The story of Lucrece's rape by Tarquin is told by Livy and Ovid, and retold by numerous others including Saint Augustine, the author of the *Gesta Romanorum*, Boccaccio, Geoffrey Chaucer, John Gower, and John Lydgate.[5] In addition to Shakespeare, it attracted Renaissance writers such as William Painter, Thomas Middleton, Thomas Heywood, and J. Quarles.[6] As set forth in the classical sources and in most subsequent versions, the story comprises four separate narrative threads: (1) the tale of Lucius Tarquinius, his assassination of Servius Tullius, usurpation, and tyrannical rule; (2) the story of the siege at Ardea, the testing of the women, the rape and suicide of Lucrece; (3) the drama of Junius Brutus pretending to be a fool and then leading the revolution against the Tarquins; (4) the record of the change in Roman government from kings to consuls. According to Livy and Ovid, the rape of Lucrece was not an isolated instance of criminal passion but a crucial incident in the fall of Tarquinian tyranny. Livy firmly places the rape in its historical context; it occupies no more than one-fifth of the narrative and receives no special emphasis. Florus likewise relegates the entire incident to a series of subordinate clauses in the lengthy sentence summarizing the story of Lucius Tarquinius's tyranny:

[5]Livy, *Historiae* I.lvii–lx; Ovid, *Fasti* II.685–852; Saint Augustine, *De Civitate Dei* I.xix; *Gesta Romanorum* (Swan trans., rev. by Hooper, 1906), Tale 135, "Of Conscience"; Boccaccio, *De Claris Mulieribus*, Ch. 46; Chaucer, *The Legend of Good Women*, 1680–1885; Gower, *Confessio Amantis* VII.4754–5130; Lydgate, *The Fall of Princes* II.1002–344.

[6]Painter, *The Palace of Pleasure* (1566–7), Novel 2; Middleton, *The Ghost of Lucrece* (1600); Heywood, *The Rape of Lvcrece* (1608). Quarles's later *The Banishment of Tarquin: Or, the Reward of Lust* (1655) is mentioned here because it was published as a continuation of Shakespeare's poem. Typical Renaissance accounts can be found in Thomas Cooper's "Dictionarivm" attached to his *Thesavrvs Lingvae Romanae & Britannicae* (1565) and in Andrea Alciati's *Emblemata cvm Commentariis* (Padua, 1621), p. 815. D. C. Allen, "Some Observations on *The Rape of Lucrece*," *ShS*, 15 (1962), 89–98, discusses various treatments of the story.

For when as Tarquinius Superbus by his prowd tyrannicall demeanure, had incurred the hatred of all men: he at last upon the forcible outrage and villanie done by Sex. Tarquinius (his sonne) in the night season upon the bodie of Lucretia: who sending for her father, Tricipitinus, and her husband Collatinus, besought them earnestly not to see her death vnrevenged, and so with a knife killed her selfe: he I say, by the meanes of Brutus, especially was driven and expelled out of Rome, when he had raigned five and twentie years.[7]

Shakespeare's principal source, Ovid's *Fasti* with the commentary of Paulus Marsus, focuses more closely and sympathetically on Lucrece, but likewise provides the historical framework.[8] Ovid begins by announcing, *Nunc mihi dicenda est regis fuga* (II.685), "Now have I to tell of the Flight of the King," and identifies the King as Tarquinius, *vir iniustus, fortis ad arma tamen* (688), "a man unjust, yet puissant in arms." After relating some of the King's misdeeds and describing Brutus as a wise man who pretends to be a fool, Ovid describes Lucrece's rape by the King's son, Sextus, and her suicide. He then tells of Brutus's oath, the exhibition of Lucrece's body, and the public rehearsal of Tarquin's foul deeds, as well as his father's, *regis facta nefanda refert* (850). Paulus Marsus glosses this phrase by recapitulating the King's crimes against the Roman people.[9] Ovid concludes the story with a quick summary of the changes in Roman government: *Tarquinius cum prole fugit, capit annua consul / iura: dies regnis illa suprema fuit* (851–2), "Tarquin and his brood were banished. A consul undertook the government for a year. That day was the last of kingly rule."

Like Ovid, but to a much greater degree, Shakespeare focuses on the rape and decks out the lustful Tarquin and the chaste Lucrece with rhetorical conceits and embellishments. And also like Ovid, Shakespeare carefully provides the traditional historical and politi-

[7]This translation of Florus's work is contained in *The Romane Historie written by T. Livivs of Padva*, trans. Philemon Holland (1600), p. 2. A check against the original Latin reveals Holland's accuracy in emphasis here.
[8]Unless otherwise noted, I have used for Latin references and English translations *Ovid's Fasti with an English Translation by Sir James George Frazer*, The Loeb Classical Library (1931).
[9]Ovid, *Fastorvm Libri Diligenti Emendatione* (Venice, 1520), fols. 69ᵛ–70.

cal context, even though such provision in his Argument conflicts with certain details of the poem.[10] Shakespeare begins the Argument by introducing the Tarquin King, "for his excessive pride surnamed / Superbus," and by recalling the cruel murder of Servius Tullius and the usurpation of the Roman throne, "contrary to / the Roman laws and customs, not requiring or staying / for the people's suffrages" (Arg. 1–2, 3–5). Shakespeare then briefly describes the siege at Ardea, the visit to the Roman wives, and the consequent rise of passion in Sextus Tarquinius, although the poem dramatizes none of this, suggesting that Collatine's boasting aroused Tarquin's lust and that Sextus had never seen Lucrece prior to the night of the rape. Shakespeare's Argument and poem agree more easily on the character of Brutus, who emerges in both as the avenger of the crime and the leader of the revolution. The Argument, however, tells us more specifically that Brutus delivered "a bitter / invective against the tyranny of the King" (Arg. 41–2), which resulted in the banishment of the Tarquins and the change in government, while the poem ambiguously mentions Brutus's speech against "Tarquin's foul offense" and "Tarquin's everlasting banishment" (1852, 1855). (Sextus? Superbus? The whole family?)[11]

On the level of plot, Shakespeare seems less interested than Livy and Ovid in the rape as the instance of Tarquinian misrule that ended Roman monarchy. But the plot in a work such as *Lucrece* is perhaps its least important element. An examination of the poem's rhetoric demonstrates that Shakespeare is aware of the larger significance of the incident. Here, as in the Roman plays, Shakespeare concentrates on characters and reveals their historical and political importance by evoking the ancient city to which they belong.

The glimpses of Roman geography that *Lucrece* affords reveal the city familiar to readers of the plays. We see the "fields of fruitful Italy" (107) around Rome, which provide a battleground

---

[10]Baldwin's demonstration of the Argument's authenticity is persuasive, *Genetics of Shakspere's Poems*, pp. 97–115. E. A. J. Honigmann, *The Stability of Shakespeare's Text* (Lincoln: University of Nebraska Press, 1965), suggests that the Argument may be based on an early outline for the narrative (p. 45); Bullough suggests that the Argument was written after the poem (Vol. I, p. 180).

[11]According to Rollins, *Poems*, the original reading of both lines was the equally ambiguous "Tarqvins."

for soldiers and a place for their camps. We catch sight of the "Capitol" (1835), that symbol of Roman government, law, and order central to the Rome of *Julius Caesar*. We glimpse also the "fair streets" (1834) of Rome, through which Lucrece's body is carried, the streets that will serve the dramatist well for scenes of revelation and confrontation. Outside Rome is Ardea, a besieged city mentioned in the first line of the poem and quickly forgotten until Lucrece sends for Collatine much later (1332). Here tossed off as an exigency of plot, the conflict between Rome and another place or people becomes later a means of articulating thematic oppositions and ironies. Shakespeare's Romans will struggle against Goths, Egyptians, Volscians, and Britons; his Rome against Alexandria, Corioles, Antium, and Britain.

The setting for most of the action in *Lucrece* is, of course, Collatia (misnamed Collatium throughout the poem). As is evident in Livy and the notes of Paulus Marsus, Collatia is a town outside Rome's walls where Collatine and Lucrece live.[12] Shakespeare follows Ovid in minimizing the distance between the town and the city and in treating the smaller as part of the larger. He calls Lucrece a "Roman dame" (51, 1628) and groups Collatine with the "noblemen of Rome" (Arg. 7) who accompany Tarquin to the siege. Shakespeare's Brutus, at the side of the dead Lucrece in Collatia, surprises the "Romans" (1811), who consider him a fool, addresses Collatine as "Thou wronged lord of Rome" (1818) and "Courageous Roman" (1828). He invokes the "Roman gods" (1831) to avenge the abominations that disgrace "Rome herself" (1833) and swears by the Capitol as well as by "country rights in Rome maintained" (1838).

So consistently is Collatia identified with Rome that one may wonder if Shakespeare was aware of the geographical distinction between the two. Whether he was or not, he chooses to depict Collatia as the private house of the Roman pair Collatine and Lucrece. He embellishes this depiction with homely, realistic details that describe the interior of the house. He tells us, for example, of the several chambers that separate Lucrece's bedroom from Tarquin's, of the various locks on the doors, and of the "unwilling

---

[12]Livy is careful to distinguish the two places throughout his account. See also Ovid, *Fastorvm*, fol. 67ᵛ.

portal" through which Tarquin passes (302ff.). The threshold grates against the opening door, and the weasels shriek in surprise (306–8). The breeze enters "through little vents and crannies" of the house walls and blows upon Tarquin's torch (310–13). On top of the rushes covering the floors lies Lucrece's glove, complete with hidden needle (317–18). The "yielding latch" of Lucrece's chamber door opens to reveal the closed curtains around her bed, her pillow, and green coverlet (339ff.). Later, the poet depicts for us the servants: a demure maid who weeps to see her mistress in sorrow; a sour-faced groom who bashfully carries the message. Collatia is envisioned not as a town unto itself, but as a part of Rome, as a private house within the precincts, if not the walls, of the great city.[13]

As a Roman household, Collatia embodies the virtues of order and propriety to an exceptional degree. Unlike the other households, whose women betake themselves to "dancing and / revelling" (Arg. 18–19) while the men fight in war, Collatia features Lucrece, the beautiful and chaste wife who spends the night spinning with her maids and worrying about her husband. Lucrece wins the praise of the Roman nobles for representing the ideal combination of domestic virtues: industry, humility, chastity, self-discipline, responsibility toward servants, solicitude for her husband. In Shakespeare's version she is not only the ideal wife, but also the good mother, concerned about her children's reputation, and the dutiful daughter who confesses the rape to her father as well as to her husband.

Such virtues may be praiseworthy in themselves, but they are also essential to the maintenance of the family and, therefore, to the proper working of the city. Lucrece resides in the middle of the Aristotelian and Ciceronian series of concentric circles that expand outward to include the family, household, city, nation, and world.[14] The subordination of selfish desires to the dictates of the individual conscience leads to a similar ordering in other parts of society and in Rome itself. Upon first seeing Lucrece, Tarquin notices the "golden age" (60) in her cheeks, this color suggesting

---

[13]This impression is confirmed by the poem's ending. What Livy describes as distinct events occurring in separate places, Collatia and Rome, Shakespeare telescopes into a continuous Roman action.

[14]See Aristotle, *Politics* 1252a–b; Cicero, *De Officiis* I.xvi–xxii.

the perfect order in her, her household, and city; and so it is that Lucrece, after the rape, immediately distrusts her servant, suspecting already the breakdown of proper relations in the home.

Tarquin's rape of Lucrece violates all the circles of social order that surround her. Most fundamentally, it violates her person and her identity as chaste wife. Attacking Lucrece, Tarquin strikes at the heart of her family, as well as at the familial structure itself. His passion, Shakespeare notes, respects "nor children's tears nor mother's groans" (431). Nor the protests of fathers and husbands. As Tarquin recognizes (232ff.), the rape is also an unlawful invasion of Collatine's household, a transgression against the laws of friendship and hospitality that govern the interaction between the household and the outside world, between the home of a private citizen and a member of the royal family. Shakespeare makes it clear that Lucrece is duty-bound to receive Tarquin as a guest. She later explains in an imaginary conversation with Collatine:

> Yet for thy honor did I entertain him;
> Coming from thee, I could not put him back,
> For it had been dishonor to disdain him.
>
> (842–4)

The rape of Lucrece also violates the principles of order and hierarchy that govern the city of Rome.[15] Shakespeare makes this point imagistically by depicting the rape of the woman as the siege of a city. Tarquin's motivation, for example, appears partly in political terms as the envy of Lucrece's "sov'reignty" (36). Later, Tarquin wonders how Collatine would react if he knew about the "siege that hath engirt his marriage" (221). "Affection" acts as a "captain," displays a "gaudy banner" (271–2), and leads Tarquin to the city walls, that is, to the various doors through which he must pass, to the closed curtains around the bed, and finally to the "ivory wall" (464) of Lucrece's body. His hand, "smoking with pride," marches on to make a stand on Lucrece's breast, "whose ranks of blue veins" leave "their round turrets destitute and pale" (438–41). Meanwhile, Lucrece's heart, "(poor citizen!) distress'd" (465–6), wounds itself to death within. Tarquin's tongue "like a

---

[15]Coppélia Kahn, "The Rape in Shakespeare's *Lucrece,*" *ShakS,* 9 (1976), 45–72, noting the patrilinear organization of Rome, discusses the specific ways in which Lucrece's rape is a threat to Roman social structure.

trumpet" sounds "a parley" (470–1) before he moves to "scale" the "never-conquered fort" (481–2), "to make the breach and enter this sweet city" (469).

The imagery of the besieged city is enhanced by the imagery of the beehive. Long a commonplace metaphor for the well-ordered commonwealth, one that Shakespeare uses early and late in his career, the image of the beehive draws upon political, literary, and iconographical traditions to reinforce the poem's controlling metaphor.[16] Lucrece laments to Collatine:

> My honey lost, and I, a drone-like bee,
> Have no perfection of my summer left,
> But robb'd and ransack'd by injurious theft.
> In thy weak hive a wand'ring wasp hath crept,
> And suck'd the honey which thy chaste bee kept.
>
> (836–40)

Here Shakespeare employs the familiar analogy between the insect and human communities to suggest the public nature of Tarquin's violation (cf. 493, 889, 1769–71). Unlike the king bee, celebrated for mildness and temperateness of behavior, the wandering wasp Tarquin terrorizes his Roman subject and plunders her home. That home, the "weak hive," no longer stands as the exemplary icon of order, productivity, and social stability; robbed and ransacked, bereft of honey, it now suggests the city under Tarquinian tyranny.

The siege of Lucrece, we observe, takes place after another siege: that of Tarquin's reason by his will.[17] As metaphors of increasing complexity imply, this siege is actually an insurrection. Tarquin's "will" (129), that is, his volition as well as his sexual desire, overcomes the "weak-built hopes" that would restrain it (130), proving itself stronger than "reason's weak removing" (243) and the powers of "frozen conscience" (247). Almost choked by Tarquin's lust, "heedful fear" (281) surrenders and

---

[16]Classical antecedents for the commonplace include Aristotle, *De Generatione Animalium* III.x.759a–60b and *Historia Animalium* V.xxi.553a–xxii.554b; Pliny, *Naturalis Historia* XI.iv–xxiii; and, of course, Vergil, *Georgics* IV. Cf. *Henry V.* I.ii.187ff. and *Troilus and Cressida* I.iii.81ff.

[17]Sam Hynes, "Rape of Tarquin," discusses this metaphor for Tarquin's inner conflict, but emphasizes the relation to Shakespeare's later tragedies, especially *Macbeth*.

joins the usurping adversary, "vows a league, and now invasion" (287). Tarquin's eye enlists the aid of the heart, which acts as a captain and leads all the "servile powers," the senses and appetites, against the forces of reason and restraint (293–8). Tarquin's eye incites his "veins" (427), the passions of the blood, to mutiny and riot:

> And they like straggling slaves for pillage fighting,
> Obdurate vassals fell exploits effecting,
> In bloody death and ravishment delighting,
> Nor children's tears nor mother's groans respecting,
> Swell in their pride, the onset still expecting.
>   Anon his beating heart, alarum striking,
>   Gives the hot charge, and bids them do their liking.
>
> (428–34)

Here the rebel passions overthrow reason and the state of man suffers an insurrection. After the rape of Lucrece, only ruins of Tarquin's inner kingdom remain. The guardian "troops of cares" gather around the "soul's fair temple," now defaced, and ask how she fares (719–21):

> She says her subjects with foul insurrection
> Have batter'd down her consecrated wall,
> And by their mortal fault brought in subjection
> Her immortality, and made her thrall
> To living death and pain perpetual.
>
> (722–6)

The siege is done, the invasion complete, and Tarquin's city destroyed.

This internal siege precipitates the external one. Throughout the poem Shakespeare depicts Tarquin as the invading barbarian who comes to raze Lucrece's city and plunder its treasure. From Ardea, Tarquin brings the "lightless fire" (4) of lust; later, he carries a torch to Lucrece's bedroom. The fire imagery gains force and cohesiveness from allusions to the archetypal siege of bright-burning Troy (1366ff.). Like the Greeks to whom he will soon be compared, Tarquin comes in stealth and cunning to reduce the city to ashes. Although he is a "Roman lord" (301), he is as alien and hostile to Lucrece as the invading Greeks were to Troy.

Images of the wild outdoors and animal predation suggest the cruel bestiality of the invading Tarquin. Lucrece's bedroom, situated at the center of the concentric circles that encompass the family, household, and city, enclosed by the laws and regulations that make civilized society possible, becomes a "wilderness where are no laws" (544). Ironically, the place of procreation, the place that should provide for the future life of the city, becomes the scene of its destruction and that of all civilized value. The images of animal predation that cluster around the rape suggest the transformation of the well-ordered city into the savage outdoors. Tarquin appears as various voracious beasts, some familiar, some exotic and mythological. He is the "night-owl" (360), the "lurking serpent" (362), the "grim lion" (421), the "falcon tow'ring in the skies" (506), the cockatrice with "dead-killing eye" (540), the gripe or griffin with "sharp claws" (543), the "rough beast" of "foul appetite" (545–6), the "foul night-waking cat" (554), the ravenous "wolf" (677), and the wild "jade" (707). After the rape he is the "full-fed hound," the "gorged hawk" (694), the "thievish dog" (736), and the "wand'ring wasp" (839). Lucrece appears often as the helpless prey. She is an unsuspecting bird "never lim'd" (88), a sleeping "dove" (360), a "new-kill'd bird" (457), a couching "fowl" (507), a "white hind" (543), a "weak mouse" (555), an "unseasonable doe" (581), a "poor lamb" (677). After the rape she is Philomela, the nightingale (1079, 1128), a "poor frighted deer" (1149), and a "pale swan in her wat'ry nest" about to die (1611). The civilized city here, as it does in Shakespeare's Roman plays, turns into a lawless jungle where only the quick strike, the sharp claw, and the keen tooth prevail.

The imagery of siege and predation cannot be dismissed as mere poetic excess, as a series of ingenious, elaborate, but merely decorative figures. It embodies in its design the historical context of the story central to the accounts of Livy and Ovid. Sextus's invasion of Lucrece recapitulates in miniature the Tarquins' invasion of Rome. Sextus's attack on the Roman family recalls Lucius Tarquinius's assassination of his father-in-law, the event that began the tyranny and that Shakespeare recollected in his Argument. Renaissance writers such as Thomas Heywood in his dramatic version of the story and Philemon Holland in his translation of Livy denounced this filial treachery, this shocking gesture of *impietas*, as they denounced Tullia, Lucius's wife, who helped plan the murder and who drove a carriage over her father's corpse.[18] Like his father, who usurped the throne "contrary to / the Roman laws and customs" (Arg. 3–4), Sextus Tarquinius, "like a foul usurper" (412), tramples on the laws and customs that hold Rome together. The savage jungle that Tarquin makes of Lucrece's home extends beyond her doors to the confines of the city where his family rules. The poetical rape of the woman and the historical rape of the city become metaphors for each other, facing mirrors that generate unending images of their own disorder.[19]

After the rape and Lucrece's declamations to Night, Opportunity, and Time, she recollects a painting or tapestry depicting the fall of Troy. This recollection, an extended *ekphrasis* of some two hundred lines, is an early and stylized example of the many allusions to Troy in the Roman plays. Such allusions are appropriate and, it may be said, inevitable, as Aeneas and the Trojan survivors were reputed in ancient legend and chronicle to be the founders of Rome. What is more, according to such Christian historiographers as Saint Augustine, the fall of the early city prefigured the fall and decay of the later. Both Troy and Rome illustrated the folly of trusting pagan gods and the vanity of the Earthly City.[20] Poetical and historical traditions thus conspired to link inextricably the

---

[18]The first scenes of Heywood's play, *The Rape of Lvcrece* (1608), focus on Tullia's unnaturalness and cruelty. Narrating the incident of the carriage and the corpse in his translation of Livy, Holland interjects a parenthetical gasp "(oh abhominable act!)" (p. 42). Livy explains also that Lucius Tarquinius killed his first wife, Tullia's younger sister, and his own brother, Arruns, before murdering Servius Tullius.

[19]A glance at the marginalia in Gabriel Harvey's copy of Livy, *Romanae Historiae Principis Decades Tres, cvm Dimidia* (Basel, 1555), indicates that at least one other contemporary regarded the story of Lucrece in the context of Roman history. After Livy's account of the rape and the expulsion of the Tarquins, Harvey notes the similarity between Roman and Hebrew history: "*Omnes primi Romanorum Reges, boni, ac validi, praeter Superbum: sicuti primi etiam Hebraeorum Reges, optimi*" (n.p.).

[20]In the opening chapters of *De Civitate Dei*, Saint Augustine discusses Troy and Rome as related incarnations of the Earthly City.

two cities in Shakespeare's imagination. Like the ghost of Hamlet's father behind Hamlet, Troy is an apparition that hovers behind Shakespeare's Rome, ever ready to be summoned into existence for point or contrast.

Shakespeare models Lucrece's recollection of Troy on passages from Vergil's *Aeneid* I and II and Ovid's *Metamorphoses* XIII.[21] The dramatic context of her recollection recalls *Aeneid* I, where Aeneas, shipwrecked on the African shore, comes upon a depiction of Troy on Juno's temple. He weeps to see again the struggles of Greeks and Trojans, the human tragedies of the war, and his civilization destroyed by foreign invaders. The scenes on the temple are carefully arranged to emphasize Greek cruelty and treachery, Trojan helplessness, and a pervasive sense of doom, *fata Troiana*.[22] They bring Aeneas to the painful realization that his city is lost forever, having already passed from reality into the realms of art, legend, and song. Paradoxically, however, the sight of Trojan woe brings comfort and relief as well as sorrow and pain. Aeneas rejoices to find a people who worship Juno, unremitting enemy of the Trojans, yet who immortalize Trojan suffering with sympathy and compassion, who may, therefore, be willing to give food, shelter, and assistance to Trojan survivors. The famous Vergilian phrase, *sunt lacrimae rerum*, repeatedly taken out of context as an expression of melancholia, is actually an expression of joy, hope, and faith in human kindness:

> en Priamus! sunt hic etiam sua praemia laudi,
> sunt lacrimae rerum et mentem mortalia tangunt.
> solve metus; feret haec aliquam tibi fama salutem.

(461–3)

[21]Shakespeare's debt to Vergil and Ovid for the Troy material has been analyzed by Baldwin, *Genetics of Shakspere's Poems*, pp. 143–6. Interestingly, the opening line of Vergil's *ekphrasis* (I.446), appears as an example in a standard grammar-school text, William Lily's *Brevissima Institutio Sev Ratio Grammatices* (1567), sig. C.v. In addition to the borrowings from Ovid for the characters of Ajax, Ulysses, Nestor, and Hecuba, Shakespeare may have gleaned the un-Vergilian detail of Priam under Pyrrhus's foot (1449) from Golding's translation of the *Metamorphoses*: "Great Troy lyes under foote" (XIII.606). Lucrece's desire to tear at Helen's beauty with her nails (1471ff.) may have been suggested by Hecuba's similar treatment of Polymestor, Ovid, *Metamorphoses* XIII.558ff.

[22]See R. D. Williams, "The Pictures on Dido's Temple (*Aeneid* I. 450–93)," *Class Q*, NS 10 (1960), 145–51.

Lo, Priam! Here, too, virtue has its due rewards; here, too,
there are tears for misfortune and mortal sorrows touch the
heart. Dismiss thy fears; this fame will bring thee some
salvation.

The dramatic context of Shakespeare's *ekphrasis*, as well as its
substance and effect, follows the Vergilian pattern. Lucrece, alone
and estranged from familiar surroundings, sees in her mind's eye a
depiction of Troy's destruction. Like Aeneas, she weeps to look on
her present sorrow pictured forth in "Troy's painted woes"
(1492). Like Aeneas, she focuses on the human tragedies of the
war, the struggles between Greeks and Trojans "from the strond
of Dardan, where they fought, / To Simois' reedy banks" (1436–
7), and the destruction of the city, bright with fire. Although
Shakespeare draws upon *Metamorphoses* XIII as well as the
Aeneid, he depicts the same Greek cruelty and treachery, the same
Trojan helplessness, and the same pervasive sense of doom. In
Shakespeare's *ekphrasis* Vergil's Achilles is joined by proud Pyrrhus and deceitful Sinon, his piteous Priam and Hector by despairing Hecuba. The vicarious experience of Trojan woe brings Lucrece, as it does Aeneas, "from the feeling of her own grief" (1578)
to a new sense of comfort and relief. She marvels at the sympathetic imagination of the "well-skill'd workman" (1520) who understands the tears of things and whose heart, like those of the Car-
thaginians and the Trojans, is touched by mortal sorrows.

Shakespeare's remembrance of Troy in *Lucrece* draws upon
Vergil's *Aeneid* II, the nightmarish *Iliupersis*, as well as *Aeneid* I.
This account, studied by generations of Elizabethan school-
children, proliferated by countless adaptations (including Ovid's
and Livy's) and references, became one of Shakespeare's most
fertile poetic acquisitions, a deep source for many future allusions.[23] In the climactic incident of the original, Pyrrhus, animated
by his father's fury, breaks through various gates and doors to
reach the innermost chambers of Priam's house:

> instat vi patria Pyrrhus: nec claustra nec ipsi
> custodes sufferre valent; labat ariete crebro

---

[23]See Harry Levin's discussion, "An Explication of the Player's Speech," reprinted from *KR*, 12 (1950), in *The Question of "Hamlet"* (New York: Oxford University Press, 1959), pp. 138–64.

ianua et emoti procumbunt cardine postes.
fit via vi.

(491–4)

On presses Pyrrhus with his father's might; no bars, no
warders even can stay his course. The gate totters under the
ram's many blows and the doors, wrenched from their
sockets, fall forward. Force finds a way.

Priam, horrified, sees Pyrrhus and prepares to defend his home:

urbis uti captae casum convolsaque vidit
limina tectorum et medium in penetralibus hostem,
arma diu senior desueta trementibus aevo
circumdat nequiquam umeris et inutile ferrum
cingitur, ac densos fertur moriturus in hostis.

(507–11)

When he saw the fall of the captured city, saw the doors of
the house wrenched off, and the foe in the heart of his
home, old as he is, he vainly throws his long-disused
armour about his aged trembling shoulders, girds on his
useless sword, and rushes to his death among his thronging
foes.

Arrogantly, Pyrrhus scorns Priam, slaughters one of his sons, Prince Polites, and then kills the aged King on one of his own altars.

The full force and power of the original must frustrate the most
skilled translator. In the lines immediately above Vergil sets up a
parallel construction with the verb *vidit* and its three direct objects, *casum, limina,* and *hostem.* The succession of long syllables
in line 507, *ŭ/tī cāp/tae cās/ūm cōn/volsă/que,* the alliteration of
the hard *c* sound, and the placement of *casum* between the perfect
participle modifying *urbis* and the one modifying *limina* all suggest the interrelatedness of the two actions described: namely, the
fall of Troy and the fall of Priam's house. *Convolsa,* like all Latin
perfect participles,[24] carries a stronger substantive force than its

[24]"The Latin perfect participle is not fully described as a verbal adjective, normally passive and past-perfect in meaning. It can be more strongly predicative,
and carry in its predication the sense of what in English would be a noun.
Mortuus Romulus is more likely to mean 'Romulus is dead,' or even more
characteristically 'the death of Romulus,' than 'dead Romulus.'" W. F. Jack-
son Knight, *Roman Vergil,* 3rd ed. (1966; rpt. New York: Barnes & Noble
Books, 1971), p. 242.

English equivalent, and so its placement before *vidit* reinforces the parallel between the smaller and larger actions. Thus Vergil presents simultaneously Pyrrhus's invasion of Priam's house and the Greek invasion of Troy.[25] The destruction of the King's private home symbolizes the destruction of the surrounding city; the murder of Priam symbolizes the fall of Troy. In *Metamorphoses* XIII, Ovid summarizes the matter pithily: *Troia simul Priamusque cadunt* (404), "Troy fell and Priam with it."

Vergil's use of the word *penetralibus* also has resonant significance. Cooper's *Thesavrvs* (1565) defines *penetrale* as "the inner parte of the house." Servius, whose commentary on the *Aeneid* Shakespeare may have read, provides an interesting gloss to Vergil's *medium in penetralibus hostem* (508):

> sane penetralia proprie deorum dicuntur, non numquam
> etiam imae et interiores partes privatarum domorum
> vocantur, unde et penum dicimus locum ubi conduntur
> quae ad vitam sunt necessaria. hic autem videtur
> opportunius penetralia de domo regis dixisse, quoniam
> reges prope suggestum imitantur deorum.[26]

Certainly the word "penetralia" refers properly to the chambers of the gods, but sometimes to the deepest and most interior parts of a private house, whence we name the place for storing food "penetralia," that is, the place where we keep all things which are necessary for life. The word seems more appropriate to the home of a king because kings are nearer to the place of gods and resemble them.

Roasted in wrath and fire, Pyrrhus invades Priam's *penetralia* and violates person, household, family, and city; he slays a son before his father, a father before his wife and daughters, a king before his subjects. This sacrilegious intrusion profanes the sacred residence of the household gods. Pyrrhus's slaughter blasphemously parodies the rituals of lawful sacrifice that regulate human interaction with the gods. The blow that sends Priam's soul to the

[25] Robert Kilburn Root, *Classical Mythology in Shakespeare,* Yale Studies in English, No. 19 (New York: Holt, 1903), notes that Shakespeare frequently uses "Ilium," another name for Troy, to refer to Priam's place (pp. 76–7).

[26] *Servianorvm in Vergilii Carmina Commentariorvm, Editio Harvardiana,* Special Publications of the American Philological Association, No. 1, Vol. II (Lancaster, Pa., 1946), p. 450.

shades below resounds not only in the household, family, and city, but in the entire universe and the heavens themselves. Pyrrhus's attack on the *penetralia* is an attack on all the physical and spiritual principles necessary for human life, *quae ad vitam sunt necessaria*. No wonder Aeneas comments, *ferit aurea sidera clamor* (488), "The din strikes the golden stars."

The importance of this climactic incident to Shakespeare's dramatic imagination and to his conception of Rome is clearly evident in *Lucrece*. The pictorial representation of Priam's death arrests Lucrece's gaze and closely mirrors her own predicament:

> Many she sees where cares have carved some,
> But none where all distress and dolor dwell'd,
> Till she despairing Hecuba beheld,
>   Staring on Priam's wounds with her old eyes,
>   Which bleeding under Pyrrhus' proud foot lies.
>
> (1445–9)

Seeing in Hecuba an image of her own grief, Lucrece assumes the identity of an onlooker and achieves some distance from her situation. However momentary and illusory, the identification with Hecuba enables her to give tongue to unspeakable sorrows. As the imaginary *ekphrasis* works its magic, she envisions herself as Priam:

> To me came Tarquin armed to beguild
> With outward honesty, but yet defil'd
>   With inward vice: as Priam him did cherish,
>   So did I Tarquin, so my Troy did perish.
>
> (1544–7)

Here Lucrece becomes the central figure in the Trojan tragedy, "slain" by the barbaric invader in the *penetralia* of her home. *Hostis ut hospes init penetralia Collatini*, wrote Ovid (*Fasti* II.787), "In the guise of a guest the foe found his way into the home of Collatinus," thus employing the resonant term *penetralia* and perhaps evoking for Shakespeare the Vergilian parallels.

The terms of the *ekphrasis* aptly cast Tarquin in the role of Pyrrhus. Like the Greek, Tarquin is a cruel and bloody usurper armed with a gleaming weapon. Like Pyrrhus, he breaks through locks and doors until he reaches the inmost recesses of his victim's home. Both invaders aim at the very center of civil stability, the midpoint of the concentric circles of social order, and both attack with the fury of their fathers. Their deeds crack the foundations of civilized life and turn the city into wilderness.

As he remembers Vergil, of course, Shakespeare transforms him. Aeneas identifies with himself in the Trojan tableau and occupies a fixed position. Lucrece, however, identifies with others, each illuminating a different aspect of her character and situation. She sees herself as the despairing Hecuba and then as the slaughtered Priam. These images fading, guilt and self-reproach cause a fleeting identification with Helen, whose "eye kindled the fire that burneth here" (1475). Lucrece's subsequent rage, the desire to tear at Helen's beauty, reflects her own wish for self-destruction and foreshadows her suicide. Soon after, Lucrece sees herself again as Priam, not as the murdered King under Pyrrhus's proud foot, but, unchronologically, as the gullible ruler who believed Sinon's lies. The various images of Troy and Trojan figures chart Lucrece's changing perception of herself from anguished onlooker to active participant in the tragedy. They provide her with objective correlatives that articulate her feelings of confusion, shock, sorrow, despair, anger, self-reproach, and finally guilt.

The shifting terms of the Trojan conceit also chart Lucrece's changing perception of Tarquin. He evolves from Pyrrhus, the cruel invader, to the anticlimactic Paris, another violator of hospitality by rape, the logical counterpart to Lucrece's Helen (1471–91). The conceit wobbles perceptibly in these lines, especially when Priam reenters as the doting father who should have restrained Paris's lust. It recovers some equilibrium as Lucrece comes to understand that Tarquin played the contemptible role of Sinon, who hid evil intent behind good appearance.[27] This understanding moves Lucrece beyond awareness of physical outrage to a horrified realization of the rapist's moral iniquity. It signifies that she has acquired the painful knowledge of experience unimagined by her former innocent self, the bird "never lim'd" (88), that she

---

[27]Commentators on Ovid provided ample precedent for this identification. See Baldwin, *Genetics of Shakspere's Poems*, pp. 144–6.

has discovered the discrepancy between appearance and reality and confronted evil incarnate.

Lucrece's response to the fall of Troy suggests the dimensions of her own fall. After the rape she no longer resides at the center of the various concentric circles of social order; instead, she exists somewhere on the outside, an exile from all she knew. The realistic details of setting that initially place her in the bedroom and home give way to images of wandering and dislocation. Like Aeneas, she voyages on the perilous ocean far from hearth, home, and country, "an unpractic'd swimmer plunging still" (1098), "deep drenched in a sea of care" (1100), while "deep woes roll forward like a gentle flood" (1118). Believing natural wilderness to be more hospitable than Rome, she wishes to find out "some dark deep desert seated from the way" (1144) and to sing sad songs there to savage beasts.

Resisting despair, however, Lucrece seeks a way to regain her former identity as "chaste wife" and her former position in the city. She ponders the question of suicide and wonders if the destruction of her body will mean the destruction of her soul as well (1154ff.). She concludes that the rape has already endangered her soul:

> Ay me, the bark pill'd from the lofty pine,
> His leaves will wither and his sap decay;
> So must my soul, her bark being pill'd away.
>
> (1167–9)

Lucrece believes that her body and soul are related organically, just as are the bark, leaves, and sap of a single tree. The only way to rescue the soul from the body's decay, she decides, is to break the organic union by committing suicide.

Despite Lucrece's plea, "let it not be call'd impiety" (1174), her decision to commit suicide has become a crux for Christian interpretation.[28] In his discussion of Lucrece, Saint Augustine poses

[28]See Roy W. Battenhouse, *Shakespearean Tragedy: Its Art and Its Christian Premises* (Bloomington: Indiana University Press, 1969), pp. 3–41; D. C. Al-

the important ethical dilemma: *si adulterata, cur laudata; si pudica, cur occisa?*, "If she was made an adulteress, why has she been praised; if she was chaste, why was she slain?"[29] He then contrasts Lucrece with outraged Christian women who patiently suffered their bodies' stain, confident that their souls were pure in God's eyes. These women, Saint Augustine notes approvingly, chose to endure *offensionem suspicionis humanae*, "the scandal of man's suspicion," rather than to evade it unlawfully.

Saint Augustine's remarks place Shakespeare's Lucrece in sharp relief from the Christians he praises. Unlike them, Lucrece does not distinguish clearly between body and soul, but believes both to be defiled.[30] She cannot rest easily in the sight of an omniscient God, secure in the justice of divine judgment, but must rely on the imperfect vision of men and seek justice in their fallible judgments. Hence, the "scandal of man's suspicion" is no trivial inconvenience to be patiently suffered; it is rather the sole moral authority by which Lucrece can measure her virtue and define her being. Her vow to commit suicide articulates the crucial terms of her moral universe:

> Mine honor be the knife's that makes my wound,
> My shame be his that did my fame confound;
>   And all my fame that lives disbursed be
>   To those that live and think no shame of me.
>
> (1201–4)

"Honor," "shame," "fame" – the opinions of others – constitute the only frame of reference by which one can judge actions in Lucrece's world, the world of Rome. Throughout the poem this cluster of secular values lies behind every major action. Lucrece's fame, her reputation for beauty and worth, first arouses Tarquin.

---

len, "Some Observations on *The Rape of Lucrece*," *ShS*, 15 (1962), 89–98. See also Malcolm Andrew, "Christian Ideas about Sin and the First Stanza of *Lucrece*," *RES*, NS 24 (1973), 179–82; and, for a dissenting view, Richard Levin, "The Ironic Reading of *The Rape of Lucrece* and the Problem of External Evidence," *ShS*, 34 (1981), 85–92.

[29]*Saint Augustine: The City of God against the Pagans*, trans. George E. Mc-Cracken et al., The Loeb Classical Library, 7 vols. (1957–72), Vol. I, pp. 88, 89. The quotation and translation below appear on pp. 90, 91.

[30]Lucrece maintains until the end, however, that she never wanted to submit to Tarquin. Thus she can claim that her "mind," as distinguished from her soul, remains unstained (1656, 1710).

After seeing her, he hesitates because he fears that the shame attached to rape will endure long after his death, forever associated with his name, forever the shame of his descendants:

> Yea, though I die, the scandal will survive,
> And be an eye-sore in my golden coat;
> Some loathsome dash the herald will contrive,
> To cipher me how fondly I did dote;
> That my posterity, sham'd with the note,
>   Shall curse my bones, and hold it for no sin
>   To wish that I their father had never been.
>
> (204–10)

Lucrece submits to the rape because Tarquin threatens to kill her and a manservant and place their corpses together in bed, thus bringing shame to her and her family: Collatine would become "the scornful mark of every open eye"; kinsmen would "hang their heads at this disdain"; her children would be "blurr'd with nameless bastardy"; and she would be remembered in verse and song as an adulteress (519–25). After the rape she fears the harsh judgment of posterity – the future nurse with child, the orator, the feast-finding minstrels (813–19). Brutus takes action later because Rome has been "disgraced" (1833). Lucrece decides to commit suicide to exonerate herself in the only court of judgment she knows – that of human opinion. In so doing, she hopes to become for all time the model of a chaste wife instead of the prototype for a fallen woman, to transform, as she puts it, her shame to fame.

Because Lucrece seeks both a reconciliation with her family and a public exoneration, she summons her father and her husband to Collatia. After commencing the session, she pleads her case, delivers the verdict, passes judgment, and proceeds to carry out the sentence:

> Even here she sheathed in her harmless breast
> A harmful knife, that thence her soul unsheathed;
> That blow did bail it from the deep unrest
> Of that polluted prison where it breathed.
> Her contrite sighs unto the clouds bequeathed
>   Her winged sprite, and through her wounds doth fly
>   Life's lasting date from cancell'd destiny.[31]
>
> (1723–9)

---

[31] I depart from Evans here and read "Life's" for "Live's."

The imagery of bondage and release signifies that Lucrece's action fulfills her intention. She frees her troubled soul from its "polluted prison" and sends it winging toward the clouds with contrite sighs. The histrionics of the suicide and of the entire scene suggest not a private gesture of guilt and despair, but a public act of self-assertion and vindication. The suicide is an exercise of *pietas,* the quintessentially Roman and Vergilian subordination of self to the obligations of family and city. It transforms Lucrece into a symbol of constancy and honor, thereby winning the fame that to her mind is an acquittal and a glorious reward.

The success of Lucrece's suicide is immediately confirmed by the reaction of its audience. The mourning of father and husband fills the air with cries of "My daughter!" and "My wife!" (1804), signaling the reinstatement of Lucrece to her proper place in the family. No longer is she the alienated wanderer in the woods, fit only for the company of beasts; now she has regained her identity, returned home, and restored order in Collatia. This restoration of order, like the violation, must extend beyond the immediate circles of family and home to the greater walls of Rome. Lucrece provides for this extension by swearing the spectators to vengeance before she dies. In a gesture that illustrates the continuity between Lucrece's action and the events that follow, Brutus plucks out the bloody knife and vows by it to "revenge the death of this true wife" (1841).[32] The subsequent bearing of Lucrece's body through Rome demonstrates that her desire for fame, for the reputation of honor, has been fulfilled: She is transformed into a symbol of chastity, fidelity, and constancy, a corporeal emblem of virtue for the people of Rome, as well as for those of other places and times.

***

Shakespeare's first full encounter with the ancient city of Rome provides a good introduction to his later dramatic works. The

[32]The perfunctory workmanship of the concluding verses, which briefly allude to the revolution of state, argues tellingly against the political interpretations of the poem advanced by E. P. Kuhl, "Shakespeare's *Rape of Lucrece, PQ,* 20 (1941), 352–60; and Michael Platt, "*The Rape of Lucrece* and the Republic for Which It Stands," *Cent R,* 19 (1975), 59–79.

poem presents the physical features of the city: its walls, Capitol, rival city, private house, and outlying fields. In addition, *Lucrece* depicts the city as a place of order and hierarchy opposed to the primitive wilderness and surging ocean. These motifs function as elements of a symbolic language that Shakespeare uses throughout his Roman canon with increasing skill and subtlety. The predominant metaphor of siege, which here fuses the personal and political conflicts, recurs with greater complexity in the plays. In *Lucrece* the moral issues raised by the siege are relatively clear-cut and straightforward. The besieging Tarquin is evil and his invasion execrable villainy; the besieged Lucrece is good, an avatar of Roman virtue. In contradistinction to *Lucrece,* the drama will derive much of its impact from moral ambiguity and paradox.

Lucrece also provides a glimpse of many themes that will occupy Shakespeare's attention in the Roman plays. We encounter *pietas,* an essential Roman virtue for Shakespeare as well as Vergil, and observe the vital relationship between Roman family and city. Here the city is the family writ large, possessing the same virtues, suffering the same injuries, embracing the same remedies. Not so later. We note as well the interplay between honor and constancy and the demands these ideals make on individual Romans. *Lucrece* also reveals the Roman body bruised to pleasure the Roman soul. The blade that pierces her breast and lets her blood reappears in various forms as Shakespeare's Romans wreak destruction on themselves for fame and glory.

The narrative method of Shakespeare's first full encounter with Rome, of course, differs fundamentally from the dramatic method of the plays. There are, however, important continuities in imaginative technique. Eclectically, Shakespeare ranges over a variety of sources to create an image of the ancient city and its citizens. Appearing here, as elsewhere, is Troy, the ancestral city whose inhabitants and history live on in Rome. Allusion to Troy in *Lucrece* is artificial and ostentatious, embodied in the formal device of *ekphrasis*. What is self-conscious and external in the poem will become subtle and integral in the plays. This dictum applies equally well to the imagery of *Lucrece,* that purple outpouring of decoration and conceit. One admires Shakespeare's fertility of invention but must wonder about his discipline. In addition to the overingenious figures and relentless moralizing, the verse exhibits a *copia* that often oppresses rather than stimulates. The much-admired image of Lucrece as a "pale swan in her wat'ry nest" (1611), for example, loses much of its luster (assuming, of course, that the reader has not yet tired of animal and bird images) when we note that essentially the same image describes Tarquin six hundred lines earlier. With time and experience Shakespeare will harness his imaginative energies to produce images of cumulative power and richness.

Lucrece provides an instructive view of Shakespeare's early conception of Rome and his imaginative technique. The narrative verse of the poem, obviously an inappropriate medium for dramatic characterization, creates distances between author, work, and reader and results in a tone best described as Ovidian. Thus we conclude where we began, with Ovid, but this time with the author of the *Metamorphoses* not the *Fasti*. For Shakespeare's story of Lucrece and her suicide resembles nothing so much as an Ovidian tale of transformation. Of course, Shakespeare is not interested in the transformation of a human being into an animal, flower, or stream, but in the transformation of a human being into a legend, into a symbol for all time. Reuben A. Brower's perceptive comments on Ovid apply equally well to Shakespeare's tale of Lucrece:

> Violence runs its full course as it must; suffering and
> vengeance lead to beautiful or pitiable or monstrous
> changes of the persons who are their victims. Ovid's is not
> a morality of comment or exemplum, but of imaginative
> vision of humanity gone astray. This is the true 'Philoso-
> phie of turnèd shapes,' not the lessons of *Ovide moralisé*.[33]

We may well wish to keep these thoughts in mind as we turn to the pitiable and monstrous changes of *Titus Andronicus*.

[33]Brower, p. 135.

III

TITUS ANDRONICUS
ROME AND THE FAMILY

Probably the most striking feature of modern critical reaction to *Titus Andronicus* is the persistent refusal to consider it one of Shakespeare's Roman plays. Early in the century, the abundant bloodletting and lurid action caused John M. Robertson to discern various hands in the play and to deny it a place in Shakespeare's canon.[1] The disintegrationist furor having died down, most critics now emphasize the importance of *Titus Andronicus* to Shakespeare's artistic development, specifically to the histories and great tragedies that follow.[2] Critics of Shakespeare's Rome generally follow the precedent of M. W. MacCallum, who relegates *Titus Andronicus* to a place apart from the Plutarchan tragedies:

> It is pretty certain then that *Julius Caesar* is the first not only of the Roman Plays, but of the great series of Tragedies. The flame-tipped welter of *Titus Andronicus*, the poignant radiance of *Romeo and Juliet* belong to Shakespeare's pupilage and youth. Their place is apart from each other and the rest in the vestibule and forecourt of his art.[3]

The vestibule has become a closet. Recent examinations of Shakespeare's Rome by Maurice Charney, Derek Traversi, J. L. Simmons, Paul A. Cantor, and Michael Platt either ignore *Titus*

Parts of this chapter appeared as an article, "*Titus Andronicus* and the Mythos of Shakespeare's Rome," *ShakS*, 14 (1981), 85–98.

[1] *Did Shakespeare Write "Titus Andronicus": A Study in Elizabethan Literature* (London: Watts, 1905). Cf. T. W. Baldwin, *On the Literary Genetics of Shakspere's Plays, 1592–1594* (Urbana: University of Illinois Press, 1959), pp. 402–20.

[2] See E. M. W. Tillyard, *Shakespeare's History Plays* (New York: Macmillan, 1946), pp. 137–41; A. C. Hamilton, *The Early Shakespeare* (San Marino, Calif.: Huntington Library, 1967), pp. 63–89 (85–9); J. C. Maxwell, ed., *Titus Andronicus*, The Arden Shakespeare, 3rd ed. (1961; rpt. London: Methuen, 1968), pp. xxxix–xlii; G. K. Hunter, "Shakespeare's Earliest Tragedies: 'Titus Andronicus' and 'Romeo and Juliet,'" *ShS*, 27 (1974), 1–9; Jimmy Lee Williams, "*Titus Andronicus* and Shakespeare's Mature Tragedies: A Study in Continuity," dissertation, Indiana University, 1971.

[3] MacCallum, p. 177.

42

Andronicus completely or skim over it.[4] Employing his three criteria for *Romanitas* – use of Roman costume, praise of suicide, source in North's Plutarch – Maurice Charney summarily dismisses *Titus Andronicus:* "Rome in *Titus Andronicus* is only the setting for a revenge play, which is based on such fictional classical themes as the Revenge of Atreus and the Rape of Philomela."[5]
The play, however, gives ample evidence of Roman character. According to T. W. Baldwin, the word "Roman" appears in the title of the chapbook, "The History of Titus Andronicus, The Renowned Roman General"; in the Stationers' Register entry, "a Noble Roman Historye of Tytus Andronicus"; and in the titles of the quartos of 1594 and 1600, "The Most Lamentable Romaine Tragedie of Titus Andronicus."[6] Moreover, as T. J. B. Spencer argues, there are many indications that Shakespeare attempts to create in *Titus Andronicus* a recognizably Roman world.[7] The city is named frequently, occurring more times in this play than in *Julius Caesar* and *Antony and Cleopatra* combined.[8] Quotations in Latin appear here along with references to Roman customs, people, political institutions, and historical events. The language reveals a conscious attempt to create a Roman style, exhibiting throughout an unusual predilection for Latinate vocabulary.[9]
What is more important, the play shows many of the Roman features that appear in *Lucrece* and in the other Roman works. Central to Shakespeare's imaginative conception is the city, defined by contrast with other landscapes and depicted once again as

[4]Platt, *Rome and Romans According to Shakespeare*, Salzburg Studies in English Literature, JDS, No. 51 (Salzburg: Institut für Englische Sprache und Literatur, 1976). Among the few who discuss *Titus Andronicus* as Shakespeare's first Roman play are Robert Adger Law, "The Roman Background of *Titus Andronicus*," *SP*, 40 (1943), 145–53; Andrew V. Ettin, "Shakespeare's First Roman Tragedy," *ELH*, 37 (1970), 325–41. Ettin's interesting discussion of Vergilian elements differs from the present one in its emphasis and conclusions.
[5]Charney, p. 207.
[6]*Genetics of Shakspere's Plays*, p. 402.
[7]"Shakespeare and the Elizabethan Romans," *ShS*, 10 (1957), 27–38 (32).
[8]A check of Martin Spevack's *Concordance*, 9 vols. (Hildesheim: Georg Olms, 1968–80) reveals that "Rome" appears 83 times in *Titus Andronicus*, 38 in *Julius Caesar*, and 30 in *Antony and Cleopatra*. Including cognates, the word appears 130 times in *Titus Andronicus*, 113 in *Coriolanus*, 73 in *Julius Caesar*, 44 in *Cymbeline*, 39 in *Antony and Cleopatra*, and 15 in *Lucrece*.
[9]See H. T. Price, "The Authorship of 'Titus Andronicus,'" *JEGP*, 42 (1943), 55–81 (67–8).

the reincarnation of Priam's Troy. As in *Lucrece,* the city wel-
comes invaders, admitting within its walls a Trojan horse that will
violate its *penetralia.* As before, Romans live and die in a restricted
ethical universe, one dominated by a military conception of honor
and by a desire for fame. And once again civil turmoil and rebellion overturn established order. Evident here is Shakespeare's
growing interest in the processes of Roman government, in the
secular problems of power and order, and in the political and
moral issues raised by the clash between private interest and public
duty. In *Titus Andronicus* the clash reverberates through all of
Rome, destroying the life of the individual, the unity of the family,
and the order in the city. Roman heroic traditions act here as a
source of strength and nobility; yet they also force Romans to lead
lives that are increasingly at odds with human instincts and needs.

⁌⚬⚬⚬⁍

Rome is the immediate focus of attention in the opening scene as
rival princes vie for the "imperial diadem" (6). References to distinguishing physical features – the Capitol (12), walls (26), Senate
(27), and Pantheon (242, 333) – construct the city in the viewer's
mind. The opening scene portrays Rome in deep distress: Having
survived wars with the "barbarous Goths" (28), it now suffers the
rise of opposing factions. Both sides defiantly approach the Senate
walls and address the senators above, thus besieging the city anew.
Despite the examples of the chapbook and *Lucrece,* Shakespeare
chooses not to dramatize the conflict between the barbarian outsiders and the city. Instead, he focuses on the political conflict
inside city walls, on the internal struggle for power that his next
Roman play, *Julius Caesar,* will explore more fully.

After the rival princes agree to abide by the decision of Titus
Andronicus, the stage clears and "Rome's best champion" (65),
having been twice announced, enters amid drums and trumpets,
surrounded by "*others as many as can be*" (s.d. 69). The ceremonious language of Titus's opening speech complements the formal pageantry on stage:

Hail, Rome, victorious in thy mourning weeds!
Lo, as the bark that hath discharg'd his fraught
Returns with precious lading to the bay
From whence at first she weigh'd her anchorage,
Cometh Andronicus, bound with laurel boughs,
To re-salute his country with his tears,
Tears of true joy for his return to Rome.

(70–6)

The paradoxical greeting to the personified city, the simile culmin-
ating in the third-person reference to himself, the repetition and
explanation of "tears," and the closing alliterative reference to
Rome are all rhetorical devices that convey the speaker's dignity,
gravity, and importance. The peremptory invocation to Jupiter
Capitolinus, "Thou great defender of this Capitol, / Stand gra-
cious to the rites that we intend!" (77–8), emphasizes Titus's
power and authority while formally commencing the burial ritual.
Titus asks the assembled citizens to behold the remainder of his
twenty-five sons, "Half of the number that King Priam had" (80).
The allusion suggests with prophetic irony that Titus is another
Priam, father of many valiant but doomed sons. After exhorting
the Romans to honor the survivors, Titus reproves himself:

Titus, unkind and careless of thine own,
Why suffer'st thou thy sons, unburied yet,
To hover on the dreadful shore of Styx?

(86–8)

As many note, this question echoes the conversation of Aeneas and
Hecate in hell. Responding to Aeneas's question about the pleading throng of souls, Hecate answers that the unburied dead (*inhu-
mata* [VI.325]) hover (*volitant* [329]) on the shores of Styx for a
hundred years. The echoing of epic and mythic passages in Titus's
speech, along with the direct address to himself and the exaggerated posture of self-reproach, threatens to turn the entire scene
into melodrama.

The portentous solemnity and formal pageantry of Titus's entrance characterize him as a figure who steps out from the sometimes grandiose, sometimes sordid welter of Roman history to
strut his hour upon the Elizabethan stage. Titus is not an indi-

45

vidual with a famous biography, as is Lucrece, Caesar, or Antony, but a composite of various characteristics vaguely conceived of as Roman. Shakespeare "seems anxious," T. J. B. Spencer remarks, "not to get it all right, but to get it all in."[10] Titus first appears manifestly larger than life: The noble Roman soldier who vanquishes the enemy outside the walls returns home to restore peace in the city. As the allusion to *Aeneid* VI suggests, Titus is a figure of Aeneas as well as Priam, even sharing with the legendary founder of Rome the epithet "pius" (23). For his fellow citizens, as well as for the people in the audience, Titus embodies *Romanitas*, here defined as a military code of honor that encompasses the virtues of pride, courage, constancy, integrity, discipline, service, and self-sacrifice. Shakespeare carefully illustrates the operation of this code in the opening funeral march: Titus does not weep tears of sorrow for his dead sons, but tears of joy for his return to Rome. So completely does he try to identify personal and civil welfare that the panoply of public triumph, theoretically at least, subsumes all private grief.

Titus's ceremonious entrance and oration function as a dramatic emblem that articulates and defines Rome. Strikingly apparent in this emblem is the centrality of the family. Here, as in *Lucrece*, the family is the fundamental unit of social structure: The family and city follow the same laws, esteem the same values, and obey the same patriarch, Titus, later called "father" of Rome (423). The Andronici protect the city and stand as avatars of its spiritual life, living symbols of Roman character and moral fiber. In the roles of wife, mother, and daughter, Lucrece embodies the feminine virtues essential to the existence of the city; victorious in mourning, Titus and his sons embody the essential masculine virtues. Prominent in center stage, the Andronici tomb joins the historical past of Rome with its living present and undreamed future. It is the focus of a communal ritual that transforms the deaths of sons and brothers into an affirmation of Roman life.

As the opening scene defines Rome for the audience, it also questions Roman values. Lucius demands a prisoner's blood in order to complete the burial ritual. As there is no precedent for this demand in the chapbook, and as Roman burial rituals did not

[10]Spencer, "Shakespeare and the Elizabethan Romans," p. 32.

require human sacrifice, one may wonder what Shakespeare is about here. A look at Lucius's language reveals the dramatic intention behind the historically inaccurate borrowing from Seneca's *Troades:*[11]

> Give us the proudest prisoner of the Goths,
> That we may hew his limbs and on a pile
> *Ad manes fratrum* sacrifice his flesh.
>
> (96–8)

Lucius's demand cuts through the ceremonious fanfare and jolts the audience.[12] The placing of the blunt and vivid English, "hew his limbs and on a pile," next to the formal Latinate phrase, "*Ad manes fratrum,*" exposes a fundamental tension in the proceedings: It suggests that Roman ritual is barbaric savagery and blood lust. The noble sentiments and hallowed abstractions of the funeral ceremony sound less grand and glorious as they lead to the death and dismemberment of a living human being, Alarbus, silent and trembling before our eyes.[13]

The perspective by which we see the masculine code of military honor embodied in Roman ritual as rigid, merciless, and predatory is developed, appropriately, by a woman. Tamora appeals to the individual persons beneath the Roman togas, to the living human beings within the historical pageant:

> Stay, Roman brethren! Gracious conqueror,
> Victorious Titus, rue the tears I shed,
> A mother's tears in passion for her son;
> And if thy sons were ever dear to thee,
> O, think my son to be as dear to me!
>
> (104–8)

Tamora's use of the word "brethren" startles us into remembering that there are some claims upon the Andronici larger and more important than those of Rome. Coming amid repetitions of the word, all referring to Andronici, the sound of "brethren" in Tam-

---

[11]See George Lyman Kittredge, ed., *The Complete Works of Shakespeare* (Boston: Ginn, 1936), p. 972. On Shakespeare's use of Seneca in this play, see Bullough, Vol. VI, pp. 26–9.

[12]For analysis of this passage I am indebted to Nicholas Brooke, *Shakespeare's Early Tragedies* (London: Methuen, 1968), pp. 22ff.

[13]It will be obvious that I, along with most modern editors, accept Rowe's addition of Alarbus to the personae named in s.d. 69, so as to make possible his exit a few moments later, s.d. 129.

ora's mouth suggests a universal brotherhood, one derived from common humanity. Tamora's brave sons are dear to her, just as Titus's are dear to him. And just as Titus's sons hope to grant their brothers eternal rest, so Tamora's sons hope to preserve Alarbus from mortal harm. Tamora challenges Roman *pietas* to encompass those brothers outside the immediate family, to recognize the human identity that transcends national disputes.

Tamora's spontaneous and stirring appeal, a marked contrast to Titus's histrionic obsequies, fails to move her audience. Titus mechanically replies that the Andronici "brethren" (122) require a sacrifice, while Lucius eagerly looks to the hewing of limbs and the burning of flesh. As Alarbus is led away, the Goths ironically remark the "cruel, irreligious piety" (130) of the Romans, and observe that Scythia never was "half so barbarous" as ambitious Rome (131).[14] In an accompanying stroke of irony, the newly bereaved brothers liken Tamora to Hecuba, Priam's sorrowing wife (136ff.). This allusion, recalling the earlier comparison of Titus to Priam, confirms Tamora's arguments by insisting upon that which Titus and sons fail to see (and which Tamora and sons soon forget): namely, that Romans and Goths share a common sorrow and a common humanity.

The tensions in Shakespeare's Rome, revealed by Lucius's speech and the confrontation with Tamora, swiftly break down the order in the family and the city. Acting with inflexible self-righteousness, adhering strictly to custom and law, Titus decides the civil dispute in favor of the elder brother, Saturninus. Consigning his daughter to the role of empress, he ceremoniously devotes himself to the new ruler:

> And here in sight of Rome to Saturnine,
> King and commander of our commonweal,
> The wide world's emperor, do I consecrate
> My sword, my chariot, and my prisoners,
> Presents well worthy Rome's imperious lord.
>
> (246–50)

The pose of humility and self-abnegation notwithstanding, Titus fully enjoys his role in the center of attention, "in sight of Rome,"

---

[14]Cf. Lear's mention of "The barbarous Scythian, / Or he that makes his generation messes / To gorge his appetite" (I.i.116–18).

and fully appreciates the value of his offerings, "Presents well worthy Rome's imperious lord." When Bassianus interrupts the ceremony of reconciliation by stealing the bride, he acts on the subversive principle that personal happiness outvalues family loyalty and civil stability; he also insults the authority and dignity of Titus himself. Titus responds immediately by drawing his sword, only to confront, however, his own sons. The ensuing melee depicts the complete disintegration of the order operative in *Lucrece,* wherein familial and civic values coincide. Here brother battles brother, and father eventually kills son, who dies calling upon his brother for help:

> *Titus:* What, villain boy,
> Barr'st me my way in Rome?
> *Mutius:* Help, Lucius, help! *Titus kills him.*
>
> (290–1)

The emblem of Roman order quickly degenerates into a vision of chaos and brutality as the Andronici create the civil division that Titus was summoned to prevent. The process of degeneration reveals fundamental weaknesses in Rome and basic paradoxes in its values. The gestalt of Roman virtues including "justice, continence, and nobility" (I.i.15), so essential to Titus's success in battle, appears inside the city walls as an intractable combination of pride, self-righteousness, and a desire for self-aggrandizement. The audience must squint especially hard to determine which shape it sees when Titus, his dead son lying on the stage, complains about not being invited to the royal wedding and about his fallen status in the city:

> I am not bid to wait upon this bride.
> Titus, when wert thou wont to walk alone,
> Dishonored thus and challenged of wrongs?
>
> (338–40)

Moreover, Roman honor, with its subordination of private feeling to public responsibility, transforms the city into barbaric chaos.[15] Titus's vision of Rome and his place in it blinds him to Alarbus, just as it blinds him to his own sons and daughter. Titus

---

[15]The crucial conflict is not simply between Rome and barbarism, as some have argued. See, for example, Alan Sommers, "'Wilderness of Tigers': Structure and Symbolism in *Titus Andronicus,*" *EIC,* 10 (1960), 275–89.

the "Pius" impiously slays a son for the unthinkable crime of standing in the way. Because the Roman family appears as the basic unit of the city, Titus's attack on Mutius is an attack on Rome itself. However necessary to the defense of the city such honor is, Shakespeare clearly shows us its disastrous consequences within city walls. He who rises above the claims of kinship and common humanity in obedience to abstract ethical principles becomes monstrous and inhuman, an enemy of Rome, not an honorable protector.

In the pleading scenes that follow Titus stubbornly refuses to grant his son burial in the family tomb; he addresses his brother as "foolish tribune" (343) and his sons as "traitors" (349). Kneeling, Marcus, Martius, and Lucius insist on their blood relationship with Titus and on the importance of natural ties:

> *Marcus:* Brother, for in that name doth nature plead –
> *Martius:* Father, and in that name doth nature speak –
>
> . . . . .
>
> *Lucius:* Dear father, soul and substance of us all –
> *Marcus:*Suffer thy brother Marcus to inter
> His noble nephew here in virtue's nest.
>
> (370–1, 374–6)

Accusing Titus of "impiety" (355), Marcus pleads, "Thou art a Roman, be not barbarous" (378). Here he articulates the paradox that results when an excess of Roman virtue becomes a vice, when Titus's subordination of natural feeling to honor begins to destroy the family and to undermine the city.

The complicated activity of the first act portrays the fall of the Andronici from power and the rise of a new royal family consisting of Saturninus, Tamora, Aaron, Demetrius, and Chiron. The new ruling clan sharply contrasts with the old one:[16] It reveals its character in furtive asides and dumb shows instead of in cere-

---

[16]See Hunter, "Shakespeare's Earliest Tragedies," p. 4.

monious pageantry; it responds to the demands of expediency instead of the dictates of conscience and tradition; it substitutes deceit, self-interest, and vindictiveness for Roman integrity, self-sacrifice, and patriotism.

As the scene shifts from city to forest, the differences between the royal family and the Andronici emerge clearly. Demetrius and Chiron, the bereaved brothers of Act I, show themselves to be ignorant, selfish louts who wrangle over the rights to Lavinia and replay the fraternal strife of Saturninus and Bassianus in a minor key. Under Aaron's tutelage, they agree to join forces and rape her, to strike the "dainty doe" to the forest floor (II.ii.26). They intend to pervert the natural, sociable, conciliatory sport of "Roman hunting" (II.ii.20) to a predatory activity, an exercise of lust, violence, and cruelty.

The scene for this perversion is, of course, the forest itself, which Aaron describes as an appropriate place for evil deeds:

> The forest walks are wide and spacious,
> And many unfrequented plots there are,
> Fitted by kind for rape and villainy.
>
> (II.i.114–16)

The pun on "plots," meaning mental schemes as well as physical locations, recalls the similar use of "path" several lines earlier:

> A speedier course than ling'ring languishment
> Must we pursue, and I have found the path.
>
> (110–11)

"Path," like "plots," refers to the plan of rape as well as to the place of execution. Both puns express Aaron's view of the forest as a region of lawless freedom where one can transform imagined schemes into reality. Unlike the court, the forest has no laws of civilization, no obstructions of custom, no censuring public voices to regulate actions. Aaron observes:

> The Emperor's court is like the house of Fame,
> The palace full of tongues, of eyes, and ears;
> The woods are ruthless, dreadful, deaf, and dull.
>
> (126–8)

Obliquely, Shakespeare alludes here to Vergil's Fama, who spread the news of Aeneas's forest encounter with Dido: *tot vigiles oculi subter (mirabile dictu),* / *tot linguae, totidem ora sonant, tot subrigit auris (Aen.* IV.182–3), "as many watchful eyes below – wondrous to tell – as many tongues, as many sounding mouths, as many pricked up ears." The allusion transfers the beast from the Carthaginian forest to the Roman court, here identified as the house of Fame. The alteration of classical myth suggests that the forest outside Rome, unlike the woods outside Carthage, is silent and secluded, safe from the spying of human and divine observers, completely "shadowed from heaven's eye" (II.i.130).

Titus's joyful aubade begins the next scene and sharply contrasts with Aaron's gloomy pastoral:

> The hunt is up, the morn is bright and grey,
> The fields are fragrant and the woods are green.
> Uncouple here and let us make a bay,
> And wake the Emperor and his lovely bride,
> And rouse the Prince, and ring a hunter's peal,
> That all the court may echo with the noise.

> (II.ii.1–6)

The alliterative imagery and sprightly rhythm, including the end rhyme in Lines 1 and 3, have the lightness and brightness of many Elizabethan pastoral lyrics. Unaware of the lurking evil, Titus sees the forest as a place of crying hounds and pealing horns, a place where the wounds of civil discord can be healed and forgotten as Romans participate in wholesome communal activity. Such innocent optimism, naive though it may be, regains for Titus some of the audience's sympathy as they know full well that dark opposing forces have already begun to cloud this idyllic vision.

In the following scene Tamora contributes two other variations on the pastoral theme. The first resembles Titus's earlier description:

> My lovely Aaron, wherefore look'st thou sad,
> When every thing doth make a gleeful boast?
> The birds chaunt melody on every bush,
> The snake lies rolled in the cheerful sun,
> The green leaves quiver with the cooling wind
> And make a checker'd shadow on the ground.
> Under their sweet shade, Aaron, let us sit,
> And whilst the babbling echo mocks the hounds,
> Replying shrilly to the well-tun'd horns,

As if a double hunt were heard at once,
Let us sit down and mark their yellowing noise.

(II.iii.10–20)

Like Titus, Tamora praises the woods in lines of lyric beauty. She appreciates the color of things, the sunlight and shadow, the sounds of nature. Unlike Titus, however, Tamora does not view the woods as a place for life-renewing reconciliation; instead, she sees them as the perfect place for an illicit rendezvous. Her description of the forest is actually a seduction ploy, a rhetorical device in service of miscegenation and adultery. Her later reference to Aeneas and Dido's "counsel-keeping cave" (24) in the Carthaginian woods recalls Aaron's earlier reference to *Aeneid* IV, thereby suggesting the coincidence of their perspectives and values.

After Bassianus and Lavinia wander onto the scene, Tamora describes the forest to her approaching sons:

A barren detested vale you see it is;
The trees, though summer, yet forlorn and lean,
Overcome with moss and baleful mistletoe;
Here never shines the sun, here nothing breeds,
Unless the nightly owl or fatal raven;
And when they show'd me this abhorred pit,
They told me, here, at dead time of the night,
A thousand fiends, a thousand hissing snakes,
Ten thousand swelling toads, as many urchins,
Would make such fearful and confused cries,
As any mortal body hearing it
Should straight fall mad, or else die suddenly.

(II.iii.93–104)

Once again Tamora uses rhetoric to fulfill her evil intentions. Now she describes the forest as a barren, detested place where the animals are harbingers of doom. At night it teems with hellish fury and echoes with the eerie shrieks and wails of Senecan phantoms.[17] Clearly, this is an appropriate if fanciful description of the

---

[17]John W. Cunliffe, *The Influence of Seneca on Elizabethan Tragedy* (1893; rpt. New York: Stechert, 1925), pp. 70–1, traces the speech to *Thyestes* 650–5, 668–73, and to *Hercules Furens* 690–2. Kittredge, *Complete Works*, cites *Thyestes* 650ff. and Ovid, *Metamorphoses* VI.521 (p. 972). Law, "Roman Background," plausibly quotes Vergil, *Aeneid* VII.561–71, as a source (p. 149).

evil place where Bassianus will be murdered and Lavinia raped. The progression of the various pastoral visions to their culmination in this nightmare of supernatural violence suggests that the forest, like the city, takes its character from the controlling figures in it. Here it becomes a region of unfettered imagination where Aaron and Tamora can freely translate their cruel visions into reality.

Demetrius and Chiron waste little time before beginning this translation. Tamora exhorts them to take revenge on Bassianus and Lavinia, "Or be ye not henceforth call'd my children" (II.iii.115). Demetrius and Chiron respond by stabbing Bassianus, thereby giving perverse witness to their ancestry and to their familial loyalty. Tamora then releases Lavinia, urging her sons to take their pleasure before they kill her. The scene grotesquely parodies the familial values depicted in the opening burial ritual. Unlike the Andronici, Tamora and her family dedicate themselves to the satisfaction of base appetites, to assisting each other in murder and in rape, "the honey," Tamora says significantly, "*we* desire" (II.iii.131) (italics mine).

Bereft of her husband, alone in the wilderness, Lavinia has no recourse but to plead for mercy. Like Lucrece with Tarquin, she beseeches Tamora to be merciful, to show some signs of natural pity, to spare her from the approaching shame. Like Lucrece's, her pleas go unheeded. As Demetrius and Chiron lead her away, Lavinia begs them to be unnatural sons to their predatory mother, the tiger,[18] to act like the gentle lion of Aesop's fable or like the legendary ravens who foster lost children. As in *Lucrece,* the animal imagery here draws ultimately a picture of bestial lust and savagery. For Demetrius and Chiron quickly prove that they are not the extraordinary animals of legend and folklore, but ravenous beasts of the wilds.

The rape of Lavinia by the new Roman princes parodies her

[18]Shakespeare's frequent mention of the tiger in this play (II.iii.142; III.i.54–5; V.iii.5, 195) recalls *Georgics* II.151, where *rabidae tigres* symbolize the savagery of the iron age. Like Vergil (*Geo.* III.248; *Aen.* IV.367; XI.577), Shakespeare uses the tiger here to suggest feminine ferocity (II.iii.142; V.iii.195). Shakespeare's image of Lavinia as a hunted deer (II.i.93, 117; II.ii.26; III.i.89) likewise invites comparison with Vergil, especially with *Aeneid* IV.68–72, where Dido is described in similar terms.

Vergilian namesake's courtship and marriage by Aeneas.[19] Like Vergil's Lavinia, Shakespeare's is initially a bride promised by her father to the future ruler of Rome. Like the betrothal in the *Aeneid,* this one leads to familial and civil discord, each Lavinia becoming an innocent *causa mali tanti* (VI.93; XI.480), "source of all that woe." Shakespeare's Lavinia, however, regrettably coarse in conversation with Tamora (II.iii.66ff.), bathetic in her injury, and desperate in her revenge, differs sharply from the shadowy figure of the *Aeneid,* who speaks not a single word in the poem, who waits, silent and suffering, for the great forces of history to decide her fate. As Creusa, the Sibyl, Anchises, Faunus, and Tiberinus prophesy, the epical Lavinia and Aeneas wed and beget children who behold *omnia sub pedibus, qua Sol utrumque recurrens / aspicit Oceanum, vertique regique* (VII.100–1), "where the circling sun looks on either ocean, the whole world roll obedient beneath their feet." Their wedding is the promised end of the epic as well as the beginning of Roman civilization and Empire. In direct contrast, the rape of Shakespeare's Lavinia is a brutal expression of savagery that signals the end of Roman civilization and the beginning of a new and barbaric dispensation. Shakespeare transforms the fruitful marriage of the destined bride into the rape and mutilation of a helpless human woman.

The turning of the peaceful forest into a jungle immediately threatens Rome and the Andronici. Aaron leads Quintus and Martius to the "loathsome pit" (II.iii.193), where Bassianus's body lies and Martius promptly stumbles into it. Quintus peers over the edge of the "subtile hole . . . Whose mouth is covered with rude-growing briers, / Upon whose leaves are drops of new-shed blood" (198, 199–200); attempting to pull his brother out, he falls into the "fell devouring receptacle, / As hateful as Cocytus' misty mouth" (235–6). As A. C. Hamilton points out, the pit becomes "an active, malignant thing," an image of hell drawn from both classical and Christian sources,[20] a visual symbol of the infernal forces embodied in Aaron and Tamora. Because it was represented on the Elizabethan stage by the trapdoor, the "blood-drinking pit"

---

[19]Law, "Roman Background," notes some of the parallels between the two Lavinias (p. 146).
[20]Hamilton, *Early Shakespeare,* p. 82.

(II.iii.224) literally replaces the tomb of Act I as the hole that swallows up Titus's sons.[21] The bumbling entrance of Titus's sons into the pit, precariously close to slapstick comedy, provides the sharpest possible contrast with the ceremonious interments of Act I, thus reflecting ironically upon them while indicating the degeneration of Roman life and death under the new regime.

⚹═⟨⋈⟩═⚹

After his sons are accused of Bassianus's murder, his daughter raped and mulilated, Titus returns to the city. The scene wherein he begs mercy for his condemned sons (III.i) diametrically opposes the opening scene wherein he refused mercy to Alarbus. Instead of standing proudly at the head of a triumphal procession, Titus the suppliant lies down before the silent, impassive judges. Instead of remaining stoically calm, Titus promises to water the earth through the seasons with his tears. Unable to quell entirely his natural affections and unable to take arms against the city, Titus becomes paralyzed, incapable of constructive action.

Not so his son Lucius, who enters Rome with sword drawn. For attempting to rescue his brothers, he is banished permanently from the city. Here Shakespeare introduces the dramatic situation of exile from Rome that recurs in *Julius Caesar* and *Coriolanus*. As in *Lucrece*, however, the moral issues in this play are simple and clear-cut. Because Rome has become a "wilderness of tigers" (III.i.54), a place where people prey upon each other, banishment is a mark of distinction, a testimony to individual rectitude. By leaving to join the Goths, Lucius actually travels to Lucrece's imaginary "dark deep desert seated from the way" (1144), to a place outside Roman walls where justice can be served. Having demonstrated loyalty to his sister and brothers, he shows in this scene courage and a capacity for action. From this time on, Lucius

---

[21]Richard David, "Drams of Eale, A Review of Recent Productions," *ShS*, 10 (1957), 126–34, observes that Peter Brook's production at Stratford, 1955, used the inner recess of a great square fluted pillar to represent the Andronici tomb as well as the forest pit (p. 126). See also Ann Haaker, "*Non sine causa*: The Use of Emblematic Method and Iconology in the Thematic Structure of *Titus Andronicus*," *RORD*, 13–14 (1970–1), 143–68.

commands respect and emerges gradually as the future hope of Rome.

The reappearance of Lavinia, ravished, her tongue cut out and hands lopped off, demonstrates the deterioration of Rome under Saturninus and Tamora. The city, like the forest, becomes a place where the good are victimized and rendered incapable of human speech and action. The enormity of the degeneration can only be expressed in emblematic and mythological terms. The sight of Lavinia wrings from Titus a reminiscence of Troy's destruction:

> What fool hath added water to the sea?
> Or brought a faggot to bright-burning Troy?
>
> (III.i.68–9)

Later, when Marcus unintentionally reminds Titus of his daughter's plight, the bereaved father again refers to the fall of Troy:

> Ah, wherefore dost thou urge the name of hands,
> To bid Aeneas tell the tale twice o'er
> How Troy was burnt and he made miserable?
>
> (III.ii.26–8)

Remembrance of Troy furnishes Titus, as it did Lucrece, an external image of personal loss and of the fall of Rome. The invasion of Troy again acts as a subtext that illuminates the rape of a Roman woman, this time by invaders who have, significantly, Greek names. As in *Lucrece* the imagery of Troy and the rape suggest the larger invasion of Rome by barbarians, the Tarquins here replaced by Tamora and her brood. Like Aeneas after Troy, the homeless Titus recalls in these lines his own unspeakable sorrow and the destruction of his beloved city.

As in *Lucrece,* images of sea wandering and dislocation accompany allusions to Troy. Like Aeneas, Titus is *multum ille et terris iactatus et alto / vi superum* (I.3–4), "that man buffeted on sea and land by violence from above." He is cut off from Rome, the dying new Troy of idealistic heroism, and adrift alone on a dark and vast ocean, surrounded by threatening waters:

> For now I stand as one upon a rock,
> Environ'd with a wilderness of sea,
> Who marks the waxing tide grow wave by wave,
> Expecting ever when some envious surge
> Will in his brinish bowels swallow him.
>
> (III.i.93–7)

Accumulating in force, water imagery recurs throughout the play, recalling the deep oceans and hostile floods of the *Aeneid*. Titus tells us that his tear-stained face resembles washed-out meadows (III.i.125–6); later he wishes that Lavinia could end her sorrows by drowning in "sea-salt tears" (III.ii.20). Images of the seas, floods, and tears gather into a universal deluge as Titus compares himself to a world overwhelmed by troubled waters:

> I am the sea; hark how her sigh doth blow!
> She is the weeping welkin, I the earth:
> Then must my sea be moved with her sighs;
> Then must my earth with her continual tears
> Become a deluge, overflow'd and drown'd.
>
> (III.i.225–9)

Titus has reached the limits of human ability to endure suffering and pain. The next horrifying revelation – that the sacrifice of his own hand has not saved his sons from death – pushes him into the realms of madness. The eerie laugh that signals the approach of insanity signals the beginning of vengeance. The old Titus, protector of the city and avatar of its virtue, dies, and a new one, crazed by grief and injustice, is born. The new Titus immediately assembles the family into a conspiratorial circle that recalls the similar circle of Brutus, Collatine, and the others around the body of Lucrece. As Brutus did earlier, and as another Brutus will do later, Titus presides over a solemn ceremony:

> You heavy people, circle me about,
> That I may turn me to each one of you,
> And swear unto my soul to right your wrongs.
> The vow is made.
>
> (III.i.276–9)

Lucius notes the similarity between the actions of the Andronici and those of the earlier rebels against Tarquinian tyranny and injustice:

> If Lucius live, he will requite your wrongs,
> And make proud Saturnine and his emperess
> Beg at the gates, like Tarquin and his queen.
>
> (III.i.296–8)

This explicit reference to the story of Lucrece's rape and Brutus's revenge points to the structural and thematic similarities between the two Roman histories as Shakespeare envisioned them. Lavinia, like Lucrece, is a chaste Roman wife wronged by barbarian insolence and revenged by a concerted familial effort. Earlier, Aaron compared the unassailable chastity of Lavinia to that of Lucrece (II.i.108–9); later, Titus will liken the violator of his daughter to the foul and secretive Tarquin who "left the camp to sin in Lucrece' bed" (IV.i.64). Lucius and Titus, the men who avenge the misdeed, find a pattern and precedent in the actions of Brutus, Collatine, and Lucrece's father, who together expelled the Tarquins from Rome. In addition to Lucius's reference to the begging Tarquin, there is also the later solemn oath and revenge ritual of Marcus:

> And swear with me, as with the woeful fere
> And father of that chaste dishonored dame,
> Lord Junius Brutus sware for Lucrece' rape,
> That we will prosecute by good advice
> Mortal revenge upon these traitorous Goths.
>
> (IV.i.89–93)

Clearly, the rape of Lucrece functions as a deep source for *Titus Andronicus*. It serves to articulate the various violations implicit in Lavinia's rape and to illuminate the revenge action, emphasizing in the process the importance of familial unity to the reordering of the savage city.

As in *Lucrece*, the sequence of events leading to the attainment of revenge features an *ekphrasis*. The work of art described is not an imaginary depiction of Troy, but the tale of Tereus, Philomela, and Procne. After the numerous Ovidian echoes and allusions, the identification of the book that Lavinia takes from young Lucius and eagerly pores over, "Grandsire, 'tis Ovid's Metamorphosis, / My mother gave it me" (IV.i.42–3), seems inevitable. Lavinia finds in the tragedy of Philomela a speaking picture of her own woe. Although she cannot weave her story into a tapestry, she can, like Io, write in the sand with a stick.

Here, as in *Lucrece,* the device of turning one work into a metaphor for another invites careful consideration. In both devices Hecuba plays an important part. Lucrece sees Hecuba as an archetype of her own suffering. Young Lucius, likewise, compares Hecuba, who "ran mad for sorrow" (IV.i.21), to grief-stricken Lavinia. This allusion recalls Demetrius's earlier comparison of Tamora to Hecuba, "the Queen of Troy" who wrought "sharp revenge / Upon the Thracian tyrant in his tent" (I.i.136, 137–8); it signals, perhaps ironically, the transfer of the revenge initiative from Tamora and the Goths to Lavinia and the Andronici. As the appearance of the *Metamorphoses* on stage implies, Shakespeare has designed *Titus Andronicus* with Ovid in mind: Demetrius and Chiron play the role of Tereus, foul rapist and mutilator; Lavinia acts the part of Philomela, the ravished innocent; Titus plays the part of Pandion, the injured father, and then that of Procne, the revenger. Titus himself notes that the forest outside Rome resembles the *sylva vetusta* of Ovid's description, "(O had we never, never hunted there!), / Pattern'd by that the poet here describes, / By nature made for murthers and for rapes" (IV.i.56–8). The dichotomy between Rome and the forest so crucial to this play descends directly from the Ovidian dichotomy between Athens, civilized home of Philomela, and the wild woods in Thrace, scene of the rape. The description of Tereus, inflamed by Philomela's beauty and by a passionate nature common to men of his region, *sed et hunc innata libido / exstimulat, pronumque genus regionibus illis / in Venerem est* (VI.458–60), is also pertinent to Shakespeare's depiction of Demetrius and Chiron, inflamed by what appears to be the congenital lust of Goths.[22]

Ovid's story of Philomela has deeper and more significant affinities with Shakespeare's *Titus Andronicus* than the resemblances in plot and character. Like Shakespeare, Ovid tells the tale of a foreign invasion that overturns all civilized order and values. Tereus is *barbarus* (VI.515), not only a foreigner, but also, as Regius explains, *a bonis moribus alienus,* "estranged from all

---

[22]Shakespeare may be drawing on contemporary notions of Greeks for his portrait of Demetrius and Chiron. See T. J. B. Spencer, " 'Greeks' and 'Merrygreeks': A Background to *Timon of Athens* and *Troilus and Cressida*," in *Essays on Shakespeare and Elizabethan Drama in Honor of Hardin Craig,* ed. Richard Hosley (Columbia: University of Missouri Press, 1962), pp. 223–33.

good customs and morals."[23] His rape of Philomela, clearly depicted as *Pandione nata,* "Pandion's daughter," as well as Procne's sister, flagrantly violates the family and the sacred bonds that tie it together. After the rape Philomela cries out to Tereus:

> "o diris barbare factis
> o crudelis" ait, "nec te mandata parentis
> cum lacrimis movere piis nec cura sororis
> nec mea virginitas nec coniugialia iura?
> omnia turbasti; paelex ego facta sororis,
> tu geminus coniunx, hostis mihi debita Procne!"
>
> (533–8)

> "Oh, what a horrible thing you have done, barbarous, cruel
> wretch! Do you care nothing for my father's injunctions,
> his affectionate tears, my sister's love, my own virginity, the
> bonds of wedlock? You have confused all natural relations:
> I have become a concubine, my sister's rival; you, a
> husband to both. Now Procne must be my enemy."

Because Philomela is the daughter of a king, the destruction of her familial bonds threatens all civil and natural order. Raphael Regius recognizes these implications, glossing her anguished *omnia turbasti* with the explanation, *omnia, inquit, iura & humana, & diuina confudisti,* "all laws, she says, both human and divine you have confounded."[24]

Like the tapestry of Troy in *Lucrece,* the story of Philomela in *Titus Andronicus* is a rich and evocative classical analog that enlarges the pathos and scope of the events portrayed. The brief mentions of Philomela in the poem (1079, 1128) foreshadow Shakespeare's use of her here as an archetypal expression of ravished innocence and suffering. Philomela, Lucrece, Lavinia, and Hecuba are all related in Shakespeare's imagination, all victims of the same injurious cruelty that undermines human relations, shakes the foundations of traditional institutions, and untunes the harmonies in the skies. Both the poem and the play present Shakespearean responses to Ovid's exclamatory question, *quantum mortalia pectora caecae / noctis habent!* (VI.472–3), "what blind night rules in the hearts of men!"

[23] *Metamorphoseon Libri XV* (Venice, 1565), p. 135.
[24] Ibid., p. 136.

Ovid, of course, answered his own question about the dark night in his description of the world's four ages (*Met.* I.89ff.). Along with Vergil's influential Fourth Eclogue, this description appeared in various forms throughout the English and Continental Renaissance, permeating, as Harry Levin illustrates, nearly every aspect of art and culture.[25] The matrix of ideas evolving from the commonplace notion that the world had degenerated from a golden past ruled by Saturn to a decadent iron present bereft of Astraea, goddess of justice, has special importance for *Titus Andronicus*. A. C. Hamilton suggests that Ovid's description of the degeneration provides a pattern for this early Shakespearean tragedy: Saturninus inverts Saturn's golden age and Titus banishes Astraea from Rome. In addition, Hamilton avers, the play parodies Vergil's Fourth Eclogue:

> in place of the age of gold that heralds a new birth of
> peace, with the earth pouring out her fruits and all beasts
> living in concord, it shows the age of Saturninus, where
> Tamora uses gold for revenge against the Andronici, and
> Rome becomes a "wilderness of tigers" (III.i.54).[26]

Frances A. Yates discerns as well the operation of this Ovidian myth in the resolution of the play. Noting that Lucius's search for Astraea leads to his hitting Virgo (i.e., Astraea) with an arrow, she suggests that the "apotheosis of Lucius at the end of the play thus perhaps represents the Return of the Virgin – the return of the just empire and the golden age."[27]

One may justifiably demur at reading the resolution of the play as an unqualified, indeed apocalyptic, victory of good over evil. Yet, the self-conscious recollection of important passages from Ovid, including Titus's "*Terras Astraea reliquit*" (IV.iii.4), create a mythological framework. Ovid's description of the four ages is one of the passages that Shakespeare and his audience are most

---

[25] *The Myth of the Golden Age in the Renaissance* (Bloomington: Indiana University Press, 1969).

[26] Hamilton, *Early Shakespeare*, pp. 70ff; the quotation appears on pp. 82–3.

[27] *Astraea: The Imperial Theme in the Sixteenth Century* (London: Routledge & Kegan Paul, 1975), p. 75. Michael Payne, *Irony in Shakespeare's Roman Plays*, Salzburg Studies in English Literature, ES, No. 19 (Salzburg: Institut für Englische Sprache und Literatur, 1974), also discusses the general relevance of the iron-age myth to *Titus Andronicus* (pp. 13–20).

likely to have read in the original, in a florilegium such as Mirandula's, or in a contemporary adaptation. And, as Harry Levin
writes, it was Ovid who crystallized the golden-age myth into a
topos, "who realigned its traditional elements in the grandly rhetorical set-piece that would be imitated, plagiarized, paraphrased,
parodied, reinterpreted, controverted, distorted, and metamor-
phosed into so many shapes" by Renaissance writers.[28] The details
of Ovid's description, as well as its general outline, would have
been familiar to most Elizabethans including Shakespeare, whose
Lucrece, we recall, has the color of the "golden age" in her cheeks
(60).

As Ovid describes it, Saturn's reign, the fabled golden age, was
remarkable for what it lacked: It contained no laws, no fear of
punishment, no harsh words engraved on brazen tablets, no suppliants trembling before the face of a judge. Then cities were not
surrounded by steep moats (Vergil says "walls"), and men had no
need for armies or the instruments of war. The earth, untilled by
human hands, supplied plenty for all: Men ate fruits, strawberries,
grains, nuts, and honey; they drank milk and nectar from flowing
streams. Spring was the only season and all were content.

After Saturn was banished, the idyllic golden age degenerated
into silver, bronze, and finally into the present age of hard iron. All
modesty, truth, and faith now give place to tricks, plots, and traps,
as well as to violence and greed. Men do not share the plenty of the
earth, but each tills his own field and digs into the ground for the
riches that provoke evil deeds. Iron forged into weapons is the
symbol of the age and gold a bane to all men. All human relations
are confounded. The corruption of *pietas*, especially the breakdown of family bonds, causes the corruption of all other relations
and the desertion of Astraea, the last divinity to leave the earth to
its bestial inhabitants.

Shakespeare's depiction of Rome in *Titus Andronicus* owes
much to Ovid's description of the world's four ages. Rome in this
play is an iron city – a military establishment protected by walls
and filled with sword-carrying soldiers such as the Andronici. In
scene after scene Shakespeare takes full advantage of the multiple
meanings of *ferrum*, the Latin word for "iron," also signifying by

[28]Levin, *Myth of the Golden Age*, p. 19.

transference any hard weapon, especially the sword. In the surviving illustration of the action in *Titus Andronicus,* the Longleat Manuscript, Titus appears with sword at side and tall spear in hand.[29] He is followed by a Roman soldier whose right hand holds a halberd and whose left rests on the hilt of his sword. Behind this man is another Roman soldier who carries a halberd and wears a sword discolored by blood. The civil strife in this play measures the distance between these Romans and the inhabitants of the golden age who shared all things and lived together in peace. Here, brother challenges brother for power and wealth, the citizens arrange themselves into armed factions, the rulers oppose the ruled. This kind of civil discord stands preeminently as a sign of the iron age for readers of the *Metamorphoses* as well as for readers of the Fourth Eclogue. Glossing Vergil's *sceleris vestigia nostri* (13), "traces of our guilt," the phrase that sums up the immorality of the present age, Servius explains:

> Vestigia autem sclerum dicit bella ciuilia,
> quae gessit Augustus contra Antonium apud Mutinam:
> contra L. Antonium fratrem huius Antonii apud Perusium:
> contra Sextum Pompeium filium Pompeii in freto
> Siciliensi: contra Brutum & Cassium in Thessalia:
> contra Antonium & Cleopatram in Epiro apud Actium
> promontorium.[30]

> The phrase "traces of guilt" refers to the civil wars which Augustus waged against Antony at Mutina, against Lucius Antony, brother of this Antony, in Perusia, against Pompey's son, Sextus Pompey, in the Sicilian Straits, against Brutus and Cassius in Thessaly, against Antony and Cleopatra in Epirus at the promontory of Actium.

The internal conflicts of the city in *Titus Andronicus* reenact the civil wars that occurred as the Augustan empire was in its birth

[29]See W. M. Merchant, "Classical Costume in Shakespearian Productions," *ShS*, 10 (1957), 71–6 (71–2). Despite the efforts of J. Dover Wilson, "'Titus Andronicus' on the Stage in 1595," *ShS*, 1 (1948), 17–22, and *TLS*, June 24, 1949, p. 413; John Munro, *TLS*, June 10, 1949, p. 385, and July 1, 1949, p. 429; and Arthur J. Perrett, *TLS*, July 1, 1949, p. 429, there has been advanced no final solution to the various problems this drawing raises.

[30]*Opera* (Venice, 1544), reprinted in *The Renaissance and the Gods*, No. 7, 2 vols. (New York: Garland, 1976), Vol. I, fol. 25. Cf. Horace, Epode 16, which associates civil war with the iron age.

pangs, the civil wars popularly understood as manifestations of the world's fall into decadence.

As the play progresses, specific incidents and passages recall details of Ovid's description. When Titus returns to Rome after the hunting trip, he appears as one of Ovid's timid suppliants, *supplex turba timebat / iudicis ora sui* (I.92–3), pleading before the impassive judge ("judges" in Shakespeare); he thus assumes the exact posture that, according to Ovid, betokens the world's degeneration. As he begs for mercy, he promises to "keep eternal spring-time" (III.i.21) on earth with his tears if only his sons can be spared execution. The desperate, fanciful conceit, turning on the Ovidian concept of *ver aeternum* (107), expresses the ardency of Titus's desire for the justice of the golden age, while at the same time suggesting the impossibility of its return. Later, when Titus resolves to "get a leaf of brass" and to inscribe it with "a gad of steel" (IV.i.102–3), he chooses a course of action that again directly recalls Ovid's description of the golden age, *nec verba minantia fixo / aere* (91–2). Because, as Ovid tells us, there were "no threatening words" inscribed in "brazen tablets" during the golden age, Titus's request gives ironic witness to the very degeneration he hopes to arrest.

The reign of Saturninus displays many salient characteristics of the iron age. In place of modesty, truth, and faith, the ruling family employs deceits, stratagems, snares, and violence: *fugere pudor verumque fidesque; / in quorum subiere locum fraudesque dolusque / insidiaeque et vis* (129–31). Saturninus and Tamora feign friendship, Demetrius and Chiron gleefully rape Lavinia and cover up their crime, Aaron plots murder and intrigue. The wicked love of gain, *amor sceleratus habendi* (131), so characteristic of the iron age in Ovid as well as in Vergil (cf. *Aen.* VIII.327), appears as a motivating principle in Saturninus, in Tamora, and in Aaron, who hopes to be bright and to "shine in pearl and gold" (II.i.19). The very action of digging into the earth for baneful wealth, *in viscera terrae . . . effodiuntur opes, inritamenta malorum* (138, 140), singled out by Ovid as a symbol of the world's decay, occurs in Act II, Scene iii. Having previously buried the gold, Aaron digs it up to incriminate Quintus and Martius in Bassianus's death, thus adding to the Ovidian emblem of avarice the dimensions of fraud and chicanery.

The myth of the four ages, then, underlies much of the action in *Titus Andronicus*. Central to the Vergilian and Ovidian conceptions of this myth is *pietas,* the ideal that encompasses familial love and respect.[31] Vergil's Fourth Eclogue, for example, celebrates the birth of a son who will study his father's deeds, *facta parentis* (26), and usher in a new race of gold. Vergil's description of Saturn's reign in *Georgics* II mentions the husbandman surrounded by loving children, *interea dulces pendent circum oscula nati* (523), "meanwhile his dear children hang upon his kisses." Domestic affection and tenderness mark the household of those Saturnian descendants, Evander and Pallas (*Aen.* VIII), just as they mark the household of Aeneas, who starts the family line that culminates in Augustus Caesar, *Divi genus, aurea condet / saecula qui rursus Latio regnata per arva / Saturno quondam* (*Aen.* VI.792–4), "son of a god, who shall again set up the Golden Age amid the fields where Saturn once reigned." The disruption of familial love characterizes the iron age, wherein *impietas* disorders the state and destroys all civilized life. Ovid concludes his account of the iron age with a chilling description of the world ruled by *impietas:*

> vivitur ex rapto: non hospes ab hospite tutus,
> non socer a genero, fratrum quoque gratia rara est;
> inminet exitio vir coniugis, illa mariti,
> lurida terribiles miscent aconita novercae,
> filius ante diem patrios inquirit in annos:
> victa iacet pietas, et virgo caede madentis
> ultima caelestum terras Astraea reliquit.

(I.144–50)

> Men lived on plunder. Guest was not safe from host, nor
> father-in-law from son-in-law; even among brothers 'twas
> rare to find affection. The husband longed for the death of
> his wife, she of her husband; murderous stepmothers
> brewed deadly poisons, and sons inquired into their fathers'
> years before the time. Piety lay vanquished, and the maiden
> Astraea, last of the immortals, abandoned the blood-soaked
> earth.

Rome in *Titus Andronicus* bears strong resemblance to the im-

[31]Cf. Ovid, *Heroides* IV.129–33; and Statius, *Silvae* I.iv.1–3, III.iii.1–7, as quoted by Arthur O. Lovejoy and George Boas, *Primitivism and Related Ideas in Antiquity* (1935; rpt. New York: Octagon, 1965), pp. 53–5.

pious iron world of Ovid's description. Queen Tamora satisfies her lust for power by betraying her country and wedding the Roman Emperor, thereby founding the royal family not on love but on self-interest and hatred for the Andronici. She satisfies her lust for sensual pleasure by taking a lover who, in turn, uses her to attain wealth and political power. Here two sets of brothers take arms against each other for personal gain;[32] one brother looks on helplessly, incapable of action, while his brother is cheated and tortured, his niece mutilated, his nephews killed or banished. During the course of the action we hear of a mother who will sell her child for gold; we see another order her bastard infant killed and encourage her full-grown sons to acts of violence. Here a Roman father murders his son and then his daughter, sacrificing both on the altar of his own personal honor. And here a rebellious Roman son, having previously drawn his sword against his father, leads a foreign army against the city and against the *pater patriae,* the Emperor himself. *Victa iacet pietas,* indeed.

Invoked by the name of Saturninus and the references to Astraea and the golden age, the great mythic personage of Saturn casts his shadow over this play. Of course, Saturninus's reign of bloodshed sharply contrasts with Saturn's reign of idyllic peace and plenty; but the figure of the god in Renaissance mythography and iconography presents other characteristics more directly pertinent to Saturninus and his Rome.[33] Cognizant of the myth that tells of Saturn's eating his sons in order to escape deposition, Renaissance mythographers and artists frequently represent the god as a child devourer. This child devouring is allegorized variously. For Stephan Batman it betokens "the wastfull spending of thinges, before they come to growth."[34] For Abraham Fraunce, as well as for Richard Linche, Lilius Giraldus, and many others, it signifies "the

---

[32]According to Catullus, fraternal strife characterizes the iron age, wherein *perfudere manus fraterno sanguine fratres,* "brothers steep their hands in fraternal blood," *Carmen* 64.399. Shakespeare's emphasis on fraternal strife in *Titus Andronicus* may owe something to Roman history, specifically to the stories of Romulus and Remus, Numitor and Amulius, and the Tarquins.

[33]Hamilton, *Early Shakespeare,* briefly discusses the importance of Saturn to the play (p. 68). See also D. J. Palmer, "The Unspeakable in Pursuit of the Uneatable: Language and Action in *Titus Andronicus,*" *CritQ,* 14 (1972), 320–39 (323–6).

[34]*The Golden Booke of the Leaden Goddes* (1577), fol. 9ᵛ.

devouring continuance of outwearing time."[35] For George Sandys, Saturn is a figure of Adam: Just as the god devoured his children, so Adam "over-threw his whole posterity" through original sin.[36] This range of possibilities is suggestive for viewers and readers of *Titus Andronicus*. In this play Saturninus rules over a city that devours its children figuratively by consigning them to the gaping maw of the Andronici tomb, and literally by serving them in the bloody banquet at the end. Significantly, Titus's son, Lucius, stops the hideous feeding, the ghastly acts of *impietas* that destroy the city. Appropriately, he is depicted as one who is gentle with his own offspring and who pointedly refuses to devour another's child – Aaron's bastard son.

Overwhelmed by the presence of evil in Rome, Titus takes no constructive action, but resorts to fanciful gesture. He sends kinsmen to seek Astraea and madly posts messages by arrow to assorted deities. As the Clown's pun on "Jupiter," "gibbet-maker," and "Jubiter" (IV.iii.80–5) suggests, Titus's plea for divine justice is actually a cry for revenge on Rome. Unlike the noble city of his earlier conception, Rome now appears to Titus as a damnable place, filled with evil and treachery. Titus's vindictive rage takes no account of the possibilities for remedy or of the good in Marcus and the common messenger, who grieves at the death of Titus's sons (III.i.239–40). Like many of Shakespeare's Romans, especially Coriolanus, Titus can conceive of the city only in absolute terms. Unable to square his former vision of Rome with the sordid reality, he becomes maniacal and destructive.

Lucius, however, provides clear contrast to Titus. Instead of

---

[35] *The Third Part of the Countesse of Pembrokes Yuychurch* (1592), fol. 7. See also Richard Linche, *The Fovntaine of Ancient Fiction* (1599), sig. Dii; Lilius Giraldus, *Historiae Deorum Gentilium* in *Opera Omnia*, Vol. I (Lugduni Batauorum, 1696), col. 135; Erwin Panofsky, *Studies in Iconology* (1939; rpt. New York: Harper & Row, 1962), pp. 73ff.

[36] *Ovid's Metamorphosis Englished, Mythologized, and Represented in Figures by George Sandys*, ed. Karl K. Hulley and Stanley T. Vandersall (Lincoln: University of Nebraska Press, 1970), p. 59.

searching the skies for a banished goddess, he turns to the Gothic warriors outside the city and organizes an invasion. The curiously neutral portrayal of the Goths, who accept Lucius as their leader without question and who behave like orderly Roman recruits, suppresses the political and moral issues that betrayal of Rome might (and will) raise.[37] We note instead that Lucius, unlike his father, embarks on a direct and purposeful course of action to combat the evil in the city.

The discovery of Aaron and his child gives Lucius a chance to show his mettle as a leader. With the same ruthlessness he displayed in demanding the blood of Alarbus, the same indifference to familial ties, and the same Anglo-Saxon bluntness, Lucius calls for the death of the child:

> First hang the child, that he may see it sprawl –
> A sight to vex the father's soul withal.
> Get me a ladder.
>
> (V.i.51–3)

Heeding Aaron's desperate promise to confess all, Lucius, however, spares the child and promises to "see it nourish'd" (V.i.60). Aaron's following confession – a gleeful recitation of foul crimes that widens into the chilling history of an evil life – rigorously tests Lucius's self-control and his promise of mercy. To his credit, Lucius's resolution does not weaken. The restraint of emotion here, the tacit recognition of higher obligations than personal satisfaction, the steady refusal to pursue a violent course of vengeance that will shed innocent blood – all suggest that Lucius has changed from an impetuous bloodthirsty youth to a man capable of wise leadership.

Meanwhile, shaken from his mythological reverie by Tamora's plot, Titus devises a counterplot for revenge. After killing Demetrius and Chiron and planning the ghastly banquet, he justifies his actions by reference to Ovid:

> For worse than Philomel you us'd my daughter,
> And worse than Progne I will be reveng'd.
>
> (V.ii.194–5)

---

[37]For an analysis of this portrayal, see Ronald Broude, "Roman and Goth in *Titus Andronicus*," ShakS, 6 (1972 for 1970), 27–34.

Titus here exchanges the role of Pandion, the injured father, for that of Procne, the revenging sister. The bloody banquet, a self-consciously Ovidian spectacle, presents the final and most grotesque parody of the opening ceremony. No longer the powerful figure who occupies the center of a Roman public place, Titus appears as a humble cook who waits upon guests in his own home. Instead of ceremoniously expressing love for Rome and loyalty to Roman ideals, he hides his hatred and treachery in the guise of hospitality.

Exactly paralleling the murder of Mutius in the opening scene is the murder of Lavinia at the banquet. After misremembering the story of rash Virginius, who killed his daughter, Titus slays the helpless Lavinia.[38] The murder appears as the act of a demented man, completely out of touch with human realities. Titus's appropriation of Roman legend as a precedent for impious murder reveals again the barbarity of Rome and Roman values. The mute witness of the Goths at the table, in addition to the memory of Aaron's recent efforts to save his own infant, provides ironic commentary on Roman action.

The climax of Titus's banquet, however, is the spectacle of a mother consuming the remains of her sons. Titus does indeed outdo Ovid here, serving up two corpses to Procne's one. Like her, and unlike his son Lucius, Titus considers this gruesome desecration of familial bonds an assertion of his own *pietas,* of the values that bind the Andronici together. The absurdity of this notion is apparent to the audience, who watches the gory eating in horror. The scene in Titus's house recalls the original scene of Procne's revenge and Ovid's description, *pars inde cavis exsultat aenis, / pars veribus stridunt; manant penetralia tabo* (VI.645–6), "part bubbles in brazen kettles, part sputters on spits; while the whole room drips with gore." This *penetralia* in turn may summon up remembrance of the other Roman *penetralia* where Tarquin raped Lucrece and, of course, the archetypal Trojan *penetralia* where vengeful Pyrrhus slew Priam and his son. Like Pyrrhus and Tarquin, Titus perverts the life-sustaining *penetralia* to a chamber of horrors. The classical antecedents for the eating also include, of

---

[38]Apparently, Titus's recollection of Virginius and his daughter represents a popular Elizabethan perversion of the original story. See Holger Nørgaard, "Never Wrong But With Just Cause," *ES,* 45 (1964), 137–41.

course, Seneca's *Thyestes*, wherein the chorus appropriately unfolds a dark vision of universal discord and confusion (789ff.). Titus's banquet also presents an extreme, cannibalistic perversion of Ovid's golden age, in which men subsisted on fruits, nuts, and grain (*Met.* XV.72ff.).

After Tamora, Titus, and Saturninus meet their violent ends, the city belongs to the younger generation. Lucius emerges to reunite Rome, "to knit again / This scattered corn into one mutual sheaf, / These broken limbs again into one body" (V.iii.70–2). The pointed reference to corn, a common iconographical attribute of Astraea,[39] suggests that Lucius is about to restore justice to the corrupt city. This restoration is not merely a return to old ways, but a new beginning. Aemilius alludes to "that baleful burning night, / When subtile Greeks surpris'd King Priam's Troy" (V.iii.83–4) and asks Lucius to tell when Sinon "hath brought the fatal engine in / That gives our Troy, our Rome, the civil wound" (86–7). This allusion culminates the Troy references and casts Lucius in the role of Aeneas, survivor of the old regime, founder of a new Rome.

Lucius immediately demonstrates to those around him that he, unlike his father, is willing to take up the scepter and control the world. He rehearses his valorous deeds and reaffirms his love for Rome:

> I am the turned forth, be it known to you,
> That have preserv'd her welfare in my blood,
> And from her bosom took the enemy's point,
> Sheathing the steel in my advent'rous body.
> Alas, you know I am no vaunter, I;
> My scars can witness, dumb although they are,
> That my report is just and full of truth.
> But soft, methinks I do digress too much,
> Citing my worthless praise. O, pardon me,
> For when no friends are by, men praise themselves.
>
> (109–18)

The appeal to the citizens' patriotism and gratitude and the elaborate show of modesty that denies what it would assert bespeak the practiced politician. After winning popular acclamation, Lucius sets about his tasks with alacrity and efficiency. First he pays

[39]On Astraea and corn, see Macrobius, *Saturnalia* I.xxi.24; and Levin, *Myth of the Golden Age*, p. 27.

homage to his dead father, leading his uncle and son in formal lamentations that recall the initial burial ceremony:

> *Lucius:* O, take this warm kiss on thy pale cold lips,
> (*Kisses Titus*)
> These sorrowful drops upon thy blood-stain'd face,
> The last true duties of thy noble son!
> *Marcus:* Tear for tear, and loving kiss for kiss,
> Thy brother Marcus tenders on thy lips.
>
> . . . . .
>
> *Boy:* O grandsire, grandsire, ev'n with all my heart
> Would I were dead, so you did live again!
>
> (153–7, 172–3)

Like the laments over Lucrece's body, these ceremonious expressions of grief unite the various generations and reconfirm the importance of *pietas* for the new regime. Lucius then orders that the Emperor be buried with his ancestors and that Titus and Lavinia "be closed in our household's monument" (194). Aaron is set breast-deep in the earth to starve, and Tamora's body is thrown to the birds and beasts – both unceremonious nonburials justly fitted endings to bestial lives. Although Astraea never returns to earth, Lucius, at least, brings new life to Rome.

Like *Lucrece, Titus Andronicus* prepares the way for Shakespeare's later dramatizations of ancient Rome. The play features two important recurring symbols: the Capitol, here merely a shadow of itself in *Julius Caesar;* and the walls, which set off the city from the wild forest and the outlying battlefields. Although the walls initially serve to define the limits of the city, to mark off the boundaries between civilization and primitive lawlessness, they come in the course of the play to enclose the city-turned-wilderness. At the end of *Titus Andronicus*, there is a siege that reverses the action of Tarquin's, a siege meant not to destroy Rome but to purge it and to restore the city to its former dignity and virtue. Shakespeare will use symbolic geography and the siege motif with increasing subtlety and complexity.

This play develops what has gone before and looks forward to Shakespeare's other Roman works. It examines the phenomenon of rebellion barely suggested by the revolt of Junius Brutus. The process outlined in *Titus Andronicus,* whereby Roman citizens form conspiratorial circles and plot against the government, receives circumspect consideration in *Julius Caesar.* Roman blood rituals, first adumbrated in Lucrece's suicide and the carrying of her body through Rome, occupy center stage here, as they often do later. Titus Andronicus, the great warrior whose vision of Rome sustains him in the battlefield but undoes him in city streets, anticipates Coriolanus, who embodies, though more powerfully, the same paradox.[40] The problematic relationship between the Roman family and city is here articulated as well. This relationship, along with the tensions generated by opposing claims of *pietas,* will be a constant Shakespearean concern. So too will be the Roman code of military honor, disturbingly evident in the noble savagery of the Andronici.

It is surely an irony worth remarking that "honor" and "fame," the two crucial terms of Lucrece's moral universe, are both invoked in *Titus Andronicus* upon occasions of burial. Titus's twice repeated "In peace and honor rest you here, my sons" (I.i.150, 156) attends the lowering of coffins into the family tomb. And the later comment, spoken by all the Andronici on stage, "No man shed tears for noble Mutius, / He lives in fame, that died in virtue's cause" (I.i.389–90), serves likewise as the eulogy for Mutius. One need not be so pragmatic as Falstaff to question such a notion of honor and those who confidently assert that a dead brother or son will live on in fame. The sheer brutality of Roman revenge, undertaken partly to make the Andronici "wonder'd at in time to come" (III.i.135), undercuts any justification based on the judgment of posterity. That which we can readily accept in *Lucrece* –violence in the name of honor – we cannot so readily tolerate in the drama, where human beings are maimed and butchered before our eyes.

The method of classical allusion in this play resembles that in *Lucrece.* Obviously fascinated by the ready wit of Ovid, the rich poignance of Vergil, and the dark power of Seneca, Shakespeare

---

[40]Bullough discusses the possible influence of Plutarch's "Coriolanus" on *Titus Andronicus* (Vol. VI, pp. 24–5).

weaves references to all three in this play.[41]Shakespeare's classicism is as self-conscious here as before, Lucrece's imaginary tapestry giving way to Young Lucius's book, her classical allusions to direct quotations and misquotations from texts. It is also extremely flexible: Titus acts the role of Pandion and then that of Procne; Lavinia recalls her Vergilian eponym as well as Philomela and Lucrece; Hecuba serves to parallel Tamora, then Lavinia; Aeneas enhances the character of Titus and then that of Lucius. This classicism is syncretic in character, variable in application; it draws upon the strands of different myths – the rape of Philomela, the fall of Troy, the banquet of Thyestes – and twists them together for increased poetic intensity and color.

The spectacle of such classicism on stage has justly prompted observers like Eugene M. Waith to comment upon the fundamental incompatibility of Ovidian narrative and drama.[42] Yet there are in *Titus Andronicus* tentative steps toward the integration of classical myth into a larger pattern of symbolic and thematic meaning. The rapes of Philomela, Lucrece, and Troy combine to suggest the civil and moral dimensions of Lavinia's rape and the barbarism of the invading Goths. The myth of the world's four ages serves as a context for the play and reveals the *impietas* of the action. The allusions to Aeneas and to the restoration of Astraea at the end of the play endow Lucius with a heroic status appropriate to the restorer of the city and to the figure popularly reputed to be the first Christian king of Britain.[43] Such mythologizing may be heavy-handed, but one cannot easily dismiss it as inappropriate decoration.

The combination of Roman history, myth, and tragedy in *Titus Andronicus* is in nobody's judgment completely felicitous.[44] The

---

[41]Emrys Jones perceptively discusses Seneca's influence on Shakespeare in general and in this play, *The Origins of Shakespeare* (Oxford: Clarendon Press, 1977), pp. 267–72. Jones argues, however, that the chief dramatic model for *Titus Andronicus* is a Latin translation of Euripides's *Hecuba* (pp. 85–107).

[42]"The Metamorphosis of Violence in *Titus Andronicus*," *ShS*, 10 (1957), 39–49.

[43]See Yates, *Astraea*, p. 75; Hamilton, *Early Shakespeare*, p. 85.

[44]Since Edward Ravenscroft compared the play to "a heap of Rubbish" in his adaptation, *Titus Andronicus, or the Rape of Lavinia* (1687), sig. A2, it has drawn a torrent of abuse. Recently, however, some have cautiously defended Shakespeare's play: Ettin, "Shakespeare's First Roman Tragedy"; Jack E. Reese, "The Formalization of Horror in *Titus Andronicus*," *SQ*, 21 (1970),

spectacle of Ovidian and Senecan horrors on stage, crudely arranged into a series of bloody climaxes, anesthetizes the audience and prevents the normal sympathetic response. The excesses of the main character arouse interest and wonder, but hardly evoke sorrow and pity. The Titus of Act I, who represents Rome in all its greatness and barbarity, degenerates into a parody of his former self, into a walking manikin stuffed with scraps from the popular revenge play and from popular notions of *Romanitas*. Tearing passion to tatters, he acts in stylized gestures and shows little capacity for spiritual maturation and growth.

Yet, despite the crudity of content and technique, *Titus Andronicus* is an important engagement with Rome and Romans. After supping full with horrors here, Shakespeare passes from the tutelage of Roman poets to that of a historian, Plutarch. In so doing, he finds a perspective that enables him to view the grand sweep and pageantry of Roman history while focusing on the tragedy of heroic individuals. The Romans to come, as we shall see, share important similarities with Titus, even as they surpass him in depth, complexity, and humanity. And though the city of Rome appears in various and shifting forms throughout these plays, the experience of *Titus Andronicus,* as well as of *Lucrece,* makes its shape a familiar and recognizable one.

77–84; D. J. Palmer, "The Unspeakable"; Albert H. Tricomi, "The Aesthetics of Mutilation in 'Titus Andronicus,'" *ShS,* 27 (1974), 11–19; also his "The Mutilated Garden in *Titus Andronicus,*" *ShakS,* 9 (1976), 89–105; S. Clark Hulse, "Wresting the Alphabet: Oratory and Action in 'Titus Andronicus,'" *Criticism,* 21 (1979), 106–18.

IV

JULIUS CAESAR
ROME DIVIDED

Shakespeare's third imaginative encounter with Rome embodies, develops, and transforms much of what has gone before. Sharply defined by recognizable localities such as the Capitol, marketplace, and walls, Rome is the central protagonist of the play. The city again shapes the lives of its inhabitants, who struggle to act according to Roman heroic traditions. As in *Lucrece* and *Titus Andronicus* the ideals of honor and constancy here make up the moral universe. And as in the earlier Roman works, Shakespeare shows continuing concern with the Roman family, though in this play women emerge more fully and the demands of Roman *pietas* become paradoxical and destructive. The barbarism inherent in Shakespeare's Rome repels us again, although the Roman ceremonies and blood rituals on this stage more effectively undercut action, provoke thought, and develop theme. As the crudely articulated revenge motif of *Lucrece* and *Titus Andronicus* changes form here, the light and incidental sketch of the city divided becomes the sharper and darker blueprint for the action.

Unlike the protagonists of the earlier works, Julius Caesar was a classical figure of commanding importance to Renaissance historians, mythographers, moralists, playwrights, and poets.[1] Shakespeare appropriates the famous story not to illustrate the evils of

---

[1] For a general survey of the growth and development of the Caesar mythos, see Friedrich Gundolph, *The Mantle of Caesar,* trans. Jacob Wittmer Hartmann (New York: Vanguard Press, 1928). For reviews of background material with special focus on Shakespeare's play, see MacCallum, pp. 168ff.; Harry Morgan Ayres, "Shakespeare's *Julius Caesar* in the Light of Some Other Versions," *PMLA,* 25 (1910), 183–227; J. Leeds Barroll, "Shakespeare and Roman History," *MLR,* 53 (1958), 327–43; Bullough, Vol. V, pp. 3–57; T. S. Dorsch, ed., *Julius Caesar,* The Arden Shakespeare (1955; rpt. Cambridge, Mass.: Harvard University Press, 1958), pp. xix–xx.

tyranny, rebellion, or both,[2] but to give his audience a look at a pivotal moment in Roman history. As Ernest Schanzer and others argue, Shakespeare here creates a play that accommodates, even insists upon, the complexity and ambivalence of Caesar's story.[3] To a greater extent than before, he, like Plutarch, focuses on the characters in the historical pageant, on the human beings who by some combination of nature's livery and fortune's star strutted or stumbled into legend and song.

The movement of living persons into legend and song constantly preoccupies the characters in the play. Imitating the past, they try to mold the present for the approval of the future. In scene after scene they recall, evaluate, assess, and judge, striving to make sense of the world around them, to find a basis for purposeful action, to win the admiration of posterity. Their struggle to impose permanent order on reality is actually an attempt to write their own history – one, the play makes clear, that is difficult and perilous. The inscriptions of these Romans, achieved at the price of blood and suffering, scatter like Sibyl's leaves, blown away by the winds of time, circumstance, and opinion.

Shakespeare portrays the struggle of Romans with history sympathetically by employing a complex network of dramatic paradoxes and ironies. Emphasizing the difference between "acting," "seeming," "appearing," "fashioning," "construing," and being,

[2]A variation of these three positions is operative in most modern interpretations of the play. For the first, see J. Dover Wilson's Cambridge edition (1949), pp. xix–xxxiii; for the second, James Emerson Phillips, Jr., *The State in Shakespeare's Greek and Roman Plays* (1940; rpt. New York: Octagon, 1972), pp. 172ff.; and for the third, Irving Ribner, "Political Issues in *Julius Caesar*," *JEGP*, 56 (1957), 10–22.

[3]Ernest Schanzer, "The Problem of *Julius Caesar*," *SQ*, 6 (1955), 297–308; Schanzer sets forth his position fully in *The Problem Plays of Shakespeare* (New York: Schocken Books, 1963), pp. 10–70. Others who insist on the complex ambiguity of the play are Adrien Bonjour, *The Structure of "Julius Caesar"* (Liverpool: Liverpool University Press, 1958); Traversi, pp. 21–75; Mildred E. Hartsock, "The Complexity of *Julius Caesar*," *PMLA*, 81 (1966), 56–62. In "Shakespeare and the Elizabethan Romans," *ShS*, 10 (1957), 27–38, T. J. B. Spencer writes that the characters of Caesar and Brutus were the "subject of constant discussion" (p. 33). Emrys Jones, *The Origins of Shakespeare* (Oxford: Clarendon Press, 1977), reminds us that Renaissance rhetorical training also fostered such reassessment and reconsideration: "The boys would be trained to find arguments for and against Brutus' act: there was no question of coming down simple-mindedly on one side" (p. 16).

the language of the play suggests the maddeningly elusive and complicated nature of reality.[4] Throughout *Julius Caesar* Shakespeare exposes the difficulty of judging truly, of distinguishing fact from fancy, of finding the truth amid conflicting appearances and reports. Despite their best efforts, the characters constantly miscalculate: Caesar puts faith in the wrong interpretation of Calphurnia's dream; Brutus believes that Antony can do no harm. The characters can no more control themselves than they can circumstances, often coming in time to resemble their own worst enemies. After the assassination, Brutus acts like thrasonical Caesar; at the funeral and after, Antony acts like rebel Brutus. No matter how hard these Romans try, no matter how much they suffer, the force of history frustrates their intentions. Instead of remaining constant as the northern star, Caesar dies at the hands of his friends; instead of restoring the Roman republic, Brutus exchanges the potential problem of Caesar for the actual tyranny of Antony and Octavius. The noble Romans who would master Clio, the play demonstrates, end up, tragically enough, by serving her.

Cinna: I dreamt to-night that I did feast with Caesar,
And things unluckily charge my fantasy.
I have no will to wander forth of doors,
Yet something leads me forth.

(III.iii.1–4)

The words of Cinna the poet before his fatal encounter with the enraged mob strike the keynote of the play. There is a curiously driven quality about the characters on stage and a peculiar inevitability about the sweep of events that leads to the Capitol and the countersweep that leads to Philippi. Throughout the play we

---

[4]A check of Martin Spevack's *Concordance*, 9 vols. (Hildesheim: Georg Olms, 1968–80) reveals that variations of the words in quotation marks appear thirty-five times in the play. Rene E. Fortin, "*Julius Caesar:* An Experiment in Point of View," *SQ*, 19 (1968), 341–7, contends that the play explores the subjectivity of perception and the limitations of human knowledge.

watch the workings of destiny and witness the grand march of history, moving slowly but ineluctably to its appointed ends.[5]

The play opens with an image of restless movement. All Rome is astir with people leaving their shops and filling the streets. The tribunes attempt to keep the commoners from the triumphal procession of Caesar, the grand march of history incarnate. Swiftly evoking the physical dimensions of the city – the "walls and battlements" (38), "tow'rs and windows" (39), "streets" (42), the "Tiber" (45, 58), and the "Capitol" (63) – the tribunes remind the people of their former affection for Pompey. Before, the commoners ran to celebrate Pompey's victories with infants in their arms (40); now they rejoice to see the slayer of Pompey's "blood" (51), that is, his sons, Romans by a Roman begotten. The tribunes suggest that active support of Caesar is a betrayal of Roman virtue, an act of *impietas* or disrespect for Roman sons, family, and city. As the abashed crowd disperses, the tribunes resolve to confront the "images" of Caesar (64) not the man, and to remove from the statues all "ceremonies" (65) or symbolic trappings.

The next scene clarifies the reason for the protest, as Caesar, crowded by a press of admirers, strides across the stage. The name "Caesar" is sounded seven times in twenty-four lines, but only once by the conqueror in a third-person reference to himself.[6] Such repetition gives a talismanic quality to the name; it appears to be a magical charm that derives potency from the faith of those who reverence it. In this scene Caesar lives up to his name: He commands Calphurnia and Antony, questions the soothsayer, and then magisterially passes judgment: "He is a dreamer, let us leave him. Pass" (24).

---

[5]Application of this view of history to *Julius Caesar* dates back to Hermann Ulrici: "Thus history appears [in *J.C.*] represented from one of its main aspects, in its inner autocratic, active and formative power, by which, although externally formed by individual men, it nevertheless controls and marches over the heads of the greatest of them." *Shakespeare's Dramatic Art: History and Character of Shakespeare's Plays*, trans. L. Dora Schmitz, 2 vols. (London: George Bell, 1876), Vol. II, p. 197.

[6]On the significance of "illeism" and on the sounding of proper names in this play, see R. A. Foakes, "An Approach to *Julius Caesar*," *SQ*, 5 (1954), 259–70 (264–70); S. Viswanathan, " 'Illeism With a Difference' in Certain Middle Plays of Shakespeare," *SQ*, 20 (1969), 407–15; Madeleine Doran, *Shakespeare's Dramatic Language* (Madison: University of Wisconsin Press, 1976), pp. 120–53.

As in *Titus Andronicus,* the Roman hero makes his entrance amid pomp and pageantry. Just as Titus carefully follows Roman burial custom for his dead sons, so Caesar carefully observes the Lupercalian traditions for his son, as yet unborn. Recalling the sayings of the "elders" (7) and instructing that no "ceremony" (11) be left out, he orders Calphurnia to stand in Antony's way so that she can be cured of barrenness. As in *Titus Andronicus,* the opening ritual creates an emblem of *Romanitas* that depicts Roman nobility but raises questions about Roman humanity. We wonder about the "unkindness" of the principal characters, about the Roman pride that leads Titus to fight his own sons and that prompts Caesar coldly and publicly to accuse his wife of a "sterile curse" (9).

That Caesar first appears participating in the Lupercalia should give the audience pause. The feast, as its name implies, commemorates the suckling of Romulus and Remus by a she-wolf; by association, it commemorates as well the founding of Rome and Roman monarchy under Romulus. In his concern with the Lupercalia, in his desire for progeny (a detail not in Plutarch), Caesar recalls Romulus, who initiated the Lupercalia and started a line of kings. Moreover, as audiences surely knew, both Caesar and Romulus slew their former partners, chief rivals for power; both gained reputations as tyrants; and both blazed in the heavens as stars after death. It required no great effort of historical imagination for Shakespeare to grasp the parallels between these two Romans. Plutarch furnished all the necessary information, Appian suggested one point of possible similarity, and both Ovid and Vergil, in passages probably familiar to Shakespeare, associated Romulus with Caesar.[7]

Other ominous undertones sound during the processional. The soothsayer voices a foreboding prophecy, and Brutus and Cassius engage in hushed conversation. Brutus contrasts himself with Antony: "I am not gamesome; I do lack some part / Of that quick

---

[7]See Plutarch's accounts of Romulus and Caesar in *Parallel Lives.* Appian, *An Avncient Historie and Exquisite Chronicle of the Romanes Warres, Both Ciuile and Foren,* trans. W. B. (1578), compares Caesar to Romulus, "who of a Kyng became a Tyranne" (p. 138). (Hereafter cited as Appian.) See also Ovid, *Metamorphoses* XV.843–70; Vergil, *Georgics* I.466–514; *Aeneid* I.286–96; and *Aeneid* VI.777–807.

spirit that is in Antony" (I.ii.28–9). Dressed *"for the course"* (s.d. I.ii), Antony appears as a man of purposeful direction, in accord with Roman tradition and in the center of Caesar's triumphal celebration. Brutus, however, appears off with Cassius, silent and brooding, out of step with the grand proceedings.[8] He is stymied, immobile, directionless. The metaphors of motion in his speech suggest his predicament. He wonders where Cassius would "lead" (63) him by having him "seek" (64) into himself; he hopes the gods will "speed" (88) him; he is wary of being "further mov'd" (167).

Unlike Brutus, Cassius has a clear plan of action and a definite direction. As did the tribunes, he proceeds by disrobing the image of Caesar, by stripping away the legends to reveal the man – flawed, fragile, human. According to Cassius, there is no special greatness in the Colossus and no special magic in Caesar's oft-sounded name. That a man of such feeble temper should get the start of the majestic world shows only how degenerate the world has become:

> Age, thou art sham'd!
> Rome, thou hast lost the breed of noble bloods!
> When went there by an age since the great flood
> But it was fam'd with more than with one man?
>
> (I.ii.150–3)

The appeal to Roman history here, complete with a glance at the story of Deucalion and Pyrrha, has special application to Brutus. Cassius goes on to mention Lucius Junius Brutus, expeller of the Tarquins:

> O! you and I have heard our fathers say
> There was a Brutus once that would have brook'd
> Th' eternal devil to keep his state in Rome
> As easily as a king.
>
> (158–61)

The arguments historical and ancestral are accompanied by the argument topographical. The once great and spacious city of

---

[8]As Emrys Jones points out, the structure of the scene enforces the sense of conspiratorial isolation. *Scenic Form in Shakespeare* (Oxford: Clarendon Press, 1971), pp. 18–23. See also J. L. Styan, *Shakespeare's Stagecraft* (Cambridge: Cambridge University Press, 1967), pp. 91–2, 133.

"wide walks" (155) has now shrunk to provide "room enough" (156) for only one man.

Cassius demythologizes Caesar by appealing to the mythos of Rome, to its proud history and physical grandeur. Continuing the attack, he recollects Caesar's humiliating illness and physical weakness, his fever in Spain and his near drowning in the "troubled Tiber" (101). Cassius's description of the latter incident presents a Caesar directly opposed to the magisterial figure who appeared on stage. In place of the assured conqueror leading the procession, Cassius depicts the helpless drowning mortal, thrashing wildly in the waters, incapable of purposeful movement. Cassius's description of the "angry flood" (103) and the roaring "torrent" (107) evokes the merciless waves of the Vergilian sea, which test Roman resolve and courage in *Lucrece* and in *Titus Andronicus*. The reference to Vergil becomes explicit as Cassius remembers his rescue of Caesar:

> I, as Aeneas, our great ancestor,
> Did from the flames of Troy upon his shoulder
> The old Anchises bear, so from the waves of Tiber
> Did I the tired Caesar.
>
> (112–15)

In so rhetorically taut and controlled a play, this allusion to Vergil demands careful consideration. As portrayed in *Aeneid* II, Aeneas asks Anchises to gather up the sacred articles and household gods; the son then takes the father on his back and carries him from the burning city:

> ergo age, care pater, cervici imponere nostrae;
> ipse subibo umeris, nec me labor iste gravabit.
> quo res cumque cadent, unum et commune periclum,
> una salus ambobus erit. mihi parvus Iulus
> sit comes, et longe servet vestigia coniunx.
>
> (707–11)

> Come then, dear father, mount upon my neck; on my own
> shoulders I will stay thee, nor will such task o'erburden me.
> However things may fall, we both shall have one common
> peril, one salvation. Let little Iülus come with me, and let
> my wife follow our steps afar.

Vergil here presents the archetypal scene of *pietas,* memorialized on Roman coins[9] and often celebrated by ancient writers such as Ovid (*Met.* XIII.624–6) and Propertius (Bk. IV.I.43–4). Speaking of the glorious contest between fathers and children, Seneca writes in *De Beneficiis:*

> Vicit Aeneas patrem, ipse eius in infantia leve
> tutumque gestamen, gravem senio per media hostium
> agmina et per cadentis circa se urbis ruinas ferens,
> cum complexus sacra ac penates deos religiosus
> senex non simplici vadentem sarcina premeret; tulit
> illum per ignes et (quid non pietas potest?) pertulit
> colendumque inter conditores Romani imperii posuit.
> (III.xxxvii.1)[10]

In Golding's translation (1578):

> *Aeneas* ouermatched his father. For wheras his father had
> borne him a Babe when he was a light and safe cariage: he
> tooke up his father heauie with age, and caried him
> through the thickest preace of his enemies, and through the
> ruines of the Citie falling doune about him, at what tyme
> the deuout old man holding his holie Relikes and household
> gods in in [*sic*] his armes, loded him with another burthen
> heuyer than himself. Yet bare he him in the fyre, yea and
> (what is not naturall loue able too doo?) he bare him
> thorough and shryned him too be woorshipped among the
> Founders of the *Romaine* Empyre.[11]

Later generations followed Seneca in regarding the carrying of Anchises as a supreme example of *pietas,* the virtuous respect for gods, country, and family.[12] Commentators on Vergil provided

---

[9]Michael Grant, *Roman Myths,* 2nd ed. (London: Penguin Books, 1973), p. 73.
[10]*Seneca: Moral Essays with an English Translation by John W. Basore,* The Loeb Classical Library, 3 vols. (1928–35), Vol. III.
[11]*The Woorke of Lucius Annaeus Seneca Concerning Benefyting,* trans. Arthur Golding (1578), p. 45.
[12]Renaissance humanists such as George Sandys in his edition of the *Metamorphoses* (1632) spoke of the Roman Empire as the reward for Aeneas's *pietas:* "This piety of *Aeneas* was rewarded in his posterity with the greatest, & longest continuing Empire, that ever virtue or fortune afforded." *Ovid's Metamorphosis Englished, Mythologized, and Represented in Figures by George Sandys,* ed. Karl K. Hulley and Stanley T. Vandersall (Lincoln: University of

appropriate glosses, ranging from the brief but touching para-
phrase of Donatus to the elaborate and learned moral essay of
Pontanus, complete with classical, medieval, and Renaissance allusions, as well as various analogs.[13] The lessons of the grammar
school on Vergilian *pietas* were reinforced by various sources: by
collectors of proverbs like Erasmus, for example; by compilers of
classical lore like Aelianus; by cataloguers of moralized antiquity
like Ravisius Textor; and by emblematists like Andrea Alciati and
Geoffrey Whitney.[14] Interestingly enough, the Vergilian emblem
was also recalled on stage by one of the characters in *The Tragedie
of Caesar and Pompey* (pub. 1607), a play often cited as a possible
source for *Julius Caesar*.[15] By the time of Shakespeare's play the
original Vergilian passage and its moral significance were commonplaces of Renaissance humanism.

In context, then, Cassius's allusion is clearly ironic. His appropriation of the well-known emblem urges not humble filial piety,
but arrogant self-assertion and murderous betrayal. Despite
Caesar's descent from Aeneas and his position as leader of state,
he here is seen as a type of Anchises – weak, old, and troublesome.

Nebraska Press, 1970), p. 608. Aeneas's exercise of *pietas* is wholly consistent
with biblical teaching, as many passages in both testaments exhort children to
love, honor, and respect their parents. Cf. Exodus 20:12, 21:17; Leviticus
20:9; Deuteronomy 5:16; Proverbs 20:20; Ecclesiasticus 3:9–18; Matthew
15:4; Mark 7:10; Ephesians 6:1–4 (Geneva Bible, 1560).

[13]Donatus writes: *pater, inquam, non tibi desunt meae ceruicis obsequia, iam
imponere humeris meis, pondus tuum deliciae meae sunt, facit pietas leue, quod
putas esse grauissimum, sarcinam tuam libēter tolerabit affectus,* "Father, I say,
my neck is willing to do its duty and lays the charge on my shoulders. Your
burden is my joy. My love and respect makes light what you consider so heavy
and will gladly bear your pack as well." *Opera* (Venice, 1544), reprinted in *The
Renaissance and the Gods*, No. 7, 2 vols. (New York: Garland, 1976), Vol. I,
fol. 230ᵛ. For the Pontanus essay, see Jacobus Pontanus (Spanmüller), *Sym-
bolarum Libri XVII Virgilii* (Augsburg, 1599), reprinted in *The Renaissance
and the Gods*, No. 18, 3 vols. (New York: Garland, 1976), Vol. II, cols. 961–4.

[14]See Erasmus, *Adagiorvm Chiliades, Omnia Opera*, Vol. II (Basel, 1536), pp.
326–7; Aelianus, *A Registre of Hystories*, trans. Abraham Fleming (1576),
fols. 39ᵛ–40; Textor, *Theatrvm Poeticvm atque Historicvm* (1609), p. 557;
Alciati, *Emblemata cvm Commentariis* (Padua, 1621), pp. 828–31; Whitney,
A Choice of Emblemes (1586), p. 163.

[15]In *The Tragedie of Caesar and Pompey, or Caesars Reuenge* (1607), Cato Jr.
says to his father (note to Senecan formulation): "Father I go with a more
willing minde, / Then did *Aeneas* when from Troyan fire, / He bare his Father,
and did so restore: / The greatest gift hee had receiued before" (sig. E).

Cassius casts himself as a new Aeneas, one unwilling to shoulder the burden of the past, but destined with Brutus to found a new Rome. Cassius's awkward repetition ("I . . . Did I . . .") suggests the fumbling impatience of his self-assertion in the conceit and in the play. He here replaces the articulated emblem of *pietas,* the image of the son saving the father, with the unarticulated emblem of *impietas,* the image of the son slaying the father.[16] To be true sons of Rome, he suggests, he and Brutus must murder the *pater patriae.*[17] Cassius's allusion to the *Aeneid* repudiates its most important virtue, one of the fundamental principles of Roman civilization – *pietas.* Unlike the clumsy stitching and patching in *Titus Andronicus,* Shakespeare here weaves Vergilian images into powerful dramatic symbols.

The encounter of Brutus and Cassius marks the midpoint of the opening action. Two pairs of parallel scenes frame the meeting: On the inside are two processional marches; on the outside are two conversations, one between the tribunes and the commoners, and the other among Casca, Brutus, and Cassius. The second procession reintroduces Caesar, who appears shrewd and perceptive but deaf in one ear, an infirmity perhaps symbolic of a fatal inability to listen. Structurally, the return procession centers Brutus and Cassius in the surrounding pageantry, but isolates them from it. After joining them, Casca remarks of the cheering mob, "But there's no heed to be / taken of them; if Caesar had stabb'd their mothers, / they would have done no less" (273–5). Thus he reiterates the tribunes' suggestion that support for Caesar impiously betrays the Roman family and city. Casca's account of Antony,

---

[16] For the legend that Brutus was Caesar's "natural" son, see Plutarch, Vol. VI, pp. 185–6, Appian, p. 137. In 2 *Henry VI* (IV.i.136–7) Suffolk refers to "Brutus' bastard hand." Shakespeare chooses not to exploit this legend in *Julius Caesar,* probably to develop more freely the larger symbolic ironies of the assassination and to enable us to sympathize with Brutus or at least experience ambivalence about him.

[17] The inscription on a pillar in Rome proclaimed Caesar the father of his country. See Suetonius, *The Historie of Twelve Caesars, Emperovrs of Rome,* trans. Philemon Holland (1606), p. 35; Richard Reynoldes, *A Chronicle of All the Noble Emperours of the Romaines* (1571), fol. 9ᵛ. Perceptively, Northrop Frye categorizes *Julius Caesar* as a tragedy of order, the central archetype of which is the slaying of the father. "My Father as He Slept: The Tragedy of Order," in *Fools of Time: Studies in Shakespearean Tragedy* (Toronto: University of Toronto Press, 1967), pp. 3–39.

Caesar, and the crown in the marketplace, his contemptuous review of the false theatrical nature of the political charade, looks
ahead to important incidents in the play. The unlocalized streets in
Titus Andronicus will here give way to the marketplace, scene of
crucial confrontations with the people. The Roman marketplace,
Casca suggests, rocks with unruly, gullible crowds buying and
selling; in it rhetorical and theatrical abilities alone determine the
value of things.

⋈⚊⊐❀⊏⚊⋉

The thunder and lightning of the storm scene appropriately accompany Casca's recital of the unnatural portents in Rome. Deriving from various sources – Plutarch's *Lives*, Vergil's *Georgics*,
Ovid's *Metamorphoses*, possibly Marlowe's Lucan – this passage
superbly exemplifies Shakespeare's synthetic imagination at
work.[18] Beyond the recognized borrowing from *Georgics* I.467ff.,
however, there is further indebtedness to Vergil. "Th' ambitious
ocean" that Casca has seen "swell, and rage, and foam" (I.iii.7) is
a Shakespearean innovation, perhaps inspired by the *Aeneid*'s vast
and troubled seas, those deep waters that continually haunt Shakespeare in the Roman plays. The lion that "glaz'd upon" Casca and
"went surly by" (21) is also Vergilian, descended probably from
the lions that appear throughout Vergil's works as symbols of
savage destructive energy. Shakespeare may be remembering specifically the yoked lions of Cybele's peaceful reign (*Aen.* III.113;
X.253) or the wild lions characteristic of the iron age (*Ecl.* IV.22;
Geo. II.151–2).

The Vergilian echoes support the initial impression that the
storm seriously threatens Roman order and civilization. The lion
by the Capitol, the screech owl in daylight, the birds and beasts
changed "from quality and kind" (I.iii.64) – all suggest the un-
leashing of bestial forces. The animal imagery continues in Cassius's remarks on Caesar's strength:

[18]See Kenneth Muir, *The Sources of Shakespeare's Plays* (New Haven: Yale
University Press, 1978), pp. 122–5.

And why should Caesar be a tyrant then?
Poor man, I know he would not be a wolf,
But that he sees the Romans are but sheep;
He were no lion, were not Romans hinds.

(103–6)

The images of predation, reminiscent of *Lucrece* and *Titus Andronicus,* anticipate Decius's remarks concerning Caesar's weakness:

I can o'ersway him; for he loves to hear
That unicorns may be betray'd with trees,
And bears with glasses, elephants with holes,
Lions with toils, and men with flatterers.

(II.i.203–6)

These images combine with the animal imagery of the storm to enhance the central imagistic pattern of the deer hunt, which culminates in the assassination of Caesar.[19] As in Shakespeare's other works, such imagery indicates the transformation of Rome into a forest. Signaling the start of this transformation, the storm heralds the birth of a conspiracy "incorporate" (I.iii.135) in Caesar's Rome just as Tamora's conspiracy is "incorporate" (I.i.462) in Saturninus's.

For Romans, however, the significance of the storm and the unnatural portents is a matter of dispute. The problem of truly assessing, interpreting, and making judgments, adumbrated by Brutus's indecision and Casca's review of the marketplace, receives restatement in the varying responses elicited by the storm.[20] Casca, breathless and horrified, sees the storm as an evil omen: It either reflects "civil strife in heaven" (I.iii.11) or portends the end of the world. Cicero refuses to interpret the wondrous events: "Indeed, it is a strange-disposed time; / But men may construe things after their fashion, / Clean from the purpose of the things

---

[19]James O. Wood, "Imitations of Actaeon in *Julius Caesar,*" *SQ,* 24 (1973), 85–8, argues plausibly that Shakespeare's linking of harts and hounds in *Julius Caesar* derives ultimately from Ovid's account of Actaeon. Shakespeare may have also taken a clue from Plutarch's account of the assassination: "He was striken at by some, and still had naked swords in his face, and was hacked and mangeled amonge them, as a wilde beaste taken of hunters" (V.68).

[20]For a full exposition of this point, see Charney, pp. 41–8. Charney goes on to note the ambivalence of two other images, blood and fire (pp. 48–66).

themselves" (I.iii.33–5). Like Brutus reading by the light of "ex-halations whizzing in the air" (II.i.44), Cicero remains unmoved by the fiery tempest and the extraordinary disruptions in nature. Cassius, however, considers the storm a pleasing sight to honest men. He believes that the "strange impatience of the heavens" (I.iii.61) manifests divine discontent with degenerate Rome, now under the sway of a single mortal "prodigious grown" (I.iii.77).

So confident is Cassius in his interpretation of the storm that he exposes himself to its fury:

> For my part, I have walk'd about the streets,
> Submitting me unto the perilous night;
> And thus unbraced, Casca, as you see,
> Have bar'd my bosom to the thunder-stone;
> And when the cross blue lightning seem'd to open
> The breast of heaven, I did present myself
> Even in the aim and very flash of it.
>
> (I.iii.46–52)

This bravado has no basis in Plutarch but probably originates in Shakespeare's remembrance of *Aeneid* V, where Aeneas bares his chest to the gods, invites the thunderbolt to strike, and witnesses as an answer to his prayers a divine tempest:

> tum pius Aeneas umeris abscindere vestem
> auxilioque vocare deos et tendere palmas:
> "Iuppiter omnipotens, si nondum exosus ad unum
> Troianos, si quid pietas antiqua labores
> respicit humanos, da flammam evadere classi
> nunc, pater, et tenuis Teucrum res eripe leto;
> vel tu, quod superest, infesto fulmine morti,
> si mereor, demitte tuaque hic obrue dextra."
> vix haec ediderat, cum effusis imbribus atra
> tempestas sine more furit tonitruque tremescunt
> ardua terrarum et campi; ruit aethere toto
> turibidus imber aqua densisque nigerrimus Austris.
>
> (685–96)

> Then good Aeneas rent the garment from his shoulders, and
> called the gods to his aid, lifting up his hands: "Almighty
> Jupiter, if thou dost not yet utterly abhor the Trojans to
> their last man, if thy loving-kindness of old hath any regard
> for human sorrows, grant to the fleet to escape the flame

even now, O Father, and snatch from doom the slender
fortunes of the Trojans! Or if I deserve it, do thou with
levelled thunderbolt send down to death the little that
remains, and here overwhelm us with thy hand." Scarce
had he uttered this when with streaming showers a black
tempest rages unrestrained; with thunder tremble hills and
plains; from the whole sky down rushes a fierce storm of
rain, pitch-black with laden south winds.

Once again Cassius casts himself in the role of Aeneas, just before
chiding Casca for not having "those sparks of life / That should be
in a Roman" (I.iii.57–8). Yet, as before, there is certain irony in
Cassius's imitation of Aeneas. Aeneas bares himself as a gesture of
piety, as an expression of his humility and his dependence on the
gods. Donatus explains:

> Cum videret Aeneas auxilio suorū, hoc est humanis
> nixibus contra tantam perniciem nauium opem competentem
> ferri non posse. tum discissa ab humeris veste, quod
> signū fuit doloris maximi, quoniā pius fuit, hoc est
> deorum purissimus cultor, superum numen restinguendo incendio
> supplice voce poscebat in auxilium.[21]

> > When Aeneas saw that with the aid of his own men, that is,
> > with human efforts, no help that would avail could be
> > brought against the great damage to his ships, then he tore
> > off the garment from his shoulders. Since he was pious, that
> > is, a most devout worshipper of the gods, he humbly
> > begged the divine powers for help in extinguishing the
> > flames.

The storm is a reward for Aeneas's piety and a sign of divine favor.
Cassius's baring of his chest after the storm has begun is an arrogant assertion of self, a gesture that brashly proclaims his own
manhood and courage, and assumes rather than petitions the
favor of the gods.

Fashioning himself as another Aeneas, Cassius seeks to return
Rome to its glorious and heroic past. To involve Brutus in the
effort, Cassius insistently recalls Junius Brutus, expeller of the
Tarquins. One of Cassius's reminders, a message attached to "old
Brutus' statue" (I.iii.146), reverses the action of undecking Cae-

---

[21]Virgil, *Opera*, Vol. I, fol. 315.

sar's statues, thereby signaling that the fates of Brutus and Caesar are inextricably but inversely linked. Cassius's strategy is successful: Brutus attempts to remake himself in the heroic image of the past:

> My ancestors did from the streets of Rome
> The Tarquin drive when he was call'd a king.
> "Speak, strike, redress!" Am I entreated
> To speak and strike? O Rome, I make thee promise,
> If the redress will follow, thou receivest
> Thy full petition at the hand of Brutus!
>
> (II.i.53–8)

Like Cassius, Brutus employs animal imagery that reflects ironically upon his high-minded intentions and noble resolutions. He muses: "It is the bright day that brings forth the adder, / And that craves wary walking" (II.i.14–15). Worrying about putting a "sting" in Caesar by crowning him, Brutus thinks him "as a serpent's egg, / Which, hatch'd, would as his kind grow mischievous" (32–3); he decides to "kill him in the shell" (34).[22]

Like many of the images in the Roman plays, Brutus's snake metaphors may derive from remembrance of Vergil. The image of the snake emerging into light depicts the terrifying Pyrrhus in *Aeneid* II:

> Vestibulum ante ipsum primoque in limine Pyrrhus
> exsultat telis et luce coruscus aëna;
> qualis ubi in lucem coluber mala gramina pastus,
> frigida sub terra tumidum quem bruma tegebat,
> nunc positis novus exuviis nitidusque iuventa
> lubrica convolvit sublato pectore terga,
> arduus ad solem, et linguis micat ore trisulcis.
>
> (469–75)

[22]The Variorum edition of *Julius Caesar*, ed. Horace Howard Furness, Jr. (Philadelphia: Lippincott, 1913), contains an interestingly pertinent gloss on Messala's lines about Error slaying its mother, Melancholy (V.iii.67ff.): "Wright: Like the brood of the adder, according to a popular belief. Compare: 'The Adders death, is her owne broode.' – Gosson, *Schoole of Abuse*, 1579 (ed. Arber, p. 46)" (p. 262). Brutus's adder, joining the other images of *impietas* including that of Messala's allegory, reflects ironically on his intentions. For an interpretation of the snake image as emblem, see John W. Velz, "Two Emblems in Brutus' Orchard," *RenQ*, 25 (1972), 307–15.

> Just before the entrance-court and at the very portal is
> Pyrrhus, proudly gleaming in the sheen of brazen arms:
> even as when into the light comes a snake, fed on poi-
> sonous herbs, whom cold winter kept swollen underground,
> now, his slough cast off, fresh and glistening in youth, with
> uplifted breast he rolls his slippery length, towering towards
> the sun and darting from his mouth a three-forked tongue!

This identification of the emerging snake and the emerging tyrant
– proud, lethal, and impious – functions as a poetic archetype in
Lucrece and *Titus Andronicus* and gives power and resonance to
Brutus's fears. Shakespeare may also have in mind a passage from
Georgics III:

> saepe sub immotis praesepibus aut mala tactu
> vipera delituit caelumque exterrita fugit,
> aut tecto adsuetus coluber succedere et umbrae
> (pestis acerba boum) pecorique adspergere virus,
> fovit humum. cape saxa manu, cape robora, pastor,
> tollentemque minas et sibila colla tumentem
> deice.
>
> $\qquad\qquad\qquad\qquad\qquad$ (416–22)

> Oft under sheds uncleansed has lurked a viper, deadly to
> touch, and shrunk in terror from the light; or an adder,
> sore plague of the kine, that is wont to glide under the
> sheltering thatch and sprinkle venom on the cattle, has
> hugged the ground. Snatch up in thy hand, shepherd,
> snatch stones and staves, and as he rises in menace and
> swells his hissing neck, strike him down!

Here again is the chilling image of the lurking snake. The intrusion
of the imperative mood at the close of Brutus's speech – "prevent"
(28), "fashion" (30), "think" (32), and "kill" (34) – strikingly
resembles Vergil's use of the imperative – *cape, cape,* and *deice.*

Evoking powerful images of tyranny and danger, the Vergilian
echoes deepen the ambivalence of Brutus's soliloquy. For Caesar,
by Brutus's own admission (28–30), has not yet proved himself to
be either Pyrrhus or a lurking viper. The entrance of the conspirators, hats plucked about their ears and faces half-buried in their
cloaks, brings the "hideous dream" (65) of Brutus's deliberation
to a climax. There is an eerie, nightmarish quality to this meeting

as Brutus faces the "monstrous visage" (81) of Conspiracy. Confusion concerning time – "I cannot by the progress of the stars / Give guess how near to day" (2–3) – matches confusion concerning place as two conspirators, Cinna and Casca, try to determine where the sun will rise. When Brutus joins the conspiracy, he transforms the phantasmal netherworld, suspended between night and day, between waking and sleeping, between the first motion and the acting of a dreadful thing, into a scene of purposeful movement. Like Lucius Junius Brutus and Titus, this Brutus presides over a conspiratorial ritual that binds together the participants, assigns to each definite parts, and validates action; he takes their hands, "one by one" (112). The striking of the clock, often jeered at as an anachronistic intrusion, marks with dramatic clarity and portentous solemnity the conspirators' exit from the limbo of indecision and their entrance into the world of history.

Several of Shakespeare's fundamental Roman themes converge in this striking scene. Having removed himself from his private household and family, Brutus acts to discharge the responsibilities levied by his public family, that is, the city of Rome and his Roman ancestry. He becomes the head of a new Roman family, one united by honor as well as common blood. He declares:

> every drop of blood
> That every Roman bears, and nobly bears,
> Is guilty of a several bastardy,
> If he do break the smallest particle
> Of any promise that hath pass'd from him.
>
> (II.i.136–40)

Both Lucrece and Titus, we recall, also deny the claims of their private families in order to fulfill the claims of Rome. The paradoxes implicit in such action, however, first sketched in Titus's barbaric slaying of his children, receive sharper delineation in this play, particularly in the coming confrontations between husbands and wives.

Also reminiscent of *The Rape of Lucrece* is the rationale behind Brutus's decision to kill Caesar. In her anguished meditation Lucrece bases the decision to commit suicide on the conviction that her chaste soul is tied to her polluted body (1156–76). Similar logic, proceeding from a similar conviction, underlies Brutus's decision to murder Caesar:

> We all stand up against the spirit of Caesar,
> And in the spirit of men there is no blood;
> O that we could come by Caesar's spirit,
> And not dismember Caesar! But, alas,
> Caesar must bleed for it!
>
> (II.i.167–71)

The inextricability of body and soul provides the basis for action. Although the action here aims at the destruction of a dangerous spirit, not a defiled body, the pagan Roman conscience defines the ethical problem in exactly the same terms and arrives at the same conclusion.

Moreover, like Lucrece and Titus Andronicus, Brutus lives according to a strict code of honor. Respect for this code and desire for fame impel him to join the conspiracy and to insist upon a ritualistic assassination instead of a bloody slaughter:

> Our course will seem too bloody, Caius Cassius,
> To cut the head off and then hack the limbs –
>
> . . . . .
>
> Let's kill him boldly, but not wrathfully;
> Let's carve him as a dish fit for the gods,
> Not hew him as a carcass fit for hounds;
> And let our hearts, as subtle masters do,
> Stir up their servants to an act of rage,
> And after seem to chide 'em. This shall make
> Our purpose necessary, and not envious;
> Which so appearing to the common eyes,
> We shall be call'd purgers, not murderers.
>
> (II.i.162–3, 172–80)

The use of blunt, vivid verbs – "cut," "hack," "kill," "carve," and especially "hew" – recalls Lucius's speech in *Titus Andronicus:*

> Give us the proudest prisoner of the Goths,
> That we may hew his limbs and on a pile
> *Ad manes fratrum* sacrifice his flesh.
>
> (I.i.96–8)

Like Lucius's language, Brutus's words reveal the savagery of the impending Roman ritual; in addition, they expose the self-delusion of the conspirators. Brutus's emphasis on the appearance of virtue "to the common eyes" raises serious questions about Roman honor and fame. Both, one uneasily realizes, may be achieved by the clever manipulator of appearances as well as by the individual of extraordinary virtue.

The ensuing conversation with Portia clarifies the conflict between Brutus's love for his private family and his allegiance to Rome. Invoking "the right and virtue" of her place, past "vows of love," and "that great vow" of marriage (II.i.269, 272), Portia asks Brutus why he has ungently stolen from her bed. Her pointed questioning insists upon her lawful status as spiritual as well as physical partner:

> Within the bond of marriage, tell me, Brutus,
> Is it excepted I should know no secrets
> That appertain to you? Am I yourself
> But, as it were, in sort or limitation,
> To keep with you at meals, comfort your bed,
> And talk to you sometimes? Dwell I but in the suburbs
> Of your good pleasure?
>
> (II.i.280–6)

Asserting that she should not reside in the suburbs of Brutus's affection, Portia articulates the thematic conflict between Brutus's private and public worlds. She envisions the marital bed (and by implication the hearth, home, and family) as a kind of city no less important than Rome. Reminding Brutus that the vow of marriage "did incorporate" and make them one (273), she directly opposes their union to the conspiratorial incorporation and insists upon the priority of the former. Brutus's Roman soul must choose between the two bodies.

Because Portia's argument derives from her lawful status as Brutus's wife, it is virtually unanswerable. Portia, however, undoes her own eloquence and abandons the solid ground of her argument; instead of asserting her identity as woman and insisting upon her rights as wife, she soon argues that her worthiness derives from association with eminent Roman men:

> I grant I am a woman; but withal
> A woman that Lord Brutus took to wife.
> I grant I am a woman; but withal
> A woman well reputed, Cato's daughter.

> Think you I am no stronger than my sex,
> Being so father'd and so husbanded?
>
> (II.i.292–7)

She denies her sex and changes from wife to comrade-in-arms:

> I have made strong proof of my constancy,
> Giving myself a voluntary wound
> Here, in the thigh; can I bear that with patience,
> And not my husband's secrets?
>
> (299–302)

The wound in the thigh, so proximate to the genitals as to become a metonym for them, is a misogynic self-mutilation that negates Portia's earlier arguments. To his discredit (and to Rome's), Brutus finds this Roman display of constancy more persuasive than the appeals based on shared love and the great vow of marriage.

The ensuing encounter of Caesar and Calphurnia further illuminates the meeting of Brutus and Portia. As Norman Rabkin's analysis indicates, Shakespeare constructs this scene as the second half of a thematic diptych on the conflict between the Roman family and city.[23] Both Brutus and Caesar give orders to servants at the outset of the scenes, both yield to their kneeling wives, both exit, after all, in the company of conspirators. Like Portia, Calphurnia appears in dishabille to oppose the claims of the marriage bed to those of Rome. She recounts the frightening portents of the night and begs Caesar to heed them. Unlike Portia, however, Calphurnia never plays the Roman warrior but remains the Roman wife, concerned for her husband's life, not his honor, possessed of acute and intimate insight into his character ("Alas, my lord, / Your wisdom is consum'd in confidence" [II.ii.48–9]). Unburdened by her ancestry and by the heroic mythos of Rome, Calphurnia does what Portia could not: She voices her fears openly and honestly and tries to impede the grand march of history to the Capitol.

Caesar's response – his resignation to the will of the gods, his stoical reflections on cowardice and courage, his brave flouting of Danger – is splendid and stirring. It might be more appropriately

---

[23]Norman Rabkin, "Structure, Convention, and Meaning in *Julius Caesar*," *JEGP*, 63 (1964), 240–54; the argument appears fundamentally unchanged in *Shakespeare and the Common Understanding* (New York: Free Press, 1967), pp. 105ff., and moves to conclusions different from those presented here.

addressed, however, to a crowd in the amphitheater than to his wife in their home. Like the conspirators, Caesar denies his private self and repudiates all domestic obligations in order to act out his public role. One is hard pressed to decide whether such denial is the necessary sacrifice of a great man or the posturing of an insufferable egocentric. The ambiguity of Caesar's character deepens when he accepts Decius Brutus's interpretation of Calphurnia's ominous dream:

> *Decius:* This dream is all amiss interpreted,
> It was a vision fair and fortunate.
> Your statue spouting blood in many pipes,
> In which so many smiling Romans bath'd,
> Signifies that from you great Rome shall suck
> Reviving blood, and that great men shall press
> For tinctures, stains, relics, and cognizance.
> This by Calphurnia's dream is signified.
> *Caesar:* And this way have you well expounded it.
>
> (II.ii.83–91)

Flattered by the image of himself as the vital source of nourishment for the city, Caesar dismisses Calphurnia and her foolish fears. Ironically, he turns away from his flesh-and-blood wife to the insubstantial image of himself as the great mother of Rome, as the *mater patriae* who will give suck to future generations.

Such turning, like the turning of Portia from herself and her womanhood, implicitly denies sexual identity, the fundamental principle of procreation and healthy family life. This denial, like the larger pattern of Roman ethical behavior, subordinates the claims of the hearth and home to those of the city. Natural affection gives way to abstract ideals; present exigencies yield to the demands of the vaunted past and to those of the imagined future. All Romans, including women, must conduct themselves like heroic men, according to their "fathers' minds" not their "mothers' spirits," as Cassius puts it (I.iii.82–3).[24] Any civilization founded on principles such as these, Shakespeare suggests, is strange, unnatural, inhuman, and doomed. Portia's betrayal of herself ends in nervous distraction, despair, and suicide. Caesar's grandiose dis-

---

[24]The expression of misogynic attitudes is a recurring feature of the play and an important sign of Roman disintegration. See also I.ii.128; II.i.122; II.i.292; II.iv.39–40.

missal of Calphurnia leads directly to the confirmation of her fears, to his assassination in the Capitol.

Shakespeare's depiction of Portia and Calphurnia in *Julius Caesar* differs significantly from his previous depictions of Roman women. These two wives represent forces and ideals crucial to the city but tragically unrecognized and unappreciated. Their anguish conveys Shakespeare's increasingly critical conception of Rome and Roman values. Both Portia and Calphurnia differ from Lucrece, who simply lives and dies by the Roman code of honor, and from Lavinia, who is simply one of its pathetic victims. They hark back not to Shakespeare's Roman works, but to Vergil's *Aeneid,* kindred in blood and spirit to Andromache, to the Trojan women who set fire to the fate-driven ships at Drepanum, to the weeping mother of Euryalus, and to all the bereaved wives and mothers of Italy.

***

The revelation of Calphurnia's dream begins a series of vignettes that portrays possible impediments to the march of history. Brutus confesses a qualm in an aside, "That every like is not the same, O Caesar, / The heart of Brutus earns to think upon!" (II.ii.128–9). Artemidorus announces his decision to give Caesar a letter exposing the conspiracy. Portia struggles to keep the secret from Lucius. The soothsayer ominously appears. Popilius Lena draws close to Caesar and engages him in private conversation. Aside from increasing dramatic tension, this focus on the potential for miscarriage underscores the inevitability of the assassination. Despite the vacillations of human will, the various warnings – both supernatural and natural – and the vagaries of circumstance, the Romans all move to the appointed place at the appointed time.[25] The

[25]Like Shakespeare, others emphasize the power of fate in bringing Caesar and the conspirators together on the ides of March. See Plutarch: "For these things, they may seeme to come by chaunce: but the place where the murther was prepared, and where the Senate was assembled, and where also there stoode up an image of Pompey dedicated by himselfe amongst other ornamentes which he gave unto the Theater: all these were manifest proofes that it was the ordinaunce of some god, that made this treason to be executed, specially in that

references to time in these scenes – to the hour as it progresses from three to eight to nine, and to the ides of March – suggest the relentlessness of history. The many references to place (to the Capitol instead of Plutarch's Senate House) present a familiar symbol of Roman government and provide a familiar focus for the action.[26]

The march of history to the Capitol and to Caesar's assassination takes the tangible form of another procession across stage. Caesar plays judge at a formal session of suits and complaints: "Are we all ready? What is now amiss / That Caesar and his Senate must redress?" (III.i.31–2). Like the earlier Lupercalian festivities and the burial ritual of *Titus Andronicus*, this Roman ceremony presents an ambivalent picture to the audience. Caesar condemns all attempts to influence his judgment as "sweet words, / Low-crooked curtsies, and base spaniel fawning" (III.i.42–3), better directed to "ordinary men" (37) than to himself. He insists upon the justice of his original decisions and likens his constancy to that of the "northern star" (60), true-fixed, unassailable, superior to all other sparks in the sky. Eloquent as such rhetoric surely is, the audience must feel discomfited by the brash assertions of superiority, especially in view of Caesar's physical disabilities, his susceptibility to Decius's flattery, and his recent vacillation concerning Calphurnia's dream. Furthermore, Cimber's suit for his banished brother, the occasion of Caesar's outbursts, evokes a similarly divided response. At first glance, the suit appears to be either an attempt to deflect the course of justice for personal rea-

---

verie place" (Vol. V, pp. 66–7); see also Vol. VI, p. 194. Appian also notes the inevitability of the movement to the Capitol: "*For it must needes come that was determined*" (p. 140). So does Velleius Paterculus, *Velleius Paterculus, Compendium of Roman History, Res Gestae Divi Augusti, with an English Translation by Frederick W. Shipley*, The Loeb Classical Library (1924): "But verily the power of destiny is inevitable; it confounds the judgement of him whose fortune it has determined to reverse" (p. 175). See also the parenthetical remark of Florus, *Lucius Annaeus Florus, Epitome of Roman History, Cornelius Nepos*, [Florus] trans. Edward Seymour Forster, The Loeb Classical Library (1929): *Quanta vis fati!*, "How powerful is fate!" (pp. 298, 299); Richard Reynoldes's marginalia, "Man purposeth and God disposeth" (*Chronicle*, fol. 8v); and Lodowick Lloid, *The Consent of Time* (1590): "destinies may be easier foreseene then auoyded, *Caesar* was that day slaine" (p. 537).

[26] On Shakespeare's conflation of the Capitol and Senate House here and elsewhere, see Lizette Andrews Fisher, "Shakspere and the Capitol," *MLN*, 22 (1907), 177–82.

sons or a ploy to get the conspirators in striking range. Yet, Cimber's plea for his banished brother touches the audience, recapitulating in miniature the conflict between family and city, between natural affection and Roman virtue.

The calculated ambivalence of this Roman ceremony suggests the problems inherent in human judgment. The audience's confusion concerning the events on stage reflects the moral confusion of the characters, who attempt to apply timeless, abstract, and universal principles to a temporal, immediate, specific (in a word, dramatic) situation. The problem of moral action thus adumbrated receives attention and articulation throughout the play by the contradictory claims of "constancy."[27] Both the conspirators and the victim invoke this virtue. Brutus exhorts his fellows to bear their purpose with "formal constancy" (II.i.227); Caesar boasts that he is as constant "as the northern star." In one context constancy signifies resolute hypocrisy and aids rebellion; in another, it signifies immovable honesty and complements authority.

Justus Lipsius's treatise, *Two Bookes of Constancie* (1595), sheds some light on contemporary understanding of this virtue. Grounding his discussion on the writings of Roman Stoics, Lipsius succinctly defines "constancy":

> CONSTANCIE is a right and immoueable strength of the
> minde, neither lifted up, nor pressed downe with externall
> or casuall accidentes.[28]

He then explains that the constant man rises above present misfortune, exhibits unshakable equanimity, and disdains all earthly striving. According to this definition, the claims of both Brutus and Caesar seem inadmissible. Both men show concern about their earthly situation, both vacillate at crucial times, both seek fame and reputation. The ironic disparity between the characters' self-

---

[27] Among the important discussions of "constancy" in this play are John S. Anson, "*Julius Caesar:* The Politics of the Hardened Heart," *ShakS,* 2 (1967 for 1966), 11–33; R. J. Kaufmann and Clifford J. Ronan, "Shakespeare's *Julius Caesar:* An Appollonian and Comparative Reading," *CompD,* 4 (1970), 18–51; Marvin L. Vawter, "'Division 'Tween Our Souls': Shakespeare's Stoic Brutus," *ShakS,* 7 (1974), 173–95. All three articles argue that the repeated claims of constancy are undercut so as to criticize the philosophy of Roman Stoicism. It should be observed also that Shakespeare's understanding of the deficiencies of Stoicism does not preclude his appreciation of its virtues.

[28] Trans. John Stradling, p. 9.

image and the reality suggests the difficulty of making disinterested moral judgments, of distinguishing between base desires and noble aspirations in oneself and in others.

The assassination scene poses dramatically the problem of assessing and evaluating character. Just after Caesar imperiously sets himself apart from men who are flesh, blood, and apprehensive, the conspirators brutally stab him to death. This climactic moment paralyzes our ability to make calm judgments. The spectacle stuns the audience, which becomes totally absorbed in the blood flowing copiously on Caesar's toga, dropping on the boards and splashing on the conspirators. The blood does not indicate whether Caesar was tyrant or king, but only that he was a mortal human being, not a marble Roman bust.[29] The assassination does not contradict preconceived notions and evaluations, but merely renders them, for the moment, peripheral.

The aftermath of the assassination transports the conspirators back to the phantasmal netherworld of uncertainty, indirection, and disorder. Cinna's triumphant shout, "Liberty! Freedom! Tyranny is dead!" (III.i.78), rings hollow amid the uproar. Directions to stand still, to ascend the pulpit, to stand fast together, to talk not of standing are barked out and ignored. The conspirators try to impose order on the chaos by participating in a blood ritual:[30]

> Stoop, Romans, stoop,
> And let us bathe our hands in Caesar's blood
> Up to the elbows, and besmear our swords;
> Then walk we forth, even to the market-place,
> And waving our red weapons o'er our heads,
> Let's all cry, "Peace, freedom, and liberty!"
>
> (III.i.105–10)

This ghastly ceremony, perhaps deriving from a detail in Plu-

---

[29]This reading is indebted to Matthew N. Proser, *The Heroic Image in Five Shakespearean Tragedies* (Princeton: Princeton University Press, 1965), pp. 10–50, who discusses the significance of the various statues in the play and the opposing pattern of blood imagery. Other perceptive discussions have been contributed by Leo Kirschbaum, "Shakespeare's Stage Blood and Its Critical Significance," *PMLA*, 64 (1949), 517–29; Foakes, "Approach to *Julius Caesar*," pp. 261–3; and Charney, pp. 48–59. (See also note 30.)

[30]See the seminal article of Brents Stirling, "Or Else This Were a Savage Spectacle," *PMLA*, 66 (1951), 765–74.

tarch's account,[31] vividly realizes Calphurnia's dream. It recalls as well the bloody slaughter of Lavinia and the Thyestean banquet of *Titus Andronicus*. In both plays the gory spectacles clash with the noble sentiments and abstract ideals producing them. Reality remains intransigently horrible, unsusceptible of transformation by the presiding masters of ceremony or by the power of the rituals. The image of the theater, introduced by Cassius and Brutus in a burst of self-congratulation, points up the falseness of the enacted charade:

> *Cassius:* Stoop then, and wash. How many ages hence
>   Shall this our lofty scene be acted over
>   In states unborn and accents yet unknown!
> *Brutus:* How many times shall Caesar bleed in sport,
>   That now on Pompey's basis lies along
>   No worthier than the dust!
> *Cassius:* So oft as that shall be,
>   So often shall the knot of us be call'd
>   The men that gave their country liberty.
>
> (III.i.111–19)

The theatrical image raises again with renewed force the disturbing host of questions concerning Roman honor, the reward of fame, and the manipulation of appearance and opinion. Shakespeare's Romans, it seems, addicted to looking backward to past glory and forward to future judgment, habitually give up their capacity for normal human response and lose what is precious and important in the present.

The city without Caesar is a city divided, "a dangerous Rome," as Antony says later (III.i.288), filled with lawless energy and the potential for violence. In such a place Brutus naturally assumes command. The striking series of parallels between the successful

---

[31]In "The Life of Marcus Brutus" Plutarch notes that Brutus "caught a blowe on his hande" and that "all the rest also were every man of them bloudied" (Vol. VI, p. 198).

rebel and his former nemesis, Caesar, suggests an ironic role reversal. After the assassination (III.i.98–100, 103–5), Brutus echoes Caesar's reflections on the inevitability of death and the folly of fear (II.ii.32–7). Like Caesar earlier, Brutus faces a kneeling suppliant in the Capitol. And with Caesarean attention to proper form, Brutus presides over the blood ritual and the arrangements for Caesar's funeral, insisting on the observance of "all true rites and lawful ceremonies" (III.i.241). After the murder, the *impietas* originally associated with Caesar becomes an attribute of Brutus, who says to Antony, "Our reasons are so full of good regard / That were you, Antony, the son of Caesar, / You should be satisfied" (III.i.224–6). The language recalls Casca's sarcastic gibe at the crowd, "if Caesar had stabb'd their mothers, / they would have done no less"; now, however, Brutus, not Caesar, appears as the violator of familial bonds, as the impious parent killer.

As Brutus becomes more like Caesar, so Antony becomes more like Brutus.[32] Formerly the loyal citizen "dressed for the course," Antony emerges as the leader of a new rebellion. As Brutus did earlier, Antony encircles himself with conspirators and takes their bloody hands:

> Let each man render me his bloody hand.
> First, Marcus Brutus, will I shake with you;
> Next, Caius Cassius, do I take your hand;
> Now, Decius Brutus, yours; now yours, Metellus;
> Yours, Cinna; and, my valiant Casca, yours;
> Though last, not least in love, yours, good Trebonius.
>
> (III.i.184–9)

Unlike Brutus, however, Antony uses the handshaking ritual to mask his true designs. His real feelings are evident in his outburst of grief and sorrow:

> Pardon me, Julius! Here wast thou bay'd, brave hart,
> Here didst thou fall, and here thy hunters stand,
> Sign'd in thy spoil, and crimson'd in thy lethe.

---

[32]Antony himself points to the role reversal: "But were I Brutus, / And Brutus Antony, there were an Antony / Would ruffle up your spirits, and put a tongue / In every wound of Caesar, that should move / The stones of Rome to rise and mutiny" (III.ii.226–30). See also John W. Velz, " 'If I were Brutus now . . . ': Role Playing in *Julius Caesar*," *ShakS*, 4 (1969 for 1968), 149–59.

O world! thou wast the forest to this hart,
And this indeed, O world, the heart of thee.
How like a deer, strooken by many princes,
Dost thou here lie!

(III.i.204–10)

As in *Lucrece* and *Titus Andronicus,* the image of the hunted deer
arouses pity for the helpless victim. In addition, Antony's use of
the image reflects ironically on Brutus's resolution to avoid hewing
Caesar as a carcass fit for hounds and on the conspirators' perception of Rome as a wild forest.

Antony's soliloquy reveals his true purpose and concludes with
a chilling prophecy of civil war, destruction, and revenge:

A curse shall light upon the limbs of men;
Domestic fury and fierce civil strife
Shall cumber all the parts of Italy;
Blood and destruction shall be so in use,
And dreadful objects so familiar,
That mothers shall but smile when they behold
Their infants quartered with the hands of war;
All pity chok'd with custom of fell deeds;
And Caesar's spirit, ranging for revenge,
With Ate by his side come hot from hell,
Shall in these confines with a monarch's voice
Cry "Havoc!" and let slip the dogs of war,
That this foul deed shall smell above the earth
With carrion men, groaning for burial.

(262–75)

Although various sources and analogs have been cited -- Appian,
Kyd's *Cornelia,* Marlowe's Lucan, the anonymous *Caesar's Revenge* – none accounts for the apocalyptic tone and frightening
power of this prophecy.[33] Shakespeare draws here upon *Aeneid* I,
where Jupiter predicts the imprisonment of *Furor impius* in Augustus Caesar's reign:

aspera tum positis mitescent saecula bellis;
cana Fides et Vesta, Remo cum fratre Quirinus
iura dabunt; dirae ferro et compagibus artis

---

[33]Bullough, Vol. V, p. 44; Muir, *Sources of Shakespeare's Plays,* pp. 119–20.

claudentur Belli portae; Furor impius intus
saeva sedens super arma et centum vinctus aënis
post tergum nodis fremet horridus ore cruento.

(291–6)

Then shall wars cease and rough ages soften; hoary Faith
and Vesta, Quirinus with his brother Remus, shall give
laws. The gates of war, grim with iron and close-fitting
bars, shall be closed; within, impious Rage, sitting on
savage arms, his hands fast bound behind with a hundred
brazen knots, shall roar in the ghastliness of blood-stained
lips.

As the allusion to Romulus (Quirinus) and Remus makes clear,
civil war is the particular horror associated with *Furor impius*.
Servius, in fact, glosses *Furor impius* by citing its manifestation in
the conflict at Philippi:

(Furor impius ītus.) Vt superius diximus, propter
bella ciuilia, que, gesta sunt contra Brutum &
Cassium ab Augusto in Philippis: cōtra Sextū
Pompeium ab Augusto in Sicilia.[34]

(Impious Rage within.) As we said earlier, because of the
civil wars that were waged against Brutus and Cassius by
Augustus at Philippi, and against Sextus Pompeius by Augustus in Sicily.

Shakespeare may also be remembering and refashioning *Aeneid*
VII, where *Furor impius* breaks loose and ravages Italy. The civil
war there described, like the one in Antony's prophecy, is started
by a female fury, Allecto, who (like Ate) comes hot from hell. The
precipitating incident, interestingly enough, is the killing of a stag
by Ascanius during a hunt. Antony's "dogs of war" may also have
their origin in Vergil, specifically in the *obscenaeque canes* (*Geo.*
I.470), "ill-boding dogs," that appear at the hour of Caesar's
death.[35] Of course, Shakespeare may be recollecting no specific
incident or passage, but remembering the general spirit and sub-

---

[34]Virgil, *Opera*, Vol. I, fol. 173.
[35]Shakespeare may also be remembering Ovid's *canes* howling the night before
the assassination (*Met.* XV.797), a possibility rendered more likely by Shakespeare's probable use of this passage for the portents. See Martha Hale
Shackford, "*Julius Caesar* and Ovid," *MLN*, 41 (1926), 172–4.

stance of the Italian civil wars. Certainly the grim, hyperbolic vision of *impietas* that Antony articulates – "mothers shall but smile when they behold / Their infants quartered with the hands of war" – sets forth an essentially Vergilian view of war, that destructive madness which cuts down so many brave sons, destroys so many innocent children, and leaves weeping so many mothers and wives.

Having been prepared by Casca's account of Caesar's theatrics, we watch the scene shift to the marketplace, where Brutus and Antony perform for the Roman crowd. Brutus's speech, filled with pious abstractions and frequent repetitions of the word "love," wins noisy but uncomprehending approval. One pleb responds, "Let him be Caesar" (III.ii.51). Antony's famous speech, eloquently demonstrating the power of language to shape reality, transforms admiration to anger. He depicts the city as a forest: "O judgment! thou art fled to brutish beasts, / And men have lost their reason" (III.ii.104–5). In so doing, Antony turns the original argument for the assassination against the conspirators. In his view their attempt to restore Rome to civilized order has brought about only bestial violence. Skillfully, he also turns the charge of *impietas* against Brutus, Cassius, and the others. In the impassioned eulogy that follows, Caesar, formerly the devouring *pater patriae,* becomes the beneficent patriarch, the generous departed father who bequeathed money, walks, private arbors, and newly planted orchards to his many Roman sons, daughters, and descendants. Through the lens of Antony's rhetoric, the assassination appears a monstrous parricide, a vicious act of *impietas,* committed by cruel, ungrateful, and treacherous sons. The countermovement of the play is thus propelled by a shrewd bargainer's manipulation of language, money, and material goods in the marketplace. Consequently, the audience must face again the problem of determining value. This scene suggests that the difficulty of judging truly derives from man's universal and indelible streak of self-interest. It casts over the noble motivations of all Romans – Caesar, Brutus, Cassius, and even Antony himself – deep and disturbing shadows.

Before descending from the pulpit and reading the will, Antony bids the plebeians to "make a ring about the corpse of Caesar" (III.ii.158). As Brutus did earlier, he takes his place in the center of a conspiratorial circle on stage. Like Brutus, he proceeds to imitate

Lucius Junius Brutus. The display of Caesar's wounds to incite rebellion recalls with savage irony the display of Lucrece's corpse (*Luc.* 1850–2). Like the conspiracy against Caesar, the new conspiracy releases a torrent of lawless energy and anarchic violence into the city. This time the scene of destruction will not be the Capitol, but the private houses of Romans:

> 1. *Plebeian:* We'll burn his body in the holy place,
>   And with the brands fire the traitors' houses.
>
> (III.ii.254–5)

Ironically, the mob's irrational desire to destroy Roman houses proves them as impious and barbaric as their enemies. Like Pyrrhus, Tarquin, and the Goths, they threaten the heart of the city, the Roman home and family.

More impious than the mob, however, are its leaders. The newly formed triumvirate – Antony, Octavius, and Lepidus – reveals its character in the first appearance on stage. The indeterminate, private setting of their meeting lends an air of furtive criminality to the proceedings. Lepidus consents to his brother's death, Antony to his nephew's. Plutarch's recollection of the Proscription appropriately glosses this impious swapping of family members, this casual trading in human lives:

> Such place tooke wrath in them, as they regarded no kinred
> nor blood, and to speake more properly, they shewed that
> no brute or savage beast is so cruell as man, if with his
> licentiousnes he have liberty to execute his will.
>
> (V.363)

The shift in setting from various localities within the city – the streets, Capitol, marketplace, and private houses – to the vast, vaguely localized battlefields marks an important development in the play.[36] Having ridden "like madmen through the gates of

---

[36]Productions of *Julius Caesar* have often made striking use of its locality changes. Herbert Beerbohm Tree's lavish 1898 production, with scenes designed by Sir Lawence Alma-Tadema, featured a Senate House wherein Caesar

Rome" (III.ii.269), Brutus and Cassius suffer the fate of the tyran-nical Tarquins, expelled by Lucius Junius Brutus at the dawn of the Republic. (Transferring the epithet *superbus*, "proud," from the Tarquin to the rebel, Lucius Junius Brutus [*Aen*. VI.817], Ver-gil shows a similar understanding of the ironies implicit in Roman rebellion.) Outside the city the struggle for power is naked and ruthless; there Romans expose what is mortal and unsure to all that fortune, death, and danger dare.

Removed from the city, center of Roman life and law, Brutus and Cassius momentarily lose sight of their public purpose and fall into a private quarrel. Cassius scolds Brutus for condemning Lu-cius Pella; Brutus stands firm in his judgment, just as Caesar did with Metellus Cimber. Brutus admonishes Cassius for not sending gold and then disdains the business of raising money "by vile means" (IV.iii.71). Noble but foolish, he admits no compromise with political necessity. We hear Caesar's thunder in his rebuke:

> There is no terror, Cassius, in your threats;
> For I am arm'd so strong in honesty
> That they pass by me as the idle wind,
> Which I respect not.

> (IV.iii.66–9)

Yet, we wonder if this is greatness or hollow rhetoric. The fallen ruler haunts the memories of both conspirators throughout the quarrel. Brutus asks, "Did not great Julius bleed for justice' sake?" (19). There is the implicit comparison of Brutus to Caesar:

---

occupied the center spot, surrounded by conspirators, and flanked on either side by rows of senators and a large statue. The "rigid symmetry" of this setting gave way to the illusion of enormous space in the forum scene, created by some 250 milling supers in multicolored costumes. In contrast, the setting for Bru-tus's tent was stark: a few strips of cloth, skin rugs, rocks, and simple furnish-ings. See John Ripley, *"Julius Caesar" on Stage in England and America, 1599–1973* (Cambridge: Cambridge University Press, 1980), pp. 150–75. (The quotation above appears on p. 160.) Witness as well the creative design of Glen Byam Shaw's 1957 production. The play opens with six majestic fluted monoliths arranged outward from Caesar. The forum scene shows the mono-liths in disarray, and the huge gap in center stage is filled only by a popular pulpit from which successive Romans harangue the multitude. Brutus's blood-red tent, once removed, leaves only the bare stage and a low ridge of cracked rock off-center. See Roy Walker, "Unto Caesar: A Review of Recent Produc-tions," *ShS*, 11 (1958), 128–35 (132–4); Ripley, *"Julius Caesar" on Stage*, pp. 256–8.

> *Cassius:* When Caesar liv'd, he durst not thus have
> mov'd me.
> *Brutus:* Peace, peace, you durst not so have tempted
> him.
>
> (58–9)

And the explicit one of Cassius to Caesar:

> *Cassius:* Strike as thou didst at Caesar; for I know,
> When thou didst hate him worst, thou lovedst him better
> Than ever thou lovedst Cassius.
>
> (105–7)

Both comparisons betray deep-seated awe and, perhaps, lingering envy of Caesar. The spirit of the ruler, as will be abundantly clear in the appearance of the ghost, has not been slain with the body, but walks abroad and through the minds of would-be assassins, mighty yet.

The quarrel scene has had great stage popularity, most commentators agree, because it displays the tragic and emotional Brutus.[37] The language, particularly the recurrent spatial metaphors, reveals Brutus's struggle to maintain his vision of the murder as the carving of a dish fit for gods. Brutus asks Cassius if he would "sell the mighty space" of their "large honors" for money (IV.iii.25). Coming from one who has recently been thrown out of Rome, the question sounds strangely misformed. In the tent on the battlefield Brutus and Cassius elbow each other for breathing room. Cassius warns Brutus not to "hedge" him in (30). Brutus later responds: "Must I give way and room to your rash choler? . . . Must I budge? . . . Must I stand and crouch / Under your testy humor?" (39, 44, 45–6).[38] The mighty space of their large honors, apparently, has not left Brutus and Cassius room enough for peaceful coexistence.

The quarrel scene also compels because of its emotional inten-

---

[37]MacCallum's discussion, pp. 255ff., has proved seminal for this interpretation. Jones, *Origins of Shakespeare,* argues that Shakespeare models this scene on the quarrel between Agamemnon and Menelaus in the beginning of Euripides's *Iphigenia in Aulis* (pp. 108–18).

[38]In the company of T. S. Dorsch I depart from G. Blakemore Evans and read "budge" instead of "bouge" (IV.iii.44), "life's" instead of "live's" (V.v.40).

sity.[39] Arising from the strain of great events, long suppressed by Roman austerity and self-control, emotions surface to reveal men of deep feeling and suffering. There is, for example, a poignant sadness and remorse in Brutus's having "worthy cause to wish / Things done undone" (IV.ii.8–9). This note is sounded as well in his mention of "great Julius," the use of the praenomen suggesting remembrance of the man, not the Colossus. We hear the wistful note again, perhaps, in Brutus's rebuke of Cassius: "You have done that you should be sorry for" (IV.iii.65). Just as surprisingly and affectingly, Cassius has a moment when he appears neither envious nor choleric, but sensitive and loving. Stung by Brutus's criticism, Cassius weeps and kneels. Once again he bares his breast, this time in a gesture of humility and self-abnegation, not pride and self-assertion:

> Come, Antony, and young Octavius, come,
> Revenge yourselves alone on Cassius,
> For Cassius is a-weary of the world;
> Hated by one he loves, brav'd by his brother.
>
> (93–6)

As in *Titus Andronicus,* the word "brother" echoes throughout the dialogue, here calling attention to the family tie that unites Brutus and Cassius against the new and impious Roman regime.

The revelations of the quarrel scene win sympathy for Brutus and Cassius, who try to maintain their vision of the assassination as a lofty scene enacted for justice's sake. This struggle continues despite mounting difficulties. Messala enters with news of the Proscription, irrefutable evidence that the attempt to save Rome has resulted only in tyranny and oppression. The news of Portia's death adds private loss to the public tragedy.[40] Like the Roman actors he praised earlier, Brutus withstands the blows with "for-

---

[39] It will be obvious that I am treating what is normally divided into two scenes, Act IV, Scenes ii and iii, as one continuous action.

[40] The debate over the double revelation of Portia's death is too well known to require documentation here. Noteworthy, however, is the evidence of revision presented by Brents Stirling, "*Julius Caesar* in Revision," *SQ*, 13 (1962), 187–205, even if his argument for retention of both passages is unconvincing. Whatever decision an editor makes about the crux, he is not likely to change materially our conception of Brutus.

mal constancy" (II.i.227). He describes his present situation and its opportunities in a rhetorical flourish:

> There is a tide in the affairs of men,
> Which taken at the flood, leads on to fortune;
> Omitted, all the voyage of their life
> Is bound in shallows and in miseries.
> On such a full sea are we now afloat,
> And we must take the current when it serves,
> Or lose our ventures.
>
> (IV.iii.218–24)

There is something at once admirable and pitiable in such heroic self-delusion. Everyone in the audience knows that the current Brutus speaks of will carry the conspirators to their deaths at Philippi, while bringing Octavius and Antony to triumphant power. As the early action moves relentlessly to the Capitol, so the later sweeps on to Philippi. As various omens – the storm, the soothsayer's prophecy, Calphurnia's dream – accompany the earlier march of history, Caesar's ghost, along with ravens, crows, and kites, now ushers the Romans along their appointed way.

The appointed way leads to the meeting of fellow Romans in battle. The messenger's notice of Brutus's army in "gallant show" (V.i.13) echoes disquietingly Brutus's description of "hollow men" a few moments earlier (IV.ii.23–4). The "flyting" preceding the battle shows Shakespeare's Romans at their worst – petty, arrogant, and boastful. Moreover, featuring enemy armies costumed alike, this scene suggests visually the intestine shock and furious close of civil butchery. The fraternal strife in *Titus Andronicus* here extends to the whole family of Rome. Shakespeare dramatizes the battle at Philippi just as Vergil envisions it: *ergo inter sese paribus concurrere telis / Romanas acies iterum videre Philippi (Geo.* I.489–90), "therefore once more Philippi saw Roman armies clash in the shock of brother weapons."[41]

---

[41]See also Book I of *De Bello Civili,* where Lucan describes the people's right hands turned against their own vitals, *populumque potentem / In sua victrici conversum viscera dextra* (2–3), hostile standard against standard, eagle against eagle, pilum against pilum, *infestisque obvia signis / Signa, pares aquilas et pila minantia pilis* (6–7). Lucan's account of the first triumvirate's internal conflicts is at many points an interesting analog to Shakespeare's portrayal of civil strife.

The image of the storm appears again after Antony, Octavius, and their forces leave the stage:

> *Cassius:* Why now blow wind, swell billow, and swim bark!
> The storm is up, and all is on the hazard.
>
> (V.i.67–8)

Although the battle will be on land, the image of the sea storm evokes the tempests of the *Aeneid* and suggests the same grand workings of destiny.[42] The subsequent conversation of Brutus and Cassius thickens with doom. Cassius compares himself to Pompey, who likewise risked all in single battle. Brutus compares himself to Cato, who committed suicide to avoid the ignominy of conquest. In their last hours, Brutus and Cassius again turn to past Romans for inspiration, but recall only Caesar's defeated enemies. Tragically, their attempt to live Roman lives can result now only in Roman deaths.

Doubting his former Epicurean philosophy, cut off from the other conspirators, Cassius faces the spirit of Caesar incarnate in Octavius and Antony. Fatally misconstruing events, he takes his own life. Brutus pointedly refuses to apotheosize Cassius's death with a Roman funeral:

> Come, therefore, and to Thasos send his body;
> His funerals shall not be in our camp,
> Lest it discomfort us.
>
> (V.iii.104–6)

Brutus no longer believes in the magical efficacy of Roman ceremony and ritual, but understands the limitations imposed by human emotion. The old high Roman way seems exhausted and near conclusion. Brutus laments:

> The last of all the Romans, fare thee well!
> It is impossible that ever Rome
> Should breed thy fellow.
>
> (99–101)

Young Marcus Cato, loudly proclaiming his name and ancestry, filled with passionate intensity, already seems to be an anachronism.

---

[42]Plutarch, who frequently compares Rome to a ship tossed by the sea, may also have suggested the image (e.g., V.30,37); cf. the similar imagery of "De Fortuna Romanorum" in the *Moralia*.

Surrounded by faces unfamiliar to the audience – Dardanius, Clitus, Strato, and Volumnius – Brutus foresees the inevitable triumph of Caesar and chooses to commit suicide. Shakespeare does not here criticize Brutus's desire to avoid dishonor or explore the irony of this Roman moral assertion. Instead, he creates a grandly moving finale by allowing Brutus a noble death.[43] Brutus takes leave of his remaining comrades in the calm, courageous accents of a Shakespearean tragic hero:

> Countrymen,
> My heart doth joy that yet in all my life
> I found no man but he was true to me.
> I shall have glory by this losing day
> More than Octavius and Mark Antony
> By this vile conquest shall attain unto.
> So fare you well at once, for Brutus' tongue
> Hath almost ended his life's history.
> Night hangs upon mine eyes, my bones would rest,
> That have but labor'd to attain this hour.
>
> (V.v.33–42)

Before holding up the sword, Strato shakes Brutus's hand, a gesture of respect and love all the more affecting for its sharp contrast with the earlier handshaking rituals. After Brutus's death, Antony's praise, "This was the noblest Roman of them all" (68), seems to acknowledge the passing of a way of life. The march of history has turned a corner; the days of the Republic are fast coming to a close, and the future of the city looms dark and uncertain ahead.

In *Julius Caesar* the places in and outside Rome take on symbolic precision and importance for the first time in Shakespeare's Ro-

[43]The recent tendency to denigrate Brutus ignores or depreciates the nobility of his last moments. See, for example, Gordon Ross Smith, "Brutus, Virtue, and Will," *SQ*, 10 (1959), 367–79, and Vawter, "'Division 'Tween Our Souls.'" Simmons's interpretation of Brutus as would-be restorer of the golden age is also unconvincing (pp. 80–6). Unlike *Titus Andronicus*, *Julius Caesar* never

man canon. The playwright here sets forth a symbolic geography consisting of city walls, the Capitol, the forum, private houses, and battlefields, all reinforced by recurrent metaphors of space and movement. These elements recombine to form new wholes and convey different meanings elsewhere. The image of the besieged city, model for the first two Roman works, gives way here to the image of the city divided by civil war. With this model the city itself fades from the play, receding before the conflicting forces that deny the fundamental principles of its existence. The next two Roman works, particularly *Coriolanus,* will realize in different ways the potential of this new model. Here Shakespeare uses the image of the divided city to explore the difficulties inherent in human judgment. As we watch Rome turn into a wilderness, we notice how limitless is man's capacity for error and self-delusion, and, surprisingly, how closely allied to it is his capacity for nobility and heroism. We sympathize with these Romans in their attempts to make sense of things and to live honorably, in their struggle with the vast force of history – powerful, mysterious, and ultimately indifferent.

The struggle between Romans and the force of history is embodied in the dramatic ironies that constitute the fabric of the play. Central to these ironies is the paradoxical effort of the Romans to use history, to imitate the heroic past for the approval of the future. Brutus and Cassius look to the ancient past, Caesar to his own past, and Antony to fallen Caesar. These would-be historians of Rome all distort by idealization, and all fail to understand the simplest, most fundamental lesson of the past; namely, that history repeats itself. Inevitably and cyclically, periods of civil war give way to periods of peace, only to be followed by more civil war. The powerless become powerful, the powerful become powerless. A fall balances every rise, and a rise accompanies every fall.[44] This lesson is implicit in the story of Pompey, the once-mighty ruler

---

evokes the myth to provide a context for action or to illuminate meaning. Brutus never shows himself a visionary egalitarian (there is no suggestion of discomfort with the rigid class system of Rome); he acts not to bring a better world into being, but to prevent the future degeneration of Rome under tyrannical rule.

[44] The point has been made and developed fully by John W. Velz, "Undular Structure in 'Julius Caesar,'" *MLR,* 66 (1971), 21–30.

who figures in the opening of the play, in the climactic assassination scene, and at the close.[45] It becomes explicit as well in the stories of Cassius, Brutus, Caesar, Antony, and even Octavius. In dramatic terms the cyclic inevitability of history manifests itself in the ironic resemblances between opposing characters, between Caesar and Brutus, and later between Brutus and Antony. These resemblances derive in part from a well-known principle of political orthodoxy, familiar to readers of Aristotle's *Politics* as well as Shakespeare's history plays: Tyrants often start out as rebels, and rebels often end up as tyrants. The slaying of Caesar only brings out the Caesar in other men.

The irony inherent in the Roman imitation of the past is also inherent in the Roman quest for future praise, in other words, in the Roman ethic of honor and its reward of fame. Shakespeare portrays this ethic uncritically in *Lucrece,* where the narrative form and decorative style suppress human realities. In *Titus Andronicus,* action committed on stage in the name of honor for a trick of fame appears shocking and barbaric. In *Julius Caesar* recurrent images of the theater, acting, and role-playing stimulate further consideration of the ethical issues at hand. From one perspective Brutus, Cassius, and Caesar are actors who use the resources of the theater for their own advancement; they are demagogic manipulators of appearance, language, and gesture, who create reality in the mind of their audience and perhaps in their own minds as well. From another perspective, however, these Romans are existential heroes, men who make life and death lock, stock, and barrel out of their bitter souls. Honor in *Julius Caesar* may be a mere scutcheon, or it may be the virtue that distinguishes Romans from lesser mortals. In a manner quite characteristic, Shakespeare increases the possibilities for criticism while enlarging the scope for admiration.

Shakespeare's conception of the Roman family also receives significant development in *Julius Caesar*. At the center of *Lucrece* and *Titus Andronicus* are violations of that family: the rape of Lucrece, the rape and mutilation of Lavinia, the slaughter of Alarbus, Mutius, and Lavinia, the Thyestean banquet. There are also

---

[45]See George Walton Williams, "Pompey the Great in *Julius Caesar*," *RenP,* 1976 (1977), 31–6.

egregious violations of the family in *Julius Caesar:* the denial of sexual identity by Portia and Caesar, the rejection of the wives by Brutus and Caesar, the recurrent misogyny, the slaying of the *pater patriae*, the casual impiety of the triumvirate. The difference is that here the notion of Roman *impietas* subtly and consistently informs the structure, language, and imagery of the play. Brutus and Cassius invoke the names of their (and Caesar's) Roman ancestors before stabbing the current father of the country, and Antony appeals to Caesar's heirs to avenge the slaying. Shakespeare's treatment of the family in *Julius Caesar* thus exposes Roman perversions of *pietas* that are bloody and destructive.

As has often been remarked, *Julius Caesar* represents a new stage in Shakespeare's continuing dialogue with classical authors, beginning a close and extended collaboration with Plutarch. *Julius Caesar* also marks an important point in Shakespeare's ongoing dialogue with Vergil. Here the poet effectively incorporates and transforms images from the *Aeneid*. During the action we glimpse Aeneas carrying Anchises and baring his chest to the gods, *Furor impius* raging in civil war, Italian families shattered by senseless violence. Vergil's Trojan mothers and wives, briefly and statically portrayed in *Lucrece* (1429–35), come to life in the powerful dramatic characters of Portia and Calphurnia. Like Shakespeare's other Roman works, *Julius Caesar* explores the tragic paradoxes implicit in Vergilian *pietas*. It is, finally, the dramatist's most compelling response to Vergil's musing, *tantae molis erat Romanam condere gentem* (*Aen.* I.33), "so vast was the struggle to found the race of Rome."

V

ANTONY AND CLEOPATRA
ROME AND THE WORLD

Shakespeare's next major encounter with Rome, *Antony and Cleopatra,* is in many ways a sequel to *Julius Caesar.* Antony's fatal infatuation with Cleopatra commanded as much attention in the Renaissance as did Caesar's assassination. In M. W. Mac-Callum's words:

> Next to the story of Julius Caesar, the story of Antony and
> Cleopatra was perhaps the prerogative Roman theme
> among the dramatists of the sixteenth century and was
> associated with such illustrious personages as Jodelle and
> Garnier in France, and the Countess of Pembroke and
> Daniel in England.[1]

In addition to the popularity of subject matter, the two plays share a focus on the same critical juncture in Roman history: the decades encompassing the dissolution of Republic and the birth of Empire. Both plays derive from Plutarch's *Lives;* both freely incorporate material from other writers, notably Appian and Vergil; both express Shakespeare's increasingly critical conception of Rome and Roman values. Like *Julius Caesar* and Shakespeare's other Roman works, *Antony and Cleopatra* examines the struggle of Romans with Rome, portrayed as a physical locality and an imagined ideal. The play explores the resulting conflict between private needs and public responsibilities by again focusing on the Roman code of honor, shame, and fame; the paradoxes implicit in Roman ceremony and ritual; the political motifs of rebellion and invasion. As do Shakespeare's previous Roman works, *Antony and Cleopatra* explores the predicament of the living human beings who must define themselves against the oppressive background of Roman tradition and history.

As is obvious to any viewer, however, *Antony and Cleopatra* is

[1]MacCallum, pp. 309–10.

a unique achievement, differing significantly from Shakespeare's other tragedies and from his other Roman works. While exposing the folly of the lovers, it celebrates the transcendent power of their love. It is preeminently a play of possibility, a daring excursus beyond the boundaries of drama and beyond those of life itself. As Una Ellis-Fermor observes, *Antony and Cleopatra* features a vast gallery of characters who range in size and color from the principals to the almost invisible Taurus, who utters but two words in his brief appearance (III.viii.2).[2] The play includes almost two hundred exits and entrances, thus presenting to the viewer's eye a continuously changing dramatic spectacle composed of infinitely malleable configurations of character, no sooner glimpsed than dissolved and re-formed.[3] Encompassing sea and land, city and field, localized and unlocalized place, the action of the play ranges between Alexandria and Rome, wandering as well to Messina, Misenum, Syria, Athens, and Actium. Remarkably, the unfolding panorama tells only part of the story. Many important incidents – the revolt and death of Fulvia, the first meeting of Cleopatra and Antony, the murders of Lepidus and Pompey, the sea battle at Actium – occur largely in report, not on stage. Rome in this play is not simply a city (the stock references to the walls, forum, Tiber, and Capitol are exceptionally few and inconspicuous), but an Empire, a world unto itself.[4]

The ten years or so that separate *Antony and Cleopatra* from *Julius Caesar* span the most creative period in Shakespeare's life and mark the height of his poetic development. It is not surprising, then, that this play differs greatly from others. And yet, the imaginative method of *Antony and Cleopatra* differs from that of the earlier works only in degree, not kind. As before, Shakespeare practices an eclectic syncretism: He borrows incidents, themes, and images from various sources – classical and contemporary – and combines them into new wholes. The fusing process remains

---

[2]"The Nature of Plot in Drama," *E&S*, NS 13 (1960), 65–81 (71–5).
[3]The figure is given by Maynard Mack in an excerpt from "*Antony and Cleopatra*: The Stillness and the Dance," reprinted in *Twentieth Century Interpretations of "Antony and Cleopatra*," ed. Mark Rose (Englewood Cliffs, N.J.: Prentice-Hall, 1977), pp. 125–6. See also Thomas B. Stroup, "The Structure of *Antony and Cleopatra*," *SQ*, 15 (1964), 289–98.
[4]See Cantor, pp. 136–8. For discussion of the recurring word "world," see Knight, pp. 208–10; Charney, pp. 79–93.

essentially the same, but the final product is different, created by a higher level of imaginative energy acting on a wider range of diverse elements. These elements – variously popular, recondite, historical, literary, iconographical, and mythological – combine to create moments of extraordinary poetic texture and resonance, moments very different from any of the parts in their making. Vergil remains an important source of image and idea, but one from which Shakespeare declares independence in a voice loud and bold.

As almost all commentators note, Philo's opening speech enunciates the central antinomy between Rome – place of order, measure, and self-control – and Egypt – place of disorder, excess, and indulgence:

> Nay, but this dotage of our general's
> O'erflows the measure. Those his goodly eyes,
> That o'er the files and musters of the war
> Have glow'd like plated Mars, now bend, now turn
> The office and devotion of their view
> Upon a tawny front; his captain's heart,
> Which in the scuffles of great fights hath burst
> The buckles on his breast, reneges all temper,
> And is become the bellows and the fan
> To cool a gipsy's lust.

> (I.i.1–10)

Few observe as well, however, that Philo's hyperbolical comparison of Antony to "plated Mars" and his description of Antony's bursting heart are curiously Egyptian terms in which to describe Roman virtue. According to the Roman point of view, apparently, one may be godlike in excess when serving honor, but not when serving love. Antony's entrance pointedly demonstrates how far removed he is from Philo's ideal. The brave soldier has become the doting lover, whose affections, he claims, reach beyond the limits of heaven and earth. Angry Mars now serves laughing Venus.

Now for the love of Love, and her soft hours,
Let's not confound the time with conference harsh;
There's not a minute of our lives should stretch
Without some pleasure now. What sport to-night?

(44–7)

The allusion to Venus and the hours, a common iconographical motif familiar to readers of Spenser's *Epithalamion,* reveals the nature of Antony's transformation.[5] Antony envisions himself as a worshipper of Venus, a figure in a mythological *pageant d'amour.* The patent artificiality of such a vision, underscored by the presence of somber Roman witnesses, suggests that the dream is delusion, the vision insubstantial and unreal.

Cleopatra commands the audience's attention just as peremptorily as she commands Antony's. Teasing him out of patience, she levels sarcastic scorn at "scarce-bearded Caesar" (21) and "shrill-tongu'd Fulvia" (32), armed with a "process" for Antony's return. Thus, she mocks Caesar's manhood, Fulvia's womanhood, and, by implication, Roman marriage. She jeers also at the Roman institutions of government and law, all appearing absurdly pompous from Egypt's hedonistic perspective. Cleopatra here shows herself to be a "wrangling queen! / Whom every thing becomes" (48–9), a paradoxical mixture of human weakness and royal power, in whose person all passions serve as ornaments, and in whose presence all things become new and strange. Infinitely variable, she is the antithesis of Roman constancy and, therefore, perfectly fitted for her role as critic of Roman values. Cleopatra's shrill mockery will fully and explicitly articulate the ironical view of Rome implicit in the opening scenes of *Titus Andronicus* and *Julius Caesar.*

The procession in this scene – the flourish followed by the entrance of "Antony, Cleopatra, *her* Ladies, *the* Train, *with eunuchs fanning her*" (s.d. 10), and the exit (s.d. 55) – resembles the procession in Act I, Scene ii of *Julius Caesar.* In both plays the ceremonial march on and off stage is punctuated by a dialogue between discontented observers who consider themselves true citizens of Rome. The Egyptian procession, however, actually par-

[5]See *Epithalamion* ll.98ff.

odies Caesar's triumphant march. The voluptuous strolling of Antony and Cleopatra, fanned by eunuchs, expresses indirection and indolence rather than purposeful direction. Instead of following the prescribed pattern of Roman ritual, Antony and Cleopatra simply follow their whims; like leisurely tourists, they "wander through the streets and note / The qualities of people" (53–4). Renouncing Rome, Antony declares his love for Cleopatra:

> Let Rome in Tiber melt, and the wide arch
> Of the rang'd empire fall! Here is my space,
> Kingdoms are clay; our dungy earth alike
> Feeds beast as man; the nobleness of life
> Is to do thus. [*embracing*]
>
> (33–7)

Antony rejects the public space of the "rang'd empire" for the private space of his lover's embrace.[6]

As in *Julius Caesar*, a soothsayer appears to utter a cryptic admonition. Ignoring the warning, Caesar shows his proud, stubborn, and imperious character; playfully delighting in ominous words, Charmian and Iras reveal their lascivious natures. If the talk of Egyptian women suggests their frivolity and fertility – natural, abundant, and irresponsible – the action of Fulvia, a Roman woman, expresses other qualities. Antony discovers that Fulvia "first came into the field" (I.ii.88) against his brother Lucius, but then joined forces with him against Caesar. Her boldness, independence, and courage are reminiscent of Lucrece, who took her life to safeguard her honor, and of Portia, who wounded herself to prove her *Romanitas*. Unlike these women, however, Fulvia does not sacrifice herself for Roman ideals, but for personal gain. As we discover later, Fulvia purposes to draw Antony back to Rome and to mend the broken marriage. As a messenger brings the news of Fulvia's death some twenty lines after the news of her

---

[6]With certain qualifications the terms "public" and "private" are admissible here. Rome is a place of public responsibility, but Romans are clearly motivated by consideration of personal gain. Egypt is, by contrast, a place of private indulgence, yet Egyptian Cleopatra thrives on public spectacle and display. For informed discussions of this matter, see Julian Markels, "The Public and Private Worlds of *Antony and Cleopatra*," in *The Pillar of the World: "Antony and Cleopatra" in Shakespeare's Development* (Ohio: Ohio State University Press, 1968), pp. 17–49; Cantor, pp. 127ff. (esp. pp. 184–208).

revolt, Shakespeare quickly passes over the problems raised by such a Roman expression of un-Roman intentions. Clearly, the playwright wishes to focus sympathetic attention on Antony and to provide an imperative reason for his return home.

The news of Fulvia's death is the climax of the reports that besiege Antony's private world and compel him to assume public responsibility. As does Brutus for Portia, Antony spends a moment of grief for Fulvia and then turns to the matter at hand.[7] The similarity here between these two Romans continues the pattern of ironic resemblance in *Julius Caesar*, a pattern that, as we shall see, becomes increasingly visible and important in this play.

Before Antony leaves for Rome, he endures Enobarbus's cynical wit and the reminder that Egyptian business cannot endure his absence. Despite Antony's gruff response, his language in this scene and elsewhere confirms Enobarbus's charge and illustrates how Egyptian the Roman triumvir has become. Antony ends their discussion with an image of spontaneous generation:

> Much is breeding,
> Which, like the courser's hair, hath yet but life,
> And not a serpent's poison.
>
> (I.ii.192–4)

This simile recalls the earlier image of weeds in the garden:

> O then we bring forth weeds
> When our quick winds lie still, and our ills told us
> Is as our earing.
>
> (I.ii.109–11)

Both metaphors look ahead to Antony's oath:

> By the fire
> That quickens Nilus' slime, I go from hence
> Thy soldier, servant, making peace or war
> As thou affects.
>
> (I.iii.68–71)

---

[7]Others have noted this parallel but not discussed its significance. See Harley Granville-Barker, *Prefaces to Shakespeare*, Vol. I (Princeton: Princeton University Press, 1946), p. 425; Brents Stirling, *Unity in Shakespearian Tragedy* (New York: Columbia University Press, 1956), p. 163.

Antony's language reflects an Egyptian awareness of nature's fecund powers and an Egyptian preoccupation with the processes of fertilization.

Antony's leave-taking of Cleopatra, carefully prepared for by the conversation with Enobarbus, allows Cleopatra to display fully her power, pettiness, temper, and theatrical talents. The scene borrows from another famous leave-taking, that of Aeneas and Dido. (Th.) Zielinski first called attention to the parallels between Act I, Scene iii of *Antony and Cleopatra* and the parting of Aeneas and Dido in Ovid's *Heroides*.[8] One verbal parallel that has since won general scholarly approval is the citation of *Heroides* VII.139 in connection with *Antony and Cleopatra* I.iii.20–1:[9]

> "Sed iubet ire deus." vellem, vetuisset adire.

> "But you are bid to go – by your god!" Ah, would he had forbidden you to come.

> *Cleopatra:* What, says the married woman you may go?
>   Would she had never given you leave to come!

Although not noticed by Zielinski, Cleopatra's needling questions about Antony's treatment of Fulvia (I.iii.27–9; 63–5; 75–8) also echo Ovid's Dido:

> omnia mentiris, neque enim tua fallere lingua
>   incipit a nobis, primaque plector ego.
> si quaeras, ubi sit formosi mater Iuli –
>   occidit a duro sola relicta viro!
>
> (81–4)

> You are false in everything – and I am not the first your tongue has deceived, nor am the first to feel the blow from you. Do you ask where the mother of pretty Iulus is? – she perished, left behind by her unfeeling lord!

As many others insist, however, Shakespeare's recollection of Aeneas and Dido draws upon sources other than Ovid's sentimen-

---

[8] "Marginalien," *Philologus*, 64, n.F. 18 (1905), 1–26 (17–19).
[9] See Baldwin, Vol. II, pp. 424–6; Gilbert Highet, *The Classical Tradition: Greek and Roman Influences on Western Literature* (New York: Oxford University Press, 1949), pp. 205–6; J. A. K. Thomson, *Shakespeare and the Classics* (New York: Barnes & Noble Books, 1952), p. 148; Ernest Schanzer, *The Problem Plays of Shakespeare* (New York: Schocken Books, 1963), p. 160.

tal version.[10] Vergil's account was a standard part of the Elizabethan grammar-school curriculum, and Shakespeare drew on memories of *Aeneid* IV throughout his career.[11] What is more, Vergil supplied an important poetic precedent for relating Dido and Cleopatra, even using the same phrase to describe their deaths.[12] Classical authorities believe that the African queens were probably perceived as parallel figures by Vergil's audiences. Both appear as proud and powerful widows, versed in the arts of black magic. Threatened on all sides by hostile forces, both Dido and Cleopatra ensnare important Roman soldiers in nets of luxury and concupiscence. Stalwart Roman virtue, embodied variously in Aeneas and in his successor, Octavius, eventually triumphs and both queens, consequently, commit suicide.[13]

[10]Ernest Schanzer, *Problem Plays,* cites also *Aeneid* IV, Chaucer's *Legend of Good Women,* and Marlowe's *Dido Queen of Carthage* (pp. 159–61). Janet Adelman, *The Common Liar: An Essay on "Antony and Cleopatra,"* Yale Studies in English, No. 181 (New Haven: Yale University Press, 1973), argues that Shakespeare knew the versions of Vergil, Chaucer, and Marlowe (pp. 68–78). The story of Dido and Aeneas was, of course, extremely popular, recurring in medieval accounts of the Troy legends, as well as in various allusions, ballads, mirrors, emblem books, mythographies, and encyclopedias. On the complicated history of the story, see Douglas Bush, *Mythology and the Renaissance Tradition in English Poetry,* rev. ed. (New York: Norton, 1963), s.v.v. "Dido," "Aeneas"; H. J. Oliver, "Introduction" to the Revels edition, *Dido Queen of Carthage and The Massacre at Paris* (Cambridge, Mass.: Harvard University Press, 1968), pp. xxxiii–xxxix; Mary Elizabeth Smith, *"Love Kindling Fire": A Study of Christopher Marlowe's "The Tragedy of Dido Queen of Carthage,"* Salzburg Studies in English Literature, ERS, No. 63 (Salzburg: Institut für Englische Sprache und Literatur, 1977), pp. 6–38, 172–6. According to Smith, six English plays and six Continental ones dramatized the story of Dido and Aeneas before 1607.

[11]A glance at Martin Spevack's *Concordance,* 9 vols. (Hildesheim: Georg Olms, 1968–80) reveals that Dido is mentioned by name in 2 *Henry VI, Titus Andronicus, Romeo and Juliet, The Merchant of Venice, Hamlet, Antony and Cleopatra, The Tempest,* and *The Two Noble Kinsmen.* See also Robert Kilburn Root, *Classical Mythology in Shakespeare,* Yale Studies in English, No. 19 (New York: Holt, 1903), pp. 56–8; Baldwin, Vol. II, pp. 456–96.

[12]Dido is described as *pallida morte futura* (IV.644), "pale at the coming of death," as is Cleopatra, *pallentem morte futura* (VIII.709). The parallel is well known to students of Vergil.

[13]C. M. Bowra may speak for many: "Virgil must have seen that, when he created Dido, his readers would remember Cleopatra and would, consciously or unconsciously, revive for Dido much of their old feeling for the Egyptian Queen and see yet another example of the dangers which the East held for the West." *From Virgil to Milton* (London: Macmillan, 1948), pp. 51–2. See also Steele Commager's "Introduction" to *Virgil: A Collection of Critical Essays*

Shakespeare turned his memory of *Aeneid* IV to good account in
Antony and Cleopatra. Antony's leave-taking of Cleopatra follows the scenic rhythm established by Vergil's Aeneas and Dido.
Dido knows (*praesensit* [IV.297]) that Aeneas is preparing to leave
before he breaks the news to her. So Cleopatra divines Antony's
intentions before he reveals them:

> *Antony:* Now my dearest queen –
> *Cleopatra:* Pray you stand farther from me.
> *Antony:* What's the matter?
> *Cleopatra:* I know by that same eye there's some good news.
> What, says the married woman you may go?
> Would she had never given you leave to come!

(I.iii.17–21)

Before Aeneas has a chance to speak, Dido berates him for betraying her love and breaking his promises:

> Dissimulare etiam sperasti, perfide, tantum
> posse nefas tacitusque mea decedere terra?
> nec te noster amor nec te data dextera quondam
> nec moritura tenet crudeli funere Dido?

(305–8)

> False one! didst thou hope also to cloak so foul a crime,
> and to pass from my land in silence? Can neither our love
> keep thee, nor the pledge once given, nor the doom of a
> cruel death for Dido?

Similarly, Cleopatra denies Antony the chance to speak and berates him for his perfidy:

> *Antony:* Cleopatra –
> *Cleopatra:* Why should I think you can be mine, and true
> (Though you in swearing shake the throned gods),
> Who have been false to Fulvia? Riotous madness,
> To be entangled with those mouth-made vows,
> which break themselves in swearing!

(26–31)

(Englewood Cliffs, N.J.: Prentice-Hall, 1966), p. 9; Kenneth Quinn, *Virgil's
"Aeneid": A Critical Description* (Ann Arbor: University of Michigan Press,
1968), p. 55; R. D. Williams, ed., *The Aeneid of Virgil, Books 1–6* (1972; rpt.
London: Macmillan, 1975), pp. 354–5. The sumptuous feasting in Shakespeare's Alexandria clearly matches that in Vergil's Carthage (I.695ff.).

Later, Dido reminds Aeneas that she granted mercy and hospitality to him, a wretched castaway and beggar (*eiectum litore, egentem* [373]). Angrily, she tells him to leave: *i, sequere Italiam ventis, pete regna per undas* (381), "Go follow Italy down the winds; seek thy kingdom over the waves." Likewise, Cleopatra reminds Antony of his former suppliance and tells him to leave:

> Nay, pray you seek no color for your going,
> But bid farewell, and go. When you sued staying,
> Then was the time for words; no going then.
>
> (32–4)

Aeneas's response is *pauca* (333), "brief" as well as "small" compared with Dido's large passion. He blames *fata* (340) for shaping his life and tells Dido to stop her rebukes:

> desine meque tuis incendere teque querellis.
> Italiam non sponte sequor.
>
> (360–1)

> Cease to fire thyself and me with thy complaints. Not of
> free will do I follow Italy!

Antony also lays the blame for his departure on an unapproachable abstraction, the "strong necessity of time" (42), and bids the angry queen, "Quarrel no more" (66). Unlike Aeneas, however, Antony does not recognize the power of the fates in the determination of his journey and his life; instead, he recognizes only the power of Cleopatra:

> but be prepar'd to know
> The purposes I bear; which are, or cease,
> As you shall give th' advice.
>
> (66–8)

The Vergilian paradigm may illuminate one of the cruxes of this scene:

> *Cleopatra:* Courteous lord, one word:
>   Sir, you and I must part, but that's not it;
>   Sir, you and I have lov'd, but there's not it;
>   That you know well. Something it is I would –
>   O, my oblivion is a very Antony,
>   And I am all forgotten.
>
> (86–91)

Zielinski suggests that Cleopatra, like Ovid's Dido, is pregnant.[14] MacCallum sensibly rejects this explanation and offers another: "If one were forced to conjecture the 'missing word,' it would be more plausible to suppose that she both wishes and hesitates to suggest marriage with Antony."[15] Shakespeare, however, probably has no one word in mind, but merely wishes to dramatize Cleopatra's love by depicting her confusion. He may well have taken his cue from Vergil's description of Dido in love: *exposcit pendetque iterum narrantis ab ore* (79), "she essays to speak and stops with the word half-spoken." Christopher Marlowe, we recall, dramatizes this image of the tongue-tied Dido in his careful reworking of *Aeneid* IV, *Dido Queen of Carthage:*

> And yet I'll speak, and yet I'll hold my peace;
> Do shame her worst, I will disclose my grief.
> Aeneas, thou art he — what did I say?
> Something it was that now I have forgot.[16]

The transfer of Dido's initial confusion to Cleopatra's leave-taking reverses the Vergilian progression from loving speechlessness to articulate anger. Shakespeare's Cleopatra progresses from articulate anger to loving speechlessness. Accordingly, she does not conclude her farewell with Dido's bitter cry to the gods for vengeance and the promise that she will haunt her lover eternally (382ff.). Instead, she asks Antony for forgiveness, exhorts the gods for his protection, and wishes him all success and honor:

> But, sir, forgive me,
> Since my becomings kill me when they do not
> Eye well to you. Your honor calls you hence,
> Therefore be deaf to my unpitied folly,
> And all the gods go with you! Upon your sword
> Sit laurel victory, and smooth success
> Be strew'd before your feet!
>
> (95–101)

---

[14]Zielinski, "Marginalien," pp. 18–19.
[15]MacCallum, p. 656.
[16]Act III, Scene iv, Lines 26–9 in H. J. Oliver's edition (cf. III.i.170–2). This parallel, along with others, has been noted by Thomas P. Harrison, "Shakespeare and Marlowe's *Dido, Queen of Carthage*," *Texas University Studies in English*, 35 (1956), 57–63 (62).

The similarities between the two leave-taking scenes do not, by any means, constitute a series of fully worked out correspondences. As is true of Shakespeare's general practice, remembrance of the earlier scene shapes the present one and produces a sequence of glancingly rapid effects.[17] The differences between *Aeneid* IV and Act I, Scene iii of *Antony and Cleopatra* remain, of course, fundamental and important. Vergil's Dido is a tragic figure who expresses broken-hearted pathos and chthonic rage. Shakespeare's Cleopatra is here essentially comic, a consummate actress whose quicksilver shifts of mood bewilder and captivate Antony. Nothing in Dido's outbursts of grief and fear, for example, compares to Cleopatra's sarcastic scorn for Roman military honor:

> *Antony:* My precious queen, forbear,
>   And give true evidence to his love, which stands
>   An honorable trial.
> *Cleopatra:* So Fulvia told me.
>   I prithee turn aside, and weep for her,
>   Then bid adieu to me, and say the tears
>   Belong to Egypt. Good now, play one scene
>   Of excellent dissembling, and let it look
>   Like perfect honor.
>
>   (73–80)

Asserting that Roman honor is merely "excellent dissembling," Cleopatra continues the ethical probing of *Julius Caesar,* wherein Romans repeatedly stage plays for "the common eyes" (II.i.179). That Shakespeare in one scene can simultaneously imitate, refashion, and then ignore a deep source illustrates the freedom and flexibility of his imaginative maturity. Such refashioning witnesses Shakespeare's continuing absorption with Vergil, but testifies to his independence, an independence crucially important to his developing vision of Rome.[18]

---

[17]See Emrys Jones, *Scenic Form in Shakespeare* (Oxford: Clarendon Press, 1971).

[18]See also Brower, who concludes that *Antony and Cleopatra* is an "imaginative sequel" to the *Aeneid* (p. 351). Adelman, *Common Liar*, suggests that *Aeneid* VIII.671–7 contributes a few details to Enobarbus's description of Cleopatra; she discusses the importance of *Fama* to both works, detects a parallel between Aeneas's "*Hic amor, haec patria est*" and Antony's "Here is my space," and makes other interesting observations in her discussion (pp. 71ff.).

The entrance of Octavius Caesar, *"reading a letter"* (s.d. I.iv), accompanied by Lepidus and a train, sharply contrasts with the entrance of Antony and Cleopatra. Unlike Antony, Caesar is eager for news, already in the process of receiving a message as he appears. Unlike Antony, Caesar dominates the scene and speaks a language of authority:

> You may see, Lepidus, and henceforth know,
> It is not Caesar's natural vice to hate
> Our great competitor. From Alexandria
> This is the news: he fishes, drinks, and wastes
> The lamps of night in revel; is not more manlike
> Than Cleopatra; nor the queen of Ptolomy
> More womanly than he; hardly gave audience, or
> Vouchsaf'd to think he had partners. You shall find there
> A man who is th' abstract of all faults
> That all men follow.
>
> (1–10)

Caesar here instructs Lepidus in the importance of being Caesar. The casual use of the subjunctive mood in the first line, implying the granting of permission, along with the third-person reference to himself, establishes the voice as one of command. The expanding sequence of parallel verbs and verb phrases, beginning with the contemptuous tricolon – "fishes, drinks, and wastes, / The lamps of night in revel" – expresses indignation while precisely listing Antony's offenses. The speech ends with a summary judgment, delivered ex cathedra, as it were, from a seat of unimpeachable rectitude.

Shakespeare here achieves the characterization of Caesar by contrast and comparison with Antony. Antony's tippling, reeling, and standing the buffet with sweaty knaves sets in relief Caesar's grim *severitas*. In an emotional direct address to the absent profligate, Caesar recalls Antony's days of glory as a Roman soldier:

> Thou didst drink
> The stale of horses and the gilded puddle
> Which beasts would cough at; thy palate then did deign
> The roughest berry on the rudest hedge;

Yea, like the stag, when snow the pasture sheets,
The barks of trees thou brows'd. On the Alps
It is reported thou didst eat strange flesh.

(61–7)

Despite their present differences, Caesar and Antony have much in common. They share a common responsibility from their common venture at Philippi, and they share a common heritage: the Roman tradition of military honor. Both express contempt for the vacillating populace: Antony speaks of "Our slippery people, / Whose love is never link'd to the deserver / Till his deserts are past" (I.ii.185–7); Caesar talks of the "common body, / Like to a vagabond flag upon the stream" (I.iv.44–5), drifting with the varying tides and rotting itself with motion. Both men also face a common peril: the rising Pompey and his pirates. From their similarities, as well as their differences, much of the drama in their conflict arises.

Unlike the contrast between Caesar and Antony, the contrast between Caesar and Cleopatra is clear-cut and unqualified. Caesar's sense of purpose and public responsibility directly opposes Cleopatra's love of idleness and luxury. At the end of Act I, Scene iv, Caesar assembles "immediate council" (75); at the beginning of Act I, Scene v, Cleopatra calls for a narcotic:

> Ha, ha!
> Give me to drink mandragora.
> *Charmian:* Why, madam?
> *Cleopatra:* . . . My Antony is away.

(3–6)

The langorous sensuality of Cleopatra's language – the dreamy murmur of *m*'s, the melodramatic alliteration of *g* and *r*, and the open-mouthed vowel sounds, especially *a* and *o* – present the opposite theme to Caesar's strong-lined Roman music. As illustrated by her joking with Mardian and by her later haling of the messenger (II.v), Cleopatra's kingdom is a garden of wicked delights where base and cruel instincts run riot. It is a kingdom of the imagination where the Queen conceives of herself as a supernatural creation – the serpent of the Nile, the paramour of Phoebus, the earthly avatar of Venus and Isis. It is a region of transshifting shapes and forms where men behave like women, women behave like men, and both act like gods. In her interview with the messenger, for example, Cleopatra sees herself as Jove, promising to rain down a "shower of gold" (II.v.45), and then threatening to use Jove's dreaded weapon: "Some innocents scape not the thunderbolt" (77).

Cleopatra's habit of mythologizing herself and her experiences focuses attention on Shakespeare's use of classical allusion in this play. Like Cleopatra, Shakespeare sees the action on stage in mythological terms, for one example, as a reenactment of the love affair of Mars and Venus. Mardian makes direct reference to the celestial affair (I.v.17–18), and scattered allusions to both deities continually recall it. As some have duly noted, the myth was popularly allegorized as a tale of harmony created by the union of opposites.[19] Yet, it is also true that Shakespeare uses different facets of this myth to suggest different facets of the earthly love affair. The myth serves likewise as a good bawdy story, the conclusion of which is highly embarrassing to Mars and highly amusing to the other gods. Ovid's version in *Metamorphoses* IV, probably one that Shakespeare knew, focuses on the cuckolded Vulcan's craft, on the successful springing of the trap, and on the resulting laughter of the gods:

> ut venere torum coniunx et adulter in unum,
> arte viri vinclisque nova ratione paratis
> in mediis ambo deprensi amplexibus haerent.
> Lemnius extemplo valvas patefecit eburnas
> inmisitque deos; ille iacuere ligati
> turpiter, atque aliquis de dis non tristibus optat
> sic fieri turpis; superi risere, diuque
> haec fuit in toto notissima fabula caelo.
>
> (182–9)

Now when the goddess and her paramour had come
thither, by the husband's art and by the net so cunningly
prepared they were both caught and held fast in each
other's arms. Straightway Vulcan, the Lemnian, opened
wide the ivory doors and let in the other gods. There lay
the two in chains, disgracefully, and some one of the merry

---

[19]See Raymond B. Waddington, "*Antony and Cleopatra:* 'What Venus did with Mars,'" *ShakS,* 2 (1967 for 1966), 210–27; Adelman, *Common Liar,* pp. 78ff.; see also Harold Fisch, "'Antony and Cleopatra': The Limits of Mythology," *ShS,* 23 (1970), 59–67.

gods prayed that he might be so disgraced. The gods
laughed, and for a long time this story was the talk of
heaven.

Mythographers such as Charles Estienne give us a similar version
of the episode – light, prurient, essentially comic.[20] Even as it
endows Antony and Cleopatra with supernatural status, then, this
myth undercuts the pretensions of the human lovers and deflates
their swelling rhetoric. By suggesting the folly of sexual appetite
and the occasionally embarrassing consequences, the Ovidian perspective increases the ambivalence of the love affair.

Sometimes reinforcing the myth of Mars and Venus, sometimes
cutting across it, sometimes running independently altogether, is
the stream of associations started by repeated reference to Hercules. Plutarch discusses Antony's relationship to this legendary
figure:

> Now it had bene a speeche of old time, that the familie of
> the Antonii were discended from one Anton, the sonne of
> Hercules, whereof the familie tooke name. This opinion did
> Antonius seeke to confirme in all his doings: not onely
> resembling him in the likenes of his bodye, as we have sayd
> before, but also in the wearing of his garments. For when
> he would openly shewe him selfe abroad before many
> people, he would alwayes weare his cassocke gyrt downe
> lowe upon his hippes, with a great sword hanging by his
> side, and upon that, some ill favored cloke.[21]

Plutarch also notes later that Cleopatra "oftentimes unarmed An-
tonius . . . as we see in painted tables, where Omphale secretlie
stealeth away Hercules clubbe, and tooke his Lyons skinne from
him."[22] Like the story of Mars and Venus, the story of Hercules

---

[20]Estienne (Stephanus), *Dictionarivm Historicvm Geographicvm, Poeticvm*
(Lyon, 1595), fol. 291. For an allegorical interpretation, see Natalis Comes,
Mythologiae, sive Explicationis Fabvlarvm, Libri Decem (Geneva, 1618), pp.
161–2.

[21]Plutarch, Vol. VI, p. 4.

[22]Ibid., Vol. VI, p. 91. The association of lions with Antony (III.xiii.94–5;
V.i.15–17) enforces the parallel with Hercules. See Giovanni Pierio Valeriano
Bolzani, *Hieroglyphica* (Lyon, 1602), reprinted in *The Renaissance and the
Gods,* No. 17 (New York: Garland, 1976), p. 11. Lions appear often in Vergil's
work as symbols of wrath and courage: e.g., *Eclogues* IV.22, V.27; *Georgics*
II.151–2; *Aeneid* VII.15, IX.339, IX.792, X.454, X.723, XII.6.

and Omphale features a heroic, godlike figure made effeminate and ridiculous by amorous desire. Both myths may gain force as well from the general association of Aeneas and Hercules (*Aen.* VIII) and from the story of Aeneas and Dido, particularly the spectacle of Aeneas armed with jewel-studded sword, costumed in Tyrian purple and gold (*Aen.* IV.261–4).[23] The combination of myths invests the motifs of clothing and sword with a symbolic significance important throughout the play, particularly in the arming-of-the-hero scene in Act IV. In addition, the myths emphasize the darker, more sinister aspects of Antony and Cleopatra's affair, suggesting as they do the loss of masculinity, military *vertu*, and heroic identity. Never before in the Roman plays has Shakespeare shown such mastery over the multiple resources of allusion; never has he combined various myths with such sure-handed subtlety and grace.

The first major movement of the play comes to a climax in the meeting of Octavius and Antony in Rome. The half-sword parley of Brutus and Cassius, with its rapid escalation of accusation and denial and quick denouement, may have provided a model for this airing of grievances between Roman competitors. Like Brutus, Antony testily defends his honor, while Caesar, like Cassius, concerns himself with the practical business of waging war. Like Brutus and Cassius, Antony and Octavius struggle to subordinate personal antipathy to public necessity. Unlike the earlier quarrel scene, however, which ends in genuine understanding and renewed friendship, this one concludes with a bargain, a political matrimony designed to hold the antagonists "staunch from edge to edge / A' th' world" (II.ii.115–16). The sounding of the word "brothers" in this scene (125, 147) is only an empty echo of the same sounding in *Julius Caesar,* that signal of Brutus's and Cas-

---

[23]Purple is also the color of Egyptian luxury. Shakespeare follows Plutarch in the description of Cleopatra's purple sails on Cydnus, an image that may gain force from the description of the Whore of Babylon in Revelation 17:4 and from depictions of *Voluptas.* On Shakespeare's general debt to Revelation, see Ethel Seaton, "*Antony and Cleopatra* and the *Book of Revelation,*" *RES,* 22 (1946), 219–24; on Cleopatra as *Voluptas,* see J. Leeds Barroll, "Enobarbus' Description of Cleopatra," *Texas University Studies in English,* 37 (1958), 61–78. Other interesting analogs to Shakespeare's depiction of Antony in female garb are Florus, *Epitomae* II.xxi.3–4, and Ovid's description of Hercules, *Fasti* II.317–26.

sius's reconciliation. The differences between the two scenes illustrate the growing venality and ignobleness of the Empire.

That the new incorporate Roman family is doomed, like those in *Titus Andronicus* and *Julius Caesar,* seems readily apparent. The making of the match directly precedes Enobarbus's description of Cleopatra on the river Cydnus and his encomium to her infinite variety. The well-known transformation of Plutarch's prose into baroque poetry – lovely, sensual, artificial, almost oversweet – seduces the audience's imagination from "admir'd Octavia." Like the attentive Agrippa, we wonder at the vision of excess, at the goddess who awakens sexual desire in the air and water. Mention of the "pretty dimpled boys, like smiling Cupids, / With divers-color'd fans, whose wind did seem / To glow the delicate cheeks which they did cool, / And what they undid did" (II.ii.202–5) recalls Philo's initial description of Antony, whose eyes "glow'd like plated Mars" and whose heart became "the bellows and the fan / To cool a gipsy's lust" (I.i.4, 9–10). The parallel depictions of Antony as Mars and Cleopatra as Venus suggest their compatibility: No woman of earthly moderation, wisdom, and beauty can hope to be so fitting a mate for Antony as Cleopatra.

The struggle for power in *Antony and Cleopatra* extends beyond Antony and Octavius to include Pompey. Depicted as the son of a famous Roman patriot, Gnaius Pompey, Pompey appears on stage *"in warlike manner"* (s.d. II.i), the enemy within who threatens the unstable Empire.[24] This fearless Roman, as both Antony and Octavius attest, commands a formidable sea power and many loyal followers. Like Lucius in *Titus Andronicus* and Octavius in *Julius Caesar,* Pompey leads an army against Rome to scourge the city for its ingratitude to his father. Pompey also resembles two

---

[24]On Shakespeare's misreading of Plutarch's error concerning the two Pompeys, see Waino S. Nyland, "Pompey as the Mythical Lover of Cleopatra," *MLN,* 64 (1949), 515–16.

other Roman rebels: In a burst of republican zeal, he identifies his revolt against Octavius with the rebellion of Brutus and Cassius:

> What was't
> That mov'd pale Cassius to conspire? and what
> Made all-honor'd, honest, Roman Brutus,
> With the arm'd rest, courtiers of beauteous freedom,
> To drench the Capitol, but that they would
> Have one man but a man? And that is it
> Hath made me rig my navy.
>
> (II.vi.14–20)

In Shakespeare's vision Roman history moves in cyclical fashion: The struggles of Pompey and Caesar at Pharsalia; of Brutus, Cassius, and Caesar in the Capitol; of Brutus, Cassius, Octavius, and Antony at Philippi are to be reenacted by members of the next generation.

Surprisingly, however, the expected conflict, like the previous one between Antony and Octavius, is aborted. Romans strike another bargain, this time the exchange of love for land, service, and tribute. The world of *Antony and Cleopatra,* unlike the worlds of *Lucrece, Titus Andronicus,* and *Julius Caesar,* is not a simple arena where Romans can hack their way to glory with swords; instead, it is a place where politic bargaining often prevails. In such a world Pompey does not remain true to the memory of his father and to the traditions of the past; he sells his birthright for Sicily and Sardinia. The warrior hero armed with strong sword and constant heart gives way to such men as Octavius, Antony, Pompey, and Lepidus – a more calculating and compromising lot than their predecessors. The false ceremony of reconciliation that follows illustrates the degeneration of Roman ideals and ethics in the Empire. While Antony carouses, Lepidus reels, and Caesar sours, Pompey wishes that Menas had cut the cables of his ship and the throats of his guests. Pompey would freely enjoy the fruits of treachery so long as he need not sully his hands with the picking.

The scene with Ventidius presents a similar variation on the theme of Roman honor. Again, the vision of Roman military heroism quickly fades to reveal a sordid world of self-interested bargaining. Again the battlefield yields to the marketplace. Ventidius enters *"as it were triumph"* (s.d. III.i), with the body of Pacorus, the conquered Parthian, before him:

> *Ventidius:* Now, darting Parthia, art thou strook, and now
> Pleas'd Fortune does of Marcus Crassus' death
> Make me revenger.
>
> (1–3)

Since Marcus Crassus was a member of the first triumvirate along with the elder Pompey, Ventidius seems to have achieved here the revenge that the younger Pompey could not. The life of the son, Pacorus, has paid for the deeds of the father, Orodes. Consequently, an officer sees for Ventidius a bright future and the Roman rewards of fame and glory: "thy grand captain, Antony, / Shall set thee on triumphant chariots, and / Put garlands on thy head" (9–11). Ventidius, however, understands that the triumphal chariot and garland are not automatically the rewards for military valor and honorable discharge of duty. If he acquires more renown, he may well arouse the jealousy of his indolent commander and earn for his pains demotion and loss of favor. The better course is the way of discretion – one part of self-deprecation; another, outright flattery:

> *Ventidius:* I'll humbly signify what in his name,
> That magical word of war, we have effected.
>
> (30–1)

The scenes with Pompey and Ventidius cast a qualifying irony over the renewed hostilities between Antony and Octavius. In Act III, Scene iv Antony bristles upon hearing of Caesar's play for power in Rome. Antony's angry declaration, "If I lose my honor, / I lose myself" (22–3), sounds pretentious and hollow in light of Pompey's fading resolution, Ventidius's politic mixing of honor and discretion, and his own dishonorable dalliance in Egypt. In Rome Caesar likewise bristles upon hearing of Antony's activities – his trading of kingdoms with Cleopatra in the marketplace, his dishonoring of Octavia, pointedly identified as Caesar's sister as well as Antony's wife (III.vi.43).[25] Preparing for war, Caesar ex-

---

[25]In a perceptive study, "The Characterization of Octavius," *ShakS*, 6 (1972 for 1970), 231–88, J. Leeds Barroll notes Caesar's hypocrisy here, observing that he had already decided to wage war against Antony before Octavia's entrance (p. 263).

presses confidence in the righteousness of his cause and in the favor of just gods:

> and the high gods,
> To do you justice, makes his ministers
> Of us and those that love you.
>
> (III.vi.87–9)

These lines echo disquietingly Pompey's earlier expression of confidence: "If the great gods be just, they shall assist / The deeds of justest men" (II.i.1–2). In so doing, they recall Pompey's ignominious behavior and undercut Caesar's claim of divine justification.

Before the outbreak of war and the battle of Actium, Shakespeare shows Antony and Octavius to be flawed and ambivalent characters. The reports of Caesar's ambitious manipulation and of Antony's profligacy are never disproved or denied, but tacitly confirmed by the subsequent action. Neither Roman, the play makes clear, is wholly virtuous and disinterested. Although both Caesar and Antony talk much about their honor, it is increasingly difficult to distinguish the operation of that virtue from the workings of vanity and self-interest. Caesar's hunger for power clearly equals Antony's hunger for pleasure. Enobarbus's reflection is accurate and prophetic:

> Then, world, thou hast a pair of chaps – no more,
> And throw between them all the food thou hast,
> They'll grind th' one the other.
>
> (III.v.13–15)

The struggle for world power, like the struggle for sensual satisfaction, appears as the grinding of jaws in service of base appetite. Sooner or later, one Roman will devour the other.

Shakespeare's portrayals of Antony and Octavius before Actium, like his earlier portrayals of Brutus, Cassius, and Caesar, illustrate how mingled a yarn is human motivation. In *Julius Caesar,* however, Romans struggle with history conceived of as a force that moves directly to its appointed ends. Here the force of history shuttles back and forth from place to place, starting and stalling with the vicissitudes of plot and vagaries of character. The emphasis is not on the powerful, straight-lined movement of time (Antony, in fact, defeats Caesar's forces in battle after Actium),

but on the sheer multiplicity of events and on the variety of mo-
tives that make up the past. In this play Shakespeare's vision of
Roman history differs greatly from Vergil's. The Roman poet saw
Actium as the apex of Roman history, as a climactic victory over
the forces of chaos and barbarism, the beginning of the hallowed
pax Augusta. There is no ambivalence in Vergil's portrayal of
Octavius before battle:

> hinc Augustus agens Italos in proelia Caesar
> cum patribus populoque, Penatibus et magnis dis
> stans celsa in puppi, geminas cui tempora flammas
> laeta vomunt patriumque aperitur vertice sidus.
>
> (*Aen.* VIII.678–81)

> Here Augustus Caesar, leading Italians to strife, with peers
> and people, and the great gods of the Penates, stands on the
> lofty stern; his joyous brows pour forth a double flame,
> and on his head dawns his father's star.

Shakespeare did not share so sanguine a vision. For him the victory of Octavius was not simply an apocalyptic triumph, nor the
defeat of Antony merely a necessary purging.

Immediately before the battle of Actium, Cleopatra tells Enobarbus that she "will / Appear there for a man" (III.vii.17–18) to lead
the Egyptians against Caesar. Like Portia's, Cleopatra's attempt to
play the man fails and results in death and disorder. And like
Brutus's, Antony's admiration for the attempt blinds him to its
inherent folly. Shakespeare's continuing interest in Brutus appears
in the repeated references to him and to Philippi (II.v.23; II.vi.13;
III.ii.56; III.xi.35ff.). In fact, Shakespeare's earlier portrait of Brutus – noble, flawed, and doomed – contributes much to his portrait of Antony before Actium. Like Brutus, Antony seeks to reenact the heroic past, hoping to fight again at Pharsalia, "Where
Caesar fought with Pompey" (III.vii.32). Like Brutus on the eve of
Philippi, Antony rejects the warnings of his comrades, repudiating
mechanically the shocked questioning of Canidius, the clear rea-

soning of Enobarbus, the forthright candor of the soldier. Brutus's rhetoric before battle — his confidence in the rising tide and his eagerness to venture out onto the flood for future glory — comes to life in dramatic action as Antony resolves to fight by sea. And once again, the resulting sea voyage proves disastrous for the hopeful Roman soldier just as it proves fortunate for Octavius.

Created by a succession of short but tense conversations, intensified by the marching of opposed armies and the off-stage noise of a sea fight, the dramatic tension leading to the battle of Actium dissipates with the report of ignominious defeat. Contemptuously, Scarus tells of Cleopatra's flight:

> Yon ribaudred nag of Egypt
> (Whom leprosy o'ertake!) i' th' midst o' th' fight,
> When vantage like a pair of twins appear'd,
> Both as the same, or rather ours the elder —
> The breeze upon her, like a cow in June —
> Hoists sail and flies.
>
> (III.x.10–15)

The description of Cleopatra as a "ribaudred nag" has rightly attracted the attention of numerous commentators, although many have focused almost exclusively on the lexical possibilities of the phrase.[26] Too often ignored is Enobarbus's puzzling aside, that prophetic bit of bawdry spoken immediately before the battle:

> Well, I could reply:
> If we should serve with horse and mares together,
> The horse were merely lost; the mares would bear
> A soldier and his horse.
>
> (III.vii.6–9)

The puns on "merely lost" and on "bear" combine to suggest that the soldier and his horse cannot attend to the business of war in the presence of females. The "mares" would simply "bear" them from their responsibilities, by laying bare their desires and by bearing them on back.

---

[26]See Horace Howard Furness's Variorum edition, *The Tragedie of Anthonie, and Cleopatra* (Philadelphia: Lippincott, 1907), pp. 217–19; M. R. Ridley, ed., *Antony and Cleopatra*, The Arden Shakespeare (1954; rpt. Cambridge, Mass.: Harvard University Press, 1956), p. 128.

Behind this fanciful figure and the "ribaudred nag" lies Vergil's
Georgics III.[27] In *Venus and Adonis* Shakespeare drew upon this
poem to illustrate the power of sexual passion.[28] For the same
purpose he returns to it here, specifically to Vergil's discussion of
rearing horses for war:

> Sed non ulla magis viris industria firmat,
> quam Venerem et caeci stimulos avertere amoris,
> sive boum sive est cui gratior usus equorum.
> atque ideo tauros procul atque in sola relegant
> pascua, post montem oppositum et trans flumina lata,
> aut intus clausos satura ad praesepia servant.
> carpit enim viris paulatim uritque videndo
> femina, nec memorum patitur meminisse nec herbae
> dulcibus illa quidem inlecebris.
>
> (209–17)

> But no care so strengthens their powers as to keep from
> them desire and the stings of secret passion, whether one's
> choice is to deal with cattle or with horses. Therefore men
> banish the bull to lonely pastures afar, beyond a mountain
> barrier and across broad rivers, or keep him well mewed
> beside full mangers. For the sight of the female slowly
> inflames and wastes his strength, nor, look you, does she,
> with her soft enchantments, suffer him to remember woods
> or pastures.

Sexual desire wastes away the strength, *vires*, needed for war and
male work. It is *caeci*, hidden and unfathomable, as well as blind
to other considerations and to its own power. Enobarbus's joking
aside draws upon this vision of sexual passion as emasculating and
antithetical to the male business of war.

In light of Vergil's *Georgics*, the "ribaudred nag" crux is intelligible and thematically significant. Vergil (no less than Shakespeare) recognizes the sexual drives of mares as well as those of
stallions. Witness his account of mare madness in the springtime:

[27]Behind it also may be Plutarch's mention of Plato's metaphor for concupiscence, the "horse of the minde" (Vol. VI, p. 36).

[28]See T. W. Baldwin, *On the Literary Genetics of Shakspere's Poems & Sonnets*
(Urbana: University of Illinois Press, 1950), pp. 23–6. Baldwin's conclusions
are rehearsed and modified by F. T. Prince in the Arden edition, *The Poems*
(1960; rpt. London: Methuen, 1968), p. 19.

scilicet ante omnis furor est insignis equarum;
et mentem Venus ipsa dedit, quo tempore Glauci
Potniades malis membra absumpsere quadrigae.
illas ducit amor trans Gargara transque sonantem
Ascanium; superant montis et flumina tranant.
continuoque avidis ubi subdita flamma medullis
(vere magis, quia vere calor redit ossibus), illae
ore omnes versae in Zephyrum stant rupibus altis
exceptantque levis auras.

(266–74)

But surely the madness of mares surpasses all. Venus herself
inspired their frenzy, when the four Potnian steeds tore
with their jaws the limbs of Glaucus. Love leads them over
the Gargarus and over the roaring Ascanius; they scale
mountains, they swim rivers. And, as soon as the flame has
stolen into their craving marrow (chiefly in spring, for in
spring the heat returns to their breasts), they all, with faces
turned to the Zephyrs, stand on a high cliff, and drink in
the gentle breezes.

Outstripping all other creatures in the frenzy of their sexual passion, mares embody aggressive and devouring female desire. Like Shakespeare's Cleopatra, they appear in association with Venus, with cruel deeds of destruction, and with reckless flight.

Furthermore, the *levis auras*, "gentle breezes," that blow on the mares in heat, blow throughout *Georgics* III and carry the maddening mating scent to eager animals:

nonne vides, ut tota tremor pertemptet equorum
corpora, si tantum notas odor attulit auras?

(250–1)

See you not how a trembling thrills through the steed's
whole frame, if the scent has but brought him the familiar
breezes?

Scarus's lines on Cleopatra, "The breeze upon her, like a cow in June – Hoists sail and flies," usually explicated by glossing the breeze as "gadfly," features these Vergilian breezes along with another animal important to *Georgics* III: namely, the cow.[29] Un-

[29]Robert G. Hunter, "Cleopatra and the 'Oestre Junonicque,'" *ShakS*, 5 (1970 for 1969), 236–9, glosses the "cow in June" passage with citation to *Georgics*

like the mare, who represents frenzied, aggressive female desire, the cow in Vergil represents quiet, receptive passivity. Able to strike up fierce desire in males, the heifer in *Georgics* III grazes peacefully while maddened bulls clash in contest for her:

> et saepe superbos
> cornibus inter se subigit decernere amantis.
> pascitur in magna Sila formosa iuvenca:
> illi alternantes multa vi proelia miscent
> volneribus crebris, lavit ater corpora sanguis,
> versaque in obnixos urgentur cornua vasto
> cum genitu; reboant silvaeque et longas Olympus.
>
> $(217-23)$

> Nay, oft she drives her proud lovers to settle their mutual
> contest with clash of horns. She is grazing in Sila's great
> forest, a lovely heifer: the bulls in alternate onset join battle
> with mighty force; many a wound they deal, black gore
> bathes their frames, amid mighty bellowing the levelled
> horns are driven against the butting foe; the woods and the
> sky, from end to end, re-echo.

Like Cleopatra, the heifer causes the battle but never participates in it. Scarus's description of Cleopatra as a mare and as a cow in June depicts her as a paradoxical creature who unites the active and passive principles of female sexuality. Not only does Cleopatra burn with the madness of sexual desire, but she causes Antony to burn with it as well.

Shakespeare effectively uses *Georgics* III in *Antony and Cleopatra*, though not so much in the way of direct or indirect allusion. The Vergilian poem functions as a poetic wellspring of image and idea, lying below the surface of Shakespeare's text, imparting life and substance to it. Although the exact paths whereby such vital connections occur ultimately remain hidden and mysterious, one can occasionally glimpse the trail of the poet's imaginative processes. In this instance it is important that *Georgics* III shares verbal and thematic similarities with Vergil's account of human passion in *Aeneid* IV,[30] much on Shakespeare's mind during the

---

III.146–56, and sees a submerged allusion in Shakespeare's text to Io and Isis. He does not discuss the passage cited here or the symbolism of Vergil's cow.
[30]See Michael C. J. Putnam, *Virgil's Poem of the Earth: Studies in the "Georgics"* (Princeton: Princeton University Press, 1979), p. 192.

writing of *Antony and Cleopatra*. It is equally important that parts of *Georgics* III inspire parts of *Venus and Adonis*, a poem that Shakespeare consciously or unconsciously transforms in *Antony and Cleopatra*.[31] Whatever the paths, Shakespeare found in Vergil a vision of sexual desire as painful and pleasurable, physical and spiritual, destructive and creative. To be sure, Shakespeare's use of images from the *Georgics* deflates the grandeur of Antony and Cleopatra by bringing them down to the level of beasts; such borrowing, however, simultaneously exalts the human lovers by suggesting that their love partakes in the natural and universal power of *eros*:

> Omne adeo genus in terris hominumque ferarumque,
> et genus aequoreum, pecudes pictaeque volucres,
> in furias ignemque ruunt: amor omnibus idem.
>
> (242–4)

> Yea, every single race on earth, man and beast, the tribes of the sea, cattle and birds brilliant of hue, rush into fires of passion: all feel the same Love.

As in *Julius Caesar*, spatial and topographical metaphors express the transfer of power, this time from Antony to Octavius. The mighty Roman who played "with half the bulk o' th' world" (III.xi.64) cannot walk the earth he once ruled: "Hark, the land bids me tread no more upon't, / It is asham'd to bear me" (III.xi.1–2). The haughty trader in kingdoms is now a vagrant who has lost his way forever and must beg the conqueror for a small space "between the heavens and earth" (III.xii.14). His good stars having "empty left their orbs, and shot their fires / Into th' abysm of hell" (III.xiii.146–7), Antony finds himself alone in a universe utterly alien and hostile. After demonstrating sovereignty

---

[31]Many have remarked the verbal and thematic connections between the early poem and the mature tragedy. See, for example, Schanzer, *Problem Plays*, pp. 161–2; Adrien Bonjour, "From Shakespeare's Venus to Cleopatra's Cupids," *ShS*, 15 (1962), 73–80; J. W. Lever, "Venus and the Second Chance," ibid., 81–8; Wayne A. Rebhorn, "Mother Venus: Temptation in Shakespeare's *Venus and Adonis*," *ShakS*, 11 (1978), 1–19.

by cutting the Ionian Sea, taking Toryne, and winning Actium, Caesar is now the indisputable ruler of worldly spaces, "universal landlord" (III.xiii.72), master of sea, earth, and still stars. In defeat and dishonor Antony "*sits down*" (s.d. III.xi.24). By contracting himself on stage to occupy the smallest physical space, he expresses his diminished stature, and, more important, his incapacity for purposeful movement in the world owned by Caesar.

Antony's rise from the nadir of misfortune and dishonor is a long spiritual process that begins with getting off the ground and ends with ascent to the tomb. Although no stage direction indicates precisely when Antony stands, he probably does so before or during his final speech in the scene, the one that measures the world lost against one of Cleopatra's tears and asserts, "Fortune knows / We scorn her most when most she offers blows" (III.xi.73–4). From this time on, Antony struggles to regain lost honor. Challenging Caesar to personal combat, he acts on the belief that heroic deeds can rectify past mistakes and win future glory:

> If from the field I shall return once more
> To kiss these lips, I will appear in blood;
> I and my sword will earn our chronicle.
>
> (III.xiii.173–5)

So speaking, Antony resembles Shakespeare's other Romans – Lucrece, Titus Andronicus, Brutus, Cassius, Caesar, Coriolanus – all of whom subscribe to the same ethical code of honor, shame, and fame and earn their chronicles with strong right arm and sword. As Shakespeare's Romans are wont to do, Antony sees himself and his struggle in epical and mythological terms. Enraged, he swears "by Jove that thunders!" (III.xiii.85); confronting Cleopatra, he refers to himself as an Aeneas manqué, as one who leaves his pillow "unpress'd in Rome" and forbears "the getting of a lawful race" (III.xiii.106–7). He vows to make Death love him by contending "even with his pestilent scythe" (III.xiii.193). Later, he refers to his comrades as "Hectors" (IV.viii.7), and declares that Scarus deserves an armor of gold, "were it carbuncled / Like holy Phoebus' car" (IV.viii.28–9). Despite the ironies implicit in such hyperbole, particularly in the reference to Hector, Antony's allusive language increases his stature and that of his exploits.

Such allusive language creates an appropriate context for the archetypal arming of the hero in Act IV, Scene iv, a scene that evokes the ghostly analogs of Aeneas receiving his shield, Hector putting on his helmet, and Achilles taking up armor. Like those warriors, Antony here assumes his responsibilities and prepares to assert his worth. His arming takes on additional resonance from the major mythic undercurrents of the play. The sword that Mars put aside for his dalliance with Venus, the armor that Hercules and Aeneas exchanged for the unmanly costumes of Omphale and Dido, are ceremoniously and pointedly reclaimed. To atone for his former indolence and effeminacy, Antony plans a blood ritual, one designed to restore his dying honor to new life:

> Or I will live,
> Or bathe my dying honor in the blood
> Shall make it live again.
>
> (IV.ii.5–7)

Antony's proposed ritual of blood, given dramatic prominence by the showing of Scarus's wounds in Act IV, Scene vii, recalls the carrying of Lucrece's corpse, Titus's Thyestean banquet, and Brutus's gory hand washing. In all instances, Shakespeare depicts the Roman body bruised to pleasure the Roman soul. Blood takes on a sacramental vitality as Romans cook, wash, and bathe in it to recover lost honor and to attain spiritual excellence. The problems implicit in such ceremonies rise here as before to confront the audience. Can success in battle and the slaughter of enemies reclaim past honor and win future glory? More important, we question the integrity of the self-appointed sacrificer, especially as he vacillates between self-deprecating remorse and self-congratulatory mirth. We wonder if Antony is striking a noble pose instead of choosing noble action, playing a heroic part instead of actually becoming a hero.

Shakespeare carefully develops the ambivalence of Antony's rejuvenation by including various perspectives on it. Cleopatra celebrates the recovery of Antony's heroic ardor, but Caesar scorns Antony's challenge and pities the aged fool. The common soldiers believe that they hear the god Hercules, "whom Antony lov'd" (IV.iii.16), leave him. Enobarbus punctures Antony's high-minded rhetoric with sharp commentary. According to him, the challenge

to Caesar demonstrates that Antony's judgment has deteriorated
with his fortunes:

> Yes, like enough! high-battled Caesar will
> Unstate his happiness, and be stag'd to th' show
> Against a sworder!

(III.xiii.29–31)

Like Cleopatra's earlier censure of Antony's "excellent dissembling," Enobarbus's caustic asides suggest that Antony's honor is
merely a charade, a public spectacle conceived by a diminished
brain.

The recurrence of animal imagery also amplifies doubts about
the nature of Antony's rejuvenation. Enobarbus compares him to
an old lion dying (III.xiii.95) and to a furious dove that will peck
at an estridge (III.xiii.196). The imagery implies that Antony's
actions are neither manly nor virtuous, but the brute instincts of
threatened beasts and birds. In a flash of ironic self-revelation,
Antony compares himself, horned and enraged, to an angry bull:

> O that I were
> Upon the hill of Basan, to outroar
> The horned herd!

(III.xiii.126–8)

The image has been traced to Psalms 22:12:[32]

> Manie yong bulles haue compassed me:
> mightie bulles of Bashán haue closed
> me about.

Clearly, Shakespeare alters the original image of the bulls as agents
of persecution and affliction. He may well be conflating the biblical image with Vergil's memorable depiction of the angry bull in
Georgics III. Having lost his love to a rival, the bull prepares for
battle and revenge:

> multa gemens ignominiam plagasque superbi
> victoris, tum quos amisit inultus amores,
> et stabula aspectans regnis excessit avitis.

---

[32]Ridley, in the Arden edition of the play, refers to Steevens, who cites the Prayer-
book versions of Psalms 48:15, 22:12 (p. 148). Below I quote from *The Geneva
Bible: A Facsimile of the 1560 edition* (Madison: University of Wisconsin
Press, 1969), p. 239.

ergo omni cura viris exercet et inter
dura iacet pernox instrato saxa cubili,
frondibus hirsutis et carice pastus acuta,
et temptat sese atque irasci in cornua discit
arboris obnixus trunco, ventosque lacessit
ictibus, et sparsa ad pugnam proludit harena.
post ubi collectum robur viresque refectae,
signa movet praecepsque oblitum fertur in hostem.

(226–36)

Much does he bewail his shame, and the blows of his
haughty conqueror, and much the love he has lost un-
avenged – then, with a wistful glance at his stall, he has
quitted his ancestral realm. Therefore with all heed he
trains his powers, and on an unstrewn couch among flinty
rocks, lies through the night, with prickly leaves and pointed sedge for fare. Anon he tests himself, and, learning to
throw wrath into his horns, charges a tree's trunk; he
lashes the winds with blows, and paws the sand in prelude
for the fray. Soon, when his power is mustered and his
strength renewed, he advances the colours, and dashes
headlong on his unmindful foe.

The similarities between Vergil's defeated bull and Shakespeare's
defeated Antony are compelling: Both lose to a haughty conqueror
and experience shame at the loss of honor; both endure exile from
ancestral realms; both gather up their forces for a return; both
charge headlong at the foe. The Vergilian echoes here, along with
the recurrent mention of animals, produce an insistently mocking
counterpoint to the grand music of heroic rhetoric.

The complexity of our reaction to Antony is continually sustained and deepened. Just when we are ready to follow Enobarbus
and desert him, Antony shows his magnanimity: He sends the
deserter "gentle adieus and greetings" (IV.v.14), along with chests
and treasure. Just when we are ready to dismiss him as a self-
deluding impostor, Antony demonstrates his courage and spirit:
He returns victorious from battle in a formal march (IV.viii). And
just when we are ready to accept the soldiers' view that Hercules
has left him forever, Antony, believing Cleopatra has betrayed
him, flies into a most Herculean rage:

The shirt of Nessus is upon me; teach me,
Alcides, thou mine ancestor, thy rage.
Let me lodge Lichas on the horns o' th' moon,
And with those hands, that grasp'd the heaviest club,
Subdue my worthiest self.

(IV.xii.43–7)

Upon receiving report of Cleopatra's death, Antony's rage turns to grief. Despite all the previous ambivalences, Shakespeare presents Antony's decision to commit suicide sympathetically. The choice of self-destruction is an act of resolution, courage, self-assertion, and transformation – the last honorable option of a Roman soldier in a base world. Events preceding and following Antony's suicide dispose the audience to pity him and admire his decision. Enobarbus's repentance and death (IV.ix), for example ("the most affecting part of the play," according to Hazlitt),[33] is a ratification of heart mysteries and a harbinger of the deaths to come. Antony's reflection on the changing clouds (IV.xiv.3ff.) expresses "a profoundly tragic sense of mutability, of the fickleness of Fortune and the fatal deceptiveness of life."[34] The later betrayal of Decretas, who takes Antony's fallen sword as a token for Caesar, confirms Antony's view of the world as an inconstant and ignoble place, filled with flatterers and time servers. Unlike the betrayals of Enobarbus, Alexas, and Canidius – honorable men corrupted by Antony's fortunes – Decretas's betrayal enhances rather than diminishes Antony's status.

Beyond the general fact that nothing so unequivocally becomes the lives of many Shakespearean Romans like the leaving, Antony's final moments share specific similarities with those of Cassius and Brutus. Cassius, we recall, asks Pindarus to fulfill the terms of his oath by assisting in the suicide:

In Parthia did I take thee prisoner,
And then I swore thee, saving of thy life,
That whatsoever I did bid thee do,
Thou shouldst attempt it. Come now, keep thine oath;
Now be a freeman.

(V.iii.37–41)

---

[33]As quoted in Furness's Variorum edition, p. 287.
[34]Markels, *Pillar of the World*, p. 168.

Similarly, Antony asks Eros to fulfill his former pledge and to hold out his sword:

> When I did make thee free, swor'st thou not then
> To do this when I bade thee? Do it at once.
>
> (IV.xiv.81–2)

Cassius's death evokes a vivid simile from Titinius:

> O setting sun,
> As in thy red rays thou dost sink to-night,
> So in his red blood Cassius' day is set!
> The sun of Rome is set. Our day is gone.
>
> (V.iii.60–3)

In Cleopatra's lament this image of the setting sun expands into a vision of apocalyptic nightfall:

> O sun,
> Burn the great sphere thou mov'st in! darkling stand
> The varying shore o' th' world![35]
>
> (IV.xv.9–11)

The similarities between the ends of Antony and of Brutus are also specific and important. Brutus declares that he "bears too great a mind" to go "bound to Rome," to be led through the streets by Caesar (V.i.111–12). Likewise, Antony refuses to become part of Caesar's triumphal procession, "with pleach'd arms, bending down / His corrigible neck, his face subdu'd / To penetrative shame" (IV.xiii.73–5). Before the final sword thrust, Brutus's comrade Strato stops for a poignant farewell: "Give me your hand first. Fare you well, my lord" (V.v.49). Similarly, Antony's comrade Eros, sword in hand, pauses for a brief but touching goodbye:

> My dear master,
> My captain, and my emperor: let me say,
> Before I strike this bloody stroke, farewell.
>
> (IV.xiv.89–91)

Both Brutus and Antony commit suicide to avoid shame and to

---

[35]These lines, of course, belong to the larger pattern of fire-and-light imagery ably explicated by Knight, pp. 240–4, and by Wolfgang H. Clemen, *The Development of Shakespeare's Imagery* (Cambridge, Mass.: Harvard University Press, 1951), pp. 162–5.

win fame; both compare death to a peaceful sleep after the toil of a long day:

> *Brutus:* Night hangs upon mine eyes, my bones would rest,
>   That have but labor'd to attain this hour.
>
>   (V.v.41−2)

> *Antony:* Unarm, Eros, the long day's task is done,
>   And we must sleep.
>
>   (IV.xiv.35−6)

After the suicide, Strato solemnly reports that "Brutus only overcame himself, / And no man else hath honor by his death" (V.v.56− 7). Looking on the dying Antony, Cleopatra says likewise, "So it should be, that none but Antony / Should conquer Antony" (IV.xv.16−17).

Shakespeare carefully depicts Antony's death in familiar dramatic terms, complete with recognizably Roman motivation, execution, and aftermath. But Antony's suicide is unique. While testifying to Roman love of honor and aversion to shame, it expresses Antony's rejection of Rome and Roman values. Before resolving to take his own life, Antony discards his armor:

>   Off, pluck off,
> The sevenfold shield of Ajax cannot keep
> The battery from my heart. O, cleave, my sides!
> Heart, once be stronger than thy continent,
> Crack thy frail case!
>
>   (IV.xiv.37−41)

The removal of armor emblematically repudiates all the demands of battlefield, Empire, and world.[36] The reference to Ajax, whose sevenfold shield cannot keep the battery from Antony's heart, suggests the limitations of military heroism. Coming hard upon Cleopatra's comparison of angry Antony to mad Ajax (IV.xiii.1−2), the classical allusion implies that the warrior has spent his heroic rage. No longer an avatar of furious Hercules or mad Telamon, Antony is the poor forked thing itself, struggling

---

[36]Charney offers a coherent discussion of the sword-and-armor imagery of the play and rightly calls attention to the significance of this disarming (pp. 125−33).

with a grief that renders all else insignificant. The prayer that his heart crack its frail case recalls unmistakably Philo's opening description of Antony as Roman warrior, "his captain's heart, / Which in the scuffles of great fights hath burst / The buckles on his breast" (I.i.6–8). Now, however, the heart bursts not in military furor but in loving grief, in service not of Rome but of Cleopatra.

Antony's suicide, then, resembles only in externals previous Roman suicides. Undertaken only partially to regain lost honor, Antony's death, at least in his mind, will bring him to Cleopatra:

> Eros! – I come, my queen! – Eros! – Stay for me!
> Where souls do couch on flowers, we'll hand in hand,
> And with our sprightly port make the ghosts gaze.
> Dido and her Aeneas shall want troops,
> And all the haunt be ours. Come, Eros, Eros!
>
> (IV.xiv.50–4)

Antony's vision of Aeneas and Dido reunited in Hades is essentially his own creation. In *Aeneid* VI the shade of Dido coldly and silently turns from Aeneas to rejoin her former husband, Sychaeus.[37] Antony's misconstruction of this Vergilian scene, whether intentional or not on Shakespeare's part, illustrates the bold reshaping of Vergilian incident and theme characteristic of this play. Unlike his famous ancestor, Antony refuses to live as fate demands and Rome requires: He decides the archetypal conflict between love and duty in favor of love.

The visual and dramatic spectacle on stage accentuates the paradoxes implicit in Antony's Roman yet un-Roman suicide. Falling on his sword, the very instrument by which he sought vindication, Antony hopes to rise to new life. The reaction of the startled guards upon seeing Antony on the ground should steer our response to admiration and pity:

> *Antony:* I have done my work ill, friends. O, make an end
>   Of what I have begun.
> *2. Guard:*   The star is fall'n.
> *1. Guard:* And time is at his period.
>
> (IV.xiv.105–7)

---

[37] J. Leeds Barroll points out, in addition, that the Elysian fields in Vergil were reserved for soldiers and patriots, not lovers. "Shakespeare and the Art of Character: A Study of Anthony," *ShakS*, 5 (1970 for 1969), 159–235 (223–4, note 16).

After word of Cleopatra's deceit arrives, the guards pick up Antony and carry him to the monument, thus creating on stage a formal march that is part funeral cortege, part triumphal procession. Appropriately, the march leads to Cleopatra's monument, the tomb that will shortly serve as marital chamber. Hoisted aloft to Cleopatra, Antony rises from the earth of Caesar and Rome. The highly charged sexual language of the scene, particularly the repeated puns on "dying," conveys its multiple paradoxes. Antony's death separates him from the world and ends his Roman life; it also unites him with Cleopatra, spiritually and sexually, and marks a new beginning.

If at the moment of death Antony proves himself a "bridegroom" (IV.xiv.100), Cleopatra has still to prove herself a bride. The questions raised by her earlier interview with Thidias, Antony's charge of betrayal (never confirmed or refuted), and her refusal to open the monument for her lover complicate judgment of her character, even as she delivers spendidly poetic protests of love and grief. After lamenting the melting of the earth's crown, the withering of the garland of war, the falling of the soldier's pole – images that suggest, among other things, the end of Roman ideals – Cleopatra faints away (s.d. IV.xv.68). Like Antony's falling on the sword, this falling begins a process of spiritual rising, an ascent that will result in transcendent reunion. And like Antony's, this rising involves a repudiation of mythological fancy and a recognition of human realities. Hoisting up the heavy body of Antony, Cleopatra remarks:

> Had I great Juno's power,
> The strong-wing'd Mercury should fetch thee up,
> And set thee by Jove's side. Yet come a little –
> Wishers were ever fools – O, come, come, come.
>
> (IV.xv.34–7)

Antony recognizes that Ajax's shield cannot protect him from the sorrows of a human heart; Cleopatra recognizes that all the strength of the Olympian gods cannot help her lift the weight of a human body. Antony learns that he is no longer a supernatural ruler, one whose sword quarters the world; Cleopatra learns to reject Iras's passionate apostrophe, "Royal Egypt! / Empress!" (IV.xv.70–1) and comes to a new understanding of her own humanity:

> No more but e'en a woman, and commanded
> By such poor passion as the maid that milks
> And does the meanest chares.
>
> (IV.xv.73–5)

Quite consciously, Cleopatra attempts to pattern her last actions after Antony's example:

> We'll bury him; and then, what's brave, what's noble,
> Let's do't after the high Roman fashion,
> And make death proud to take us.
>
> (IV.xv.86–8)

She expresses the same horror of Caesar's triumph and humiliation by the "shouting varlotry / Of censuring Rome" (V.ii.56–7). And she speaks with the same music of resolution and triumph in her voice:

> And it is great
> To do that thing that ends all other deeds,
> Which shackles accidents and bolts up change,
> Which sleeps, and never palates more the dung,
> The beggar's nurse and Caesar's.
>
> (V.ii.4–8)

Cleopatra here renounces the incessant motion of the sublunary world – the ebb and flow of the Nile, the rise and fall of Fortune, the natural processes of propagation and dissolution. Her vision of dung as "the beggar's nurse and Caesar's" expresses her world weariness, her disenchantment with the natural cycle of begetting, consuming, and decaying, and her desire for death.

The incidents of the last act draw upon Shakespeare's experience in the Roman plays and elsewhere to create scenes of power and resonance. The Roman soldiers who enter behind Cleopatra and capture her in her own monument reenact an important archetype in Shakespeare's Roman vision: the invasion of private

space by the impious and destructive outsider. The archetype originates with Vergil's account of Pyrrhus in Priam's *penetralia* and in
Shakespeare's Roman canon takes various forms in order to ex-
foliate various moral and political meanings. Tarquin's rape of
Lucrece, for example, violates the values of family, household,
city, and world. The rape of Lavinia by the Goths symbolizes their
invasion of Rome and the barbarism of the world in the iron age.
The assassination of Caesar may also draw upon the archetype,
especially as the stabbing is recounted in Antony's metaphor:

> Mark how the blood of Caesar followed it,
> As rushing out of doors to be resolv'd
> If Brutus so unkindly knock'd or no.
>
> (III.ii.178–80)

In *Antony and Cleopatra* the locked monument represents the
private space; Cleopatra, the helpless victim; and Caesar's soldiers, the violent outsiders.[38] Caesar, who had previously demonstrated brotherly affection for his sister, now threatens to slaughter Cleopatra's children (V.ii.128–33). No less impious than
Pyrrhus, Tereus, Tarquin, Chiron, Demetrius, Brutus, and the conspirators, Caesar appears as the barbaric invader who menaces the
helpless family.

The scene with Seleucus, despite comic overtones, features another Roman motif important to Shakespeare. As Brutus, Cassius,
and the conspirators betray Caesar, and as Enobarbus, Alexas,
Canidius, and Decretas betray Antony, so Seleucus turns against
Cleopatra, his mistress and benefactor.[39] Cleopatra denounces the
exposure of her deceit as self-serving treachery:

> See, Caesar! O, behold,
> How pomp is followed! Mine will now be yours,
> And should we shift estates, yours would be mine.
>
> (V.ii.150–2)

Betrayal from within thus accompanies invasion from without.
This time, however, no Roman suffers betrayal, only Cleopatra.

[38]See Richard Hosley, "The Staging of the Monument Scenes in *Antony and
Cleopatra*," *LC*, 30 (1964), 62–71.
[39]The possibility of collusion between Cleopatra and Seleucus seems remote,
especially in light of Brents Stirling's persuasive discussion, "Cleopatra's Scene
with Seleucus: Plutarch, Daniel, and Shakespeare," *SQ*, 15 (1964), 299–311.

Like the Roman invasion, the Egyptian betrayal portrays the conquering Caesar as enemy and the conquered Cleopatra as pitiable victim.

Cleopatra's death, no less than Antony's, fuses Roman and non-Roman elements. Despite her desire to imitate the Roman fashion, Cleopatra dies like a true Egyptian: She stages her own suicide as an erotic pageant, complete with costume and admiring spectators:

> Now, Charmian!
> Show me, my women, like a queen; go fetch
> My best attires. I am again for Cydnus
> To meet Mark Antony.

> (V.ii.226–9)

Unlike the earlier pageant of Enobarbus's description, this one takes place on stage. For prologue Cleopatra sings a rhapsody to Antony, who crested the world, shook the orb, and dropped realms and islands from his pocket (V.ii.79ff.). Dolabella's quiet skepticism reminds us that Cleopatra's vision of herself as Venus and of Antony as Mars is not fact but vision. Shakespeare qualifies the proceedings further by the appearance of the Clown, who talks of lying women: "but he / that will believe all that they say, shall never be sav'd / by half that they do" (V.ii.255–7). The precarious balance between low comedy – realistic and deflating – and operatic passion – splendid, poetical, excessive – makes the scene curiously homely and credible, yet glorious.

The mythic undertones that Shakespeare uses throughout the play resound in Cleopatra's final moments. The story of Dido and Aeneas, continually evoked at crucial points, figures importantly in the conclusion as Dido's death scene enriches Cleopatra's. Both women decide to commit suicide because they suffer from broken hearts and fear imminent conquest. Dido's companions help prepare a purgation ritual; Cleopatra's handmaids help prepare a sacrificial rite. Dido retreats into the locked *penetralia* that contains Aeneas's sword, clothing, and the familiar bed, *notumque cubile* (648); Cleopatra withdraws into the monument, also an epithalamial tomb, a place of marriage and self-immolation. Before dying, both queens recall the first meeting with their lovers,

both receive kisses and loving ministrations from their companions, and both give the lie to Mercury's cruel jeer, *varium et muta-
bile semper / femina* (569–70), "a fickle and changeful thing is
woman ever."[40] Whereas Dido dies bitterly and tragically, however, Cleopatra dies triumphantly and joyfully. Cleopatra's glazed
rapture (V.ii.76ff.) replaces Dido's grim curse (607ff.). And Antony's transformation from guest to husband ("Husband, I come!
/ Now to that name my courage prove my title!" [V.ii.287–8])
neatly reverses Aeneas's degeneration from husband to guest:
hospes, / hoc solum nomen quoniam de coniuge restat (323–4),
"O guest – since that alone is left from the name of husband."

The rich tableau of Cleopatra with the asps at her breast draws
upon various iconographical and mythological traditions. In
Christian terms Cleopatra is Eve, the first woman to take a serpent
to her bosom; in classical terms she is "alma Venus," the nurtur-
ing goddess of love and beauty.[41] Martha Hester Golden notes the
intersection of other traditions in this scene:

> We have been prepared by Enobarbus' description to per-
> ceive the Queen in state as an entrancing quean, or Volup-
> tas; a woman with vipers at her breasts is the sign of
> Luxuria; and the serpents' teeth seem to bring only drowsy
> pleasure. At the same time Cleopatra becomes maternal at
> last, speaking to the creatures as babes nursing at her
> breasts, transforming herself into a Madonna or Charity. In
> this one obstinately ambivalent scene, as throughout the
> play, Cleopatra remains faithful to all the contradictory
> extremes of her own nature and of human love itself.[42]

Reviewing classical and neoclassical lore, Janet Adelman describes
the serpent as a strange divinity, "who simultaneously kills and
gives life, is old and young, moves and is motionless." She suggests
that Shakespeare's transfer of the serpent bite from Cleopatra's

[40]L. J. Mills, "Cleopatra's Tragedy," *SQ*, 11 (1906), 147–62, suggests plausibly
that Cleopatra's "I am marble-constant; now the fleeting moon / No planet is
of mine" (V.ii.240–1) reflects the contemporary popularity of Mercury's remark (p. 158, note 24).

[41]On "alma Venus," see *Aeneid* I.618, X.332; Andrea Alciati, *Emblemata cvm
Commentariis* (Padua, 1621), pp. 832–4; Rebhorn, "Mother Venus."

[42]*The Reader's Encyclopedia of Shakespeare*, ed. Oscar James Campbell and
Edward G. Quinn (New York: Crowell, 1966), p. 820.

arm, where Plutarch locates it, to her breast also borrows "the force of an ancient image for Terra, the generative mother earth, who was frequently portrayed nourishing serpents."[43]

Also pertinent here is the symbolism of serpents in Cesare Ripa's *Iconologia*. The emblem for suffering, *Dolore*, features a bound man with a serpent at his naked chest.[44] The serpent is *sempre male*, "always evil," and causes pain and sorrow. Similarly, the emblem for sin, *Peccato*, shows a figure enwrapped with evil serpents; the worm of conscience, *uerme della conscienza*, eats at the heart. Ripa's serpents and worm, symbols of suffering, sin, and guilt, may lie behind Shakespeare's portrayal of Cleopatra in death. Unlike the figures in the emblems, however, Cleopatra does not ache with grief, pain, and remorse, but with hope, joy, and longing. The biting of her serpents is immortal in both senses of the Clown's pun, bringing death and an end to woe as well as "better life" (V.ii.2). Here Shakespeare transforms the emblems of worldly and spiritual affliction into an image of transcendence.

That Shakespeare used Ripa in Cleopatra's death scene is all the more possible given the contemporary practice of his friend and rival, Ben Jonson. For Jonson relied heavily on Ripa in the construction of his masques, those elaborate courtly entertainments coming into vogue at about the time of *Antony and Cleopatra*.[45] Although many recognize masque elements in Shakespeare's final plays (where, as Stephen Orgel puts it, "seeing is believing, and specifically, believing the impossible"),[46] no one has yet discussed masque elements in *Antony and Cleopatra*.[47] The

[43]Adelman, *Common Liar*, pp. 61ff. The quotations appear on pp. 63, 64.

[44]Cesare Ripa, *Iconologia* (Padua, 1611), reprinted in *The Renaissance and the Gods*, No. 21 (New York: Garland, 1976), pp. 125–6. For the emblem of *Peccato*, see pp. 407–9.

[45]On Jonson's use of Ripa, see Allan H. Gilbert, *The Symbolic Persons in the Masques of Ben Jonson* (1948; rpt. New York: AMS Press, 1969), s.v. "Ripa."

[46]Stephen Orgel and Roy Strong, *Inigo Jones: The Theatre of the Stuart Court*, 2 vols. (Berkeley and Los Angeles: University of California Press, 1973), Vol. I, p. 10. See the excellent opening discussion, "The Poetics of Spectacle," to which I am indebted for my account of the theory and staging of the Jonsonian masque.

[47]Past productions, however, have often emphasized to excess the visual and spectacular elements of the play. Witness the Drury Lane revival (1873), complete with Roman festival, Amazonian procession, boy chorus, ballets, extravagant settings, and gorgeous costumes. George C. D. Odell, *Shakespeare from Betterton to Irving*, 2 vols. (New York: Scribner, 1920), Vol. II, pp. 304–6. See also Margaret Lamb, *"Antony and Cleopatra" on the English Stage* (Ruther-

final scenes of this play feature the artificially contrived pageantry and the gorgeous, regal, and symbolic costuming of the Jonsonian masque. Here also is the triumph of the revels over the antimasque – ugly, discordant, and threatening – represented by Caesar and the armed guards who enter Cleopatra's monument (s.d. V.ii.34, 110). One wonders if Shakespeare was influenced by Jonson's *Hymenaei,* performed January 5, 1606, wherein eight men issue from a huge globe "with a kind of contentious music" and approach Hymen's altar with drawn swords.[48]

The final meaning of a Jonsonian masque, we should observe, inheres not simply in the antithesis between revels and antimasque, but in the creative tension between them. Orgel's comments on the ending of a Jonsonian masque apply incisively to the conclusion of *Antony and Cleopatra:*

> Neither Comus nor Daedalus presides over the court in which we find ourselves at the end of *Pleasure Reconcild to Vertue.* Rather, it is a middle realm, existing somewhere between the extremes of the antimasque's misrule and the revels' order, but including both as possibilities. Indeed, this masque asserts with equal strength both the power of the individual will to overcome disorder and the insubstantiality of the ideal vision.[49]

Just so.

The invasion of *"the* Guard *rustling in"* (s.d. V.ii.319) breaks the poignant quietness of Cleopatra's death and Charmian's eulogy for the "lass unparallel'd." These soldiers are soon followed by Dolabella and by "Caesar *and all his* Train, *marching"* (s.d. 332). Even as Caesar realizes that he has been cheated of his triumph, the sight of Cleopatra, "bravest at the last" and "royal"[50] (335–6), wrings

---

ford, N.J.: Fairleigh Dickinson University Press, 1980), passim (esp. pp. 72–98).

[48] *Ben Jonson: The Complete Masques,* ed. Stephen Orgel, The Yale Ben Jonson (New Haven: Yale University Press, 1969), p. 79.

[49] Stephen Orgel, *The Jonsonian Masque* (Cambridge, Mass.: Harvard University Press, 1965), p. 190.

[50] Furness's Variorum edition contains an interesting gloss on this word. A deer that escaped from the hunt of the king or queen was called a "hart-royal" (p. 373). The image of Cleopatra as a hunted deer continues the pattern of hunting imagery in Shakespeare's Roman works (especially *Julius Caesar*) and in the *Aeneid,* especially the description of Dido (IV.68–73).

from him words of wonder and praise: "she looks like sleep, / As she would catch another Antony / In her strong toil of grace" (346–8). The phrase "toil of grace" evocatively recalls Cleopatra's reference to her lover uncaught by Caesar, the "world's great snare" (IV.viii.18), and thereby suggests that she alone has the power to catch Antony, Mars among men. Saddened but undeterred, Caesar orders a solemn funeral rite and the return to Rome. As he expects, his return to the city will commence his triumphant reign over the Roman Empire and the world; but, as Caesar can only dimly perceive, the world he now rules is a changed one, ineffably diminished and impoverished by what it has lost.

⟨══⟩MK⟨══⟩

Despite frequent allusions to its streets, Rome in *Antony and Cleopatra* is not a city of definite dimensions and familiar landmarks, but an Empire that spans vast spaces. Initially, Rome appears to be a place of *gravitas* in conflict with Egyptian *voluptas*, but the dichotomy between these places and these values does not remain absolute and unqualified. Rather, as much recent criticism cogently argues, the tension between Rome and Egypt exposes the strengths as well as the weaknesses of each.[51] Rome in *Antony and Cleopatra* is a kingdom divided against itself in bloody civil war. More important, however, the Empire is in spiritual conflict with itself, caught between its profession of honorable ideals and its sordid, self-serving practice. Perceptively, Norman Rabkin distinguishes between the two pictures of Rome that the play presents:

[51]Variations of this view, sometimes called "complementarious," can be found in many places. See Benjamin T. Spencer, "*Antony and Cleopatra*" and the Paradoxical Metaphor," *SQ*, 9 (1958), 373–8; Traversi, pp. 79–203; Stephen A. Shapiro, "The Varying Shore of the World: Ambivalence in *Antony and Cleopatra*," *MLQ*, 27 (1966), 18–32; Norman Rabkin, *Shakespeare and the Common Understanding* (New York: Free Press, 1967), pp. 184–8; Markels, *Pillar of the World* passim; Sidney R. Homan, "Divided Response and the Imagination in *Antony and Cleopatra*," *PQ*, 49 (1970), 460–8; Howard Felperin, *Shakespearean Representation: Mimesis and Modernity in Elizabethan Tragedy* (Princeton: Princeton University Press, 1977), pp. 107–12.

> One is of the world that Antony loses in choosing
> Cleopatra: a world in which honor is the watchword,
> military men are giants who can survive superhuman trials,
> and fame is the spur to noble men's ambition. But the other
> picture is of a vicious political arena where honor is
> meaningless and comes only to men who do not deserve it;
> a general atmosphere of treachery and triviality makes
> Rome seem hardly worth the contemning.[52]

Clearly, the struggle between the principal Romans, Caesar and Antony, is not simply a conflict between Rome and Egypt, virtue and vice, honor and love, or reason and passion. Caesar, for example, is more complex and ambivalent than many recognize.[53] Calculating in his intention to lead Cleopatra in triumph, ruthless in his handling of Alexas, Pompey, and Lepidus, politic in his manipulation of Octavia, he shows at times warm affections and strong emotions. We have no reason to suspect his sincerity when he expresses love for his sister (III.ii.24ff.), especially as he does so well after the political match is made. Nor need we doubt the authenticity of his grief for Antony (V.i.14ff.), the man whom he praised earlier for strength and courage. Antony, of course, is equally complex and paradoxical. From one perspective, he is a middle-aged libertine who shirks his duties in order to glut himself with the pleasures of power, wine, food, and sex. Yet Antony appears throughout the play as an avatar of Roman virtue: Philo, Demetrius, and Enobarbus recall his great captaincy; Caesar remembers his heroic exploits; Pompey fears him as his "soldiership / Is twice the other twain" (II.i.34–5). The deliberate echoes of Brutus and Cassius in Antony's death scene are also to the point. Valiantly vanquished by himself, Antony resembles in part those noble bygone Romans who committed suicide for the sake of honor.

Antony's struggle to maintain a noble conception of himself –

---

[52]Rabkin, *Shakespeare and the Common Understanding*, p. 186. Cf. Ben Jonson's picture of sordid Imperial politics in *Sejanus* (1603).

[53]Compare the resigned graciousness of Shakespeare's Caesar in the final scene with the frantic desperation of the conqueror in other portrayals. The Caesars of Suetonius and Dio Cassius, for example, employ Psyllian snake charmers to suck the poison from Cleopatra's wounds in an attempt to revive her for the triumphal procession (*De Vita Caesarum* II.xvii.4; *Historia Romana* LI.xiv. 3–4).

wholly admirable and wholly ridiculous though it appear by turns – is the struggle of Shakespeare's Rome writ small. Like the city in Shakespeare's conception, Antony is torn between the demands of pulsing blood and those of Roman tradition – marmoreal, imposing, unyielding. Like many of Shakespeare's Romans – Lucrece, Titus, Cassius, Brutus, Portia, Pompey, Coriolanus, Volumnia – Antony looks to the past and sees an intimidating gallery of austere Roman portraits, frozen in immemorial postures of virtue for posterity to admire and imitate. Although Antony tries hard to strike the required pose through rhetoric and ritual, he finds, as do many others, that he cannot maintain the position for very long. The body yearns for pleasure; emotions seek expression; life demands movement. Unlike the past (at least as conceived by these self-appointed Roman historians), the present exhibits a bewildering array of opportunities for compromise and demands flexibility. Inflexible adherence to yesterday, especially when coupled with blindness to present realities, leads increasingly in Shakespeare's Rome to disorder and destruction.

As we have seen, the forms of such destruction are many. Typically, Shakespeare depicts Roman destructiveness by focusing on the ironic disparity between intention and deed and by portraying Roman action as *impius,* as a flagrant violation of Vergilian *pietas.* Hence the recurring images of shattered families and perverted family relations. For the most part, however, Shakespeare abandons this strategy in *Antony and Cleopatra,* where mention of family relations is systematically suppressed and the perspective that such mention offers ignored. Both Plutarch and Appian, for example, discuss at length Antony's relationship with Fulvia and describe her revolt in detail. Both also emphasize the motherhood of Octavia, who selflessly cares for Antony's many children, and that of Cleopatra, who worries about the survival of her children. Shakespeare, however, unlike Robert Garnier and Samuel Daniel, dramatizes none of this, retaining only a few glancing references to hint at the presence of family obligations. Perhaps thinking that emphasis on the lovers' family ties would have been too incriminating or distracting, Shakespeare here departs radically from his past perspective and practice.

Such independence on the playwright's part is also evident in the characterization of Cleopatra, brought to full and pulsing life from the thin shadows in Plutarch. Initially she appears as the incarnate spirit of the other earthly world, that place in dramatic and military opposition to Rome. In Shakespearean terms she is allied with the Ardeans in *Lucrece,* the Goths in *Titus Andronicus,* the pirates in *Antony and Cleopatra,* the Volscians in *Coriolanus.*[54] Yet, for all this, Cleopatra is Roman too, sharing important similarities with Shakespeare's Roman women. Like Calphurnia, Cleopatra opposes the Roman military and masculine code of honor and asserts the importance of personal obligations. Like Portia, she abandons this opposition and tries to follow the Roman fashion. Like Lucrece, she finally asserts her loyalty and her love through suicide, an act of marriage as well as self-destruction. In Vergilian terms Cleopatra is Dido, Circe, Amata, and Juno – the exotic and powerful female who threatens the march of Roman history. But if she is Vergil's Dido, Cleopatra is finally Vergil's Lavinia, the destined Roman bride who embodies the promise and possibility of a peaceful future. Least Roman of all Shakespearean women, Cleopatra is, paradoxically, most Roman as well.

The rich texture of *Antony and Cleopatra,* created by the experienced dramatist from various strands of myth, history, and legend, strenuously resists reductive analysis. No single-minded moral or political approach can satisfactorily elucidate its action and reveal its meaning.[55] The taking of such approaches has often

---

[54]In contrast to the Cleopatras of Vergil (*Aen.* VIII.678ff.), Horace (*Carmina* I.37), Lucan (*De Bello Civili* X.53ff.), and others, however, Shakespeare's Cleopatra is not politically motivated. She is not out to conquer Rome and to expand her empire.

[55]For various moral readings, see Dolora G. Cunningham, "The Characterization of Shakespeare's Cleopatra," *SQ,* 6 (1955), 9–17; Franklin M. Dickey, *Not Wisely But Too Well: Shakespeare's Love Tragedies* (San Marino, Calif.: Huntington Library, 1957), pp. 144–202; J. Leeds Barroll, "Shakespeare and Roman History," *MLR,* 53 (1958), 327–43; Robert E. Fitch, "No Greater Crack?" *SQ,* 19 (1968), 3–17; Simmons, pp. 109–63; Michael Platt, *Rome and Romans According to Shakespeare,* Salzburg Studies in English Literature, JDS, No. 51 (Salzburg: Institut für Englische Sprache und Literatur, 1976), pp. 246ff.; Andrew Fichter, "'Antony and Cleopatra': 'The Time of Universal Peace,'" *ShS,* 33 (1980), 99–111. For political readings, see Daniel Stempel, "The Transmigration of the Crocodile," *SQ,* 7 (1956), 59–72; James Emerson Phillips, Jr., *The State in Shakespeare's Greek and Roman Plays* (1940; rpt. New York: Octagon, 1972), 188–205; Paul Lawrence Rose, "The Politics of *Antony and Cleopatra,*" *SQ,* 20 (1969), 379–89. The two categories, of course, often overlap.

required outright or de facto glorification of Caesar, viewed either as the Emperor who ushers in the fourth temporal monarchy and the birth of Christ, as the leader who ends Roman civil wars and reinstates the institution of kingship, or as both. Renaissance auditors, we are solemnly assured, would have remembered Christ was born in Augustus's reign, a halcyon time of peace and political stability.

The Caesar who comes to power in Shakespeare's play, however, little resembles the hallowed Augustus of such legend.[56] Moreover, Cleopatra's withering sarcasm and final triumph over the "ass / Unpolicied" (V.ii.307–8) leave the audience little disposed to ring in the new millennium. When considered along with *Julius Caesar*, history in *Antony and Cleopatra* appears to be undular and cyclical rather than teleological; it seems to repeat itself rather than to move in a linear progression to consummation in the reign of Augustus. Caesar follows Pompey, Brutus follows Caesar, Antony follows Brutus, Caesar follows Antony. The ironic pattern of resemblances between Julius Caesar and Brutus is sustained in the similar pattern of resemblances between Brutus and Antony. The Caesar who first "bore the palm alone" is finally succeeded by his adopted son, "sole sir of the world." This vacillating rhythm may be part of some greater harmony; it may also be merely the movement of the varying tide that rots all things with incessant motion.[57] Caesar's visionary optimism about his future reign, "the time of universal peace" (IV.vi.4), is balanced and undercut by Cleopatra's ominous reflection on his luck, "which the gods give men / To excuse their after wrath" (V.ii.286–7).

The city of Rome has clearly undergone major transformation in *Antony and Cleopatra*. No longer the central focus of our attention, Rome is relegated at the end of the play to the status of its

[56] A recent study argues that Elizabethans drew sharp distinctions between the ascendant Octavius, often depicted as deceitful, ambitious, and tyrannical, and the crowned Augustus. See Robert P. Kalmey, "Shakespeare's Octavius and Elizabethan Roman History," *SEL*, 18 (1978), 275–87. Surprisingly, Kalmey does not mention Seneca, who provided an important *locus classicus* for this dual conception in *De Clementia* I.xi.1–3.

[57] The first view is well known and influential; for the second, see MacCallum, who observes of the play that "there is no moral cement to hold together this ruinous world" (p. 348); and Cantor, who refers to the "bedrock of nihilism" underlying the lovers' mountainous passion (p. 166).

former opponents. Cleopatra's monument in Alexandria finally occupies the center of our interests and sympathies, and the entering Romans appear as impious invaders. Shakespeare could go no further in depicting the problematic relationship between Rome and the world outside it. The way ahead in *Coriolanus* leads back into the city and to a closer examination of what Antony and Cleopatra have left behind.

VI

CORIOLANUS
ROME AND THE SELF

For all their obvious differences, *Coriolanus* shares important similarities with *Antony and Cleopatra*. Alfred Harbage observes that both plays feature a struggle for power that "goes against a naturally superior man because of his failure to accommodate himself to reality."[1] J. Dover Wilson writes that Coriolanus and Antony "were soldiers, both cast in the heroic mould, both subject to fits of vehement passion which in the end brought them to disaster."[2] Geoffrey Bullough suggests that Antony and Coriolanus are parallel portraits of concupiscence and irascibility – the Aristotelian complements.[3] Norman Rabkin treats the plays as "opposite halves of the same statement" about the possibilities of heroism and self-fulfillment in this world.[4] Both Antony and Coriolanus suffer in exile from Rome and both die in the tragic attempt to return home. The Romes that these soldiers struggle against, though radically different in political organization, present one and the same paradox: In both plays Rome is a noble place of high heroic deeds and honor, as well as a sordid center of selfish scheming and political infighting.

Despite these similarities, the far-flung empire of *Antony and Cleopatra* little resembles the constricted and constrictive city in *Coriolanus*.[5] This *urbs,* again an image of Troy, is sharply defined by outlying battlefields, rival towns, and its own vividly realized topography – its walls, gates, Capitol, Tiber, Tarpeian rock, forum, private houses, and streets. The action inside Rome, as T. J. B.

[1]*William Shakespeare: A Reader's Guide* (New York: Farrar, Straus, 1963), p. 437.

[2]J. Dover Wilson, ed., *The Tragedy of Coriolanus,* (Cambridge: Cambridge University Press, 1960), p. xvii.

[3]Bullough, Vol. V, pp. 454–5.

[4]"*Coriolanus:* The Tragedy of Politics," *SQ,* 17 (1966), 195–212. The quotation appears on p. 212.

[5]See Cantor, pp. 57, 136–7.

Spencer notes,[6] is depicted with unusual attention to local color, as if Shakespeare hoped that the precise rendering of concrete detail would yield forth the abstract principles and problems there embodied, as if careful representation of Rome's body would reveal its soul. The contrast between the vast, indefinable, and expansive world of *Antony and Cleopatra* and the clearly circumscribed city of *Coriolanus* suggests the movement of Shakespeare's concern to Rome itself, specifically, to the political organization of the earthly city. This is not to say that Shakespeare wishes to take sides in the ongoing quarrel about preferable forms of government, but that he seeks in *Coriolanus* to explore the purpose, nature, and problems of political order.[7] By focusing on a figure who embodies uncompromisingly the Roman ideal of honor, he exposes the paradoxes inherent in the civilized community, especially those deriving from the differences between private virtue and the public good, or as Aristotle put it, between the good man and the good citizen.[8]

Of course, interest in Roman politics, its familial origins, its ceremonies and rituals is nothing new to Shakespeare's Roman canon. But whereas *Lucrece* culminates in the founding of the Republic, *Titus Andronicus* in a new regime, *Julius Caesar* in a new triumvirate, and *Antony and Cleopatra* in the unification of Empire, *Coriolanus* portrays no such political change. The tri-

---

[6]"Shakespeare and the Elizabethan Romans," *ShS*, 10 (1957), 27–38 (34–5). But see John W. Draper, "The Realism of Shakespeare's Roman Plays," *SP*, 30 (1933), 225–42 (237–9). Also pertinent is Gail Kern Paster's suggestion that the architecture of the city provides images for assessing the spiritual state of the characters. "To Starve with Feeding: The City in *Coriolanus*," *ShakS*, 11 (1978), 123–44 (130ff.).

[7]Like *Julius Caesar*, *Coriolanus* has a rich critical and theatrical history of partisan interpretation. For an introduction to the latter, see Philip Brockbank, ed., *Coriolanus*, The Arden Shakespeare (London: Methuen, 1976), pp. 74–89. My approach to the politics is similar to that of A. P. Rossiter, *Angel with Horns* (London: Longmans, 1961), pp. 235–52, who argues that the play is not about class war or the Tudor theory of order, but about politics, power, and the state, broadly conceived.

[8]F. N. Lees, "*Coriolanus*, Aristotle, and Bacon," *RES*, NS 1 (1950), 114–25, first suggested that Aristotle's *Politics* provides illuminating glosses on Shakespeare's play, though he unwisely argued for direct influence through I. D.'s 1598 translation. Rodney Poisson, "Coriolanus as Aristotle's Magnanimous Man," in *Pacific Coast Studies in Shakespeare*, ed. Waldo F. McNeir and Thelma N. Greenfield (Eugene: University of Oregon Press, 1966), pp. 210–24, interprets the play with reference to Aristotle's *Ethics*.

bunacy is established at the outset of action, and the play dramatizes instead rebellions and invasions, the conflicts within and the
threats from without the city. Once again Shakespeare returns to
Vergil for image and idea, though this time he reaches for Homer
as well. A. C. Bradley observed that the audience does not see
much into the hearts and minds of the characters, or hear much of
the supernatural.[9] Instead, we fix our gazes firmly on the earth-
bound city, on the increasingly alien Romans who move in and out
of its gates, trying to preserve it from others as well as from
themselves.

The first few scenes of *Coriolanus* introduce its main conflicts and
major themes. The play opens in tumult as angry citizens march on
stage "*with staves, clubs, and other weapons*" (s.d. I.i). The First
Citizen fans the flames of rebellion by a series of questions culmin-
ating in the "verdict" that Caius Martius be killed and corn dis-
tributed freely (I.i.10–11). Shakespeare portrays the unreasoning
violence of mob action by the noisy bustle on stage, the brash
demagoguery of the First Citizen, and the quick choice of a scape-
goat (we think of Cinna the poet). The irony attaching to the word
"verdict," a word normally implying dispassionate consideration
and legal procedure, further suggests the lawlessness of the mob.

As in the opening of *Julius Caesar*, an antagonist who seeks to
return the people to their homes and shops abruptly halts the
movement of citizens to the Capitol. Menenius Agrippa does not
hear complaints but insists on the folly of defying Roman authority and on the impossibility of altering Roman destiny:

> For your wants,
> Your suffering in this dearth, you may as well
> Strike at the heaven with your staves as lift them
> Against the Roman state, whose course will on
> The way it takes, cracking ten thousand curbs
> Of more strong link asunder than can ever
> Appear in your impediment.

(I.i.66–72)

[9]"*Coriolanus*," PBA, 5 (1913 for 1911–12), 457–73 (458–60). Cf. Plutarch's
soothsayer and speaking statue, Vol. II, pp. 179–80, 187.

Grand assertions, but patently false. As the play makes clear, an angry crowd has just altered Roman politics and destiny by expelling the Tarquins; another, even as Menenius speaks, wrings an important political concession from the aristocracy, namely, the establishment of the tribunacy. Ironically, Menenius's mention of the "dearth" strikes up sympathy for the starving people, giving credence to the First Citizen's protest that he speaks "in hunger for bread, not in thirst / for revenge" (I.i.24–5). Menenius's assertion that the "helms o' th' state" care for the people "like fathers" (77), a flagrant but effective mixing of stock political metaphors, evokes a list of grievances:

> 1. *Citizen:* Care for us? True indeed! They ne'er
> car'd for us yet. Suffer us to famish, and their
> store-houses cramm'd with grain; make edicts for
> usury, to support usurers; repeal daily any wholesome
> act establish'd against the rich, and provide more
> piercing statutes daily to chain up and restrain the
> poor. If the wars eat us not up, they will; and there's
> all the love they bear us.
>
> (79–86)

As no one ever confirms or refutes these charges, they increase the ambivalence of the scene by suggesting the gravity of the situation and by tempering our initial repulsion from the mob.

In response to the citizen, Menenius reverts to another ancient political metaphor, the body politic. His rehearsal of the belly fable does not directly answer the grievances; instead, it makes a general but pointed statement about civic interdependence. The senators of Rome, Menenius avers, are like the good belly which appears to be idle and greedy but which actually distributes nutrition to the entire body. As related members of the incorporate state, then, plebs and patricians must cooperate with each other, just as all parts of the body must cooperate to preserve the health of the individual.[10] This fable pithily articulates basic political

---

[10]Shakespeare's version of the fable derives from various sources: North's Plutarch (1579 or a later edition), Holland's Livy (1600), Camden's *Remaines* (1605), William Averell's *A Marvailous Combat of Contrarieties* (1588), and possibly Sidney's *Apology* (1595) and Camerarius's *Fabellae Aesopicae* (1573). See Baldwin, Vol. I, p. 622; Kenneth Muir, "Menenius's Fable," *NQ*, 198 (1953), 240–2; Bullough, Vol. V, p. 459; Brockbank, *Coriolanus,* pp. 29–30.

truths and succeeds in quieting the crowd; yet, the patrician's application disturbs. One wonders about the comparison of senators to the stomach instead of the "kingly-crowned head" (115), center of reason, deliberation, and judgment. And one questions the propriety of defending a full stomach to a crowd of empty ones, especially as the crowd accuses the Senate of failing to distribute corn.

In this opening scene Shakespeare carefully maintains a balance in audience reactions. Initially, the crowd appears as another version of the furious mob in *Julius Caesar,* which seeks to pluck down "forms, windows, any thing" (III.ii.259); as the scene progresses, however, the people claim more of our sympathy. Through the ambivalences of the encounter with Menenius (and the following encounter with Coriolanus), Shakespeare poses fundamental questions about the organization of the *urbs* and the rights of individuals within it. Aristotle explained that the city exists to satisfy the needs of its citizens and to provide them not only with life, but with *good* life.[11] Glossing Aristotle, Le Roy defined the "chiefest good" of civil organization as "soueraigne felicitie or welfare, consisting both in the publique and in the priuat fruition of all kind of goods both of soule and bodie, and also of fortune."[12] As the fable instructs, however, citizens can achieve this "soueraigne felicitie" only by sacrificing certain goods and by subordinating self-interest to public welfare. In the opening scenes of *Coriolanus* the tension of this paradox threatens to destroy civilized life in Rome.

The entrance of Caius Martius – proud, powerful, and contemptuous – develops the emerging conflict between the self and the city. Scornfully Martius harangues the abashed crowd and, like Octavius and Antony in *Antony and Cleopatra,* ridicules their inconstancy:

> Hang ye! Trust ye?
> With every minute you do change a mind,

Perceptive critical discussions are offered by David G. Hale, "*Coriolanus:* The Death of a Political Metaphor," *SQ,* 22 (1971), 197–202; Andrew Gurr, "'Coriolanus' and the Body Politic," *ShS,* 28 (1975), 63–9; Paster, "To Starve with Feeding."

[11]*Politics* 1252b–1253a. Cf. Plato, *The Republic* II.368ff.; Cicero, *De Re Publica* I.xxv.39; *De Legibus* I.vi.18–xiii.39.

[12]*Aristotles Politiqves,* translated from Loys Le Roy by I. D. (1598), p. 1.

And call him noble, that was now your hate;
Him vild, that was your garland.

(181–4)

Caius Martius is a "true-bred" Roman (243), one whose prowess
on the field has earned for him glory in the city. Like Titus Andronicus, Julius Caesar, and Mark Antony before Cleopatra, Martius proves his *Romanitas* through military exploits, each scar a
sign of constancy and courage, a symbol of his identity. After
hearing of the Volscian preparation for attack, Martius disdain-
fully dismisses the citizens and readies himself to act the part of the
soldierly arm, defender of the body politic.

The stage history of *Coriolanus* gives ample witness to the dramatic power of Martius's grand entrance and ringing denuncia-
tions.[13] Amazement at the Colossus on stage, however, does not
preclude criticism and questioning. Martius's contempt for the
"poor itch" (165) of the people's "opinion" discomfits us. Fame,
the tribunes justly observe, is the spur to his actions and the good
opinion of others the reward for his deeds (263–72). Martius's
ostensible concern for Rome, moreover, ill sorts with his out-
spoken hatred of Roman citizens:

> Would the nobility lay aside their ruth
> And let me use my sword, I'd make a quarry
> With thousands of these quarter'd slaves, as high
> As I could pick my lance.

(197–200)

Surely this thundering is strident and excessive. However ardently
Martius defends Rome, his loyalty to the city is problematical.
Implicit in his speeches there are prophetic hints of tension between the demands of his own honor and those of Rome. Com-
menting on the establishment of the tribunacy he swears:

> 'Sdeath,
> The rabble should have first unroof'd the city
> Ere so prevail'd with me.

(217–19)

[13]See the account of Kemble's entrance in the New Variorum edition, *The Tragedie of Coriolanus,* ed. Horace Howard Furness, Jr. (Philadelphia: Lippincott,
1928), p. 55. See also Arthur Colby Sprague, *Shakespeare and the Actors: The
Stage Business in His Plays (1660–1905)* (Cambridge, Mass.: Harvard University Press, 1944), pp. 326–7.

Martius rather contemplates the destruction of the city than the swaying of his own firm judgment. Later, speaking of Tullus Aufidius, he declares:

> Were half to half the world by th'ears, and he
> Upon my party, I'd revolt, to make
> Only my wars with him.
>
> (233–5)

More loyal to self than city, Martius envisions himself revolting from common cause for individual honor. Thinking so, Martius, no less than the crowd he reviles, contradicts the belly fable and its insistence on civic cooperation for the greater good of all.

Martius's appearance in the first scene continues Shakespeare's probing of the *urbs*. Extending the examination of the city's purpose and ends, Martius the soldier suggests the necessity of defense. Aristotle, of course, recognized the importance of a strong defense to the *polis*. Although he did not go so far as Machiavelli, who considered self-defense the primary cause for most political organization, he censured Plato for not giving defense its due in *The Republic*.[14] Shakespeare here represents the abstract political necessity through use of a concrete and specific example: the Volscian invasion. In one complex opening scene, then, he juxtaposes the two dominant political motifs of the Roman canon: rebellion and invasion. In so doing, he assembles from various Roman fragments the image of a complex and living city, complete with a wide range of problems and responsibilities.

Opposed to the energetic movements of citizens in the streets is the stationary domesticity of Volumnia and Virgilia, sitting and sewing at home (I.iii). Volumnia quickly identifies herself as a Roman matron, fiercely proud of her son's exploits, wholly devoted to the ideal of military honor.[15] She declares:

> Hear me pro-
> fess sincerely: had I a dozen sons, each in my love
> alike, and none less dear than thine and my good

[14]*Politics* 1291a. Machiavelli's ideas on the origins of political organization can be found in *Discorsi* I.i.

[15]Brockbank in the Arden edition of *Coriolanus* suggests that Shakespeare's Volumnia may owe something to Plutarch's description of Spartan women in *Moralia* and *Lives* (p. 42).

Martius, I had rather had eleven die nobly for their
country than one voluptuously surfeit out of action.

(21–5)

Volumnia's preference for her offspring's honorable death before
dishonorable life recalls Titus Andronicus, who gladly buried his
sons nobly slain, but who refused burial for the defiant Mutius. In
both instances the consignment of Roman sons to the soldier's
tomb is too easy and untroubled. To be sure, civic demands must
occasionally take precedence over family bonds in any city, but the
situation in Rome appears unnatural. If Coriolanus had died in
battle, Volumnia avers, "his good report should have been my /
son; I therein would have found issue" (20–1). Virgilia's shocked
silence suggests the perversity of such regard for fame. Moreover,
Volumnia's language reflects her essential unnaturalness as woman and mother; she habitually equates images of birth and battle.
Her joy in producing a "man-child," for example, is matched by
her joy in his proving "himself a man" (16–17). When Virgilia
recoils at the thought of her husband wounded and bleeding, Volumnia angrily dismisses her with an extravagant simile:

> Away, you fool! it more becomes a man
> Than gilt his trophy. The breasts of Hecuba,
> When she did suckle Hector, look'd not lovelier
> Than Hector's forehead when it spit forth blood
> At Grecian sword, contemning.
>
> (39–43)

The association of Hecuba's milk-filled breast with Hector's
blood-spitting forehead, of course, is meant to shock, and it does.
Yet, in its strained insistence on the similarity between a mother's
breast and a wound, the conceit suggests the perversion of Volumnia's values and the pathological excesses of Roman honor. Furthermore, the figures of Hecuba and Hector appear here, as they
do in *Lucrece, Titus Andronicus,* and *Antony and Cleopatra,* to
stir our subconscious memories of Troy: They foreshadow ever so
faintly the future grief of the mother, Volumnia, and the future
doom of the brave warrior son, Coriolanus. By this point in his
Roman canon Shakespeare has attained full mastery over the subtle art of allusion.

The unnaturalness of Volumnia's Roman ethos is also suggested by the description of her grandson, child of the "confirm'd" (and woeful) countenance (59–60). In one of his "father's moods" (66) the boy catches a gilded butterfly, lets it go, and catches it again, only to tear it to pieces in the end. Like his father's pursuit of honor and fame, this chase leads to frustration and senseless destruction. The comedy inherent in the boy's puerile imitation of his father is mock heroic and double-edged: It cuts backward to expose in all heroic action a core of juvenile bad temper. Not only does the child appear ridiculous, but so does his father, who will likewise "set his teeth" (64) and mammock that which he seeks.

Throughout this scene and the play, Virgilia opposes the Roman code and its incarnation in Volumnia. Caius Martius is her husband, not a trophy to be gilt with blood or a picture to be stirred to life by renown (9–12, 39–40). Consequently, she is repelled by the thought of his wounds and horrified at the prospect of his death. She does not "freelier rejoice in that absence / wherein he won honor than in the embracements of his / bed" (3–5), but fervently hopes for his safe return. Like another chaste Roman wife, Lucrece, Virgilia sits home, spins, and worries about her husband's safety. No less than seven times in about forty lines does she refuse to accompany Volumnia and Valeria out of doors (69–111). The insistent emphasis on her remaining at home sets up here the familiar antithesis between private, enclosed space and the public outdoors, between Brutus's garden or Caesar's bedroom and the wide walkways to the Capitol, between Cleopatra's embrace and the world of Rome. Like Portia, Calphurnia, Cleopatra, and their prototypes in *Aeneid*,[16] Virgilia suggests the importance of private space and human love, even for proud and honorable Romans.

As the action moves from the city to the outlying battlefields, specifically to the grounds outside Corioles, there appears to be

---

[16]A particularly suggestive analog for this scene is Vergil's portrait of Euryalus's mother, likewise sewing, who drops her shuttle and thread when she hears of her son's death (*Aen.* IX.475–83).

little difference between Rome and the opposing city. Both have walls and both possess mighty champions who walk onto the stage covered with blood (s.d. I.iv.61; s.d.I.x). What is more, both subscribe to the same strict code of military honor. Aufidius, for example, exhorts the senators to keep their "honors safe" (I.ii.37). Before battle the First Senator vouches for the steadfast courage of each Volscian soldier (I.iv.14−15); the stage reverberates for several scenes with the noise and action of an equal battle.

Interestingly, the Roman siege of Corioles prevents the expected Volscian siege of Rome: The invaders become the invaded; the defenders, the attackers. This exchange of roles and this change in focus from besieged Rome to besieged Corioles are rife with political and dramatic ironies. Rome, apparently, can survive and prosper only by conquest of other cities, however like Rome they may be. Unwittingly, Titus Lartius speaks of Rome as well as Corioles when he remarks, "If we lose the field, / We cannot keep the town" (I.vii.4−5). Accordingly, the individual Roman can gain success and honor only by conquering fellow warriors, his spiritual kindred in courage and in moral perspective. The Roman city and the Roman self thrive in the encouragement and glorification of martial energy, energy that will prove as uncontrollable and menacing as it is necessary for preservation from external threats.

The siege enacted on stage in *Coriolanus* recalls the other sieges in the Roman works: the siege of Lucrece by Tarquin, the siege of Rome by Lucius and the Goths, the siege of Caesar by the conspirators, the siege of Cleopatra by Octavius. Here, however, the emphasis is almost exclusively external. In so far as is possible in drama, Shakespeare seems intent on portraying an epic struggle, complete with prebattle parley, siege, invasion, duel, and aftermath. The sights and sounds on stage summon up a host of Homeric and Vergilian analogs. In the bold and bloody figure of the invading Martius we see, for example, Achilles, proud, fierce, and inexorable opponent of the archetypal walled city, Troy. We see his son Pyrrhus, avatar of *impietas, multo Priami de sanguine Pyrrhus, / gnatum ante ora patris, patrem qui obtruncat ad aras* (*Aen.* II.662−3), "Pyrrhus, steeped in the blood of Priam − Pyrrhus who butchers the son before the father's eyes, the father at the altars." We also recognize Hector, invader of the Greek camp in

Iliad XII, and Turnus, the brave warrior who, like Coriolanus, fights inside enemy walls in solitary courage and glory (*Aen.* IX).[17]

Of the epic invasions recapitulated in Martius's attack on Corioles, two are especially significant. Hector's invasion of the Greek camp provides a prototype of the defender turned invader for the rewards of fame and glory. Remembrance of Hector's action in *Iliad* XII or some later retelling may have combined in Shakespeare's imagination with Vergil's reworking of the incident in *Aeneid* IX, where Turnus invades the invading Trojans, temporarily ensconced in Latinus's territory. John W. Velz notes the pertinence of *Aeneid* IX to *Coriolanus* and suggests that Shakespeare's portrayal of Coriolanus owes much to Vergil's Turnus, the warrior hero who belongs on the battlefield, not in the more complex if less exalted space within city walls.[18] Surely this suggestion is apt. And surely Vergil's covert allusions to Hector in the last six books of the *Aeneid* ironically reflect upon Turnus's boasts and deeds, just as Shakespeare's allusions to Hector ironically reflect on Martius's.[19] We recall Volumnia's strained simile (I.iii.40–3) and Aufidius's later taunt:

[17]Noteworthy among those who have written about the epic qualities of the play and its main character are Brower, pp. 354–81; Richard C. Crowley, "*Coriolanus* and the Epic Genre," in *Shakespeare's Late Plays: Essays in Honor of Charles Crow*, ed. Richard C. Tobias and Paul G. Zolbrod (Athens: Ohio University Press, 1974), pp. 114–30; Howard Felperin, *Shakespearean Representation: Mimesis and Modernity in Elizabethan Tragedy* (Princeton: Princeton University Press, 1977), pp. 113–14; See also J. R. Mulryne, "*Coriolanus* at Stratford-upon-Avon: Three Actors' Remarks," *SQ*, 29 (1978), 323–32 (324). Paul A. Jorgensen has suggested a different context for the play, that of Elizabethan soldiership, in "Shakespeare's Coriolanus: Elizabethan Soldier," *PMLA*, 64 (1949), 221–35, and *Shakespeare's Military World* (Berkeley and Los Angeles: University of California Press, 1956), passim. Presumably, Homer and Vergil were more familiar to Elizabethans than Robert Barret and Barnaby Rich.

[18]"Cracking Strong Curbs Asunder: Roman Destiny and the Roman Hero in *Coriolanus*," *ELR*, 13 (1983), 58–69.

[19]On Vergil's subtle and ironic use of Homer, see William S. Anderson, "Vergil's Second *Iliad*," *Transactions of the American Philological Association*, 88 (1957), 17–30; also his *The Art of the Aeneid*, Landmarks in Literature (Englewood Cliffs, N.J.: Prentice-Hall, 1969), pp. 75–80. Anderson brilliantly demonstrates that Vergil undercuts Turnus's Achillean pretensions by modeling him on Hector.

174

> Wert thou the Hector
> That was the whip of your bragg'd progeny
> Thou shouldst not scape me here.
>
> (I.viii.11–13)

Shakespeare's allusions to Hector in this play, as we shall see, greatly increase the drama and poignance of Coriolanus's struggle.

Throughout the battle scenes that make up the rest of Act I Martius moves with epic power. After spurring the Romans on to victory, he swears by "battles," "blood," and "vows" (I.vi.56–7), and sets out to face Aufidius and the Antiates. Having affrighted the enemies with his "grim looks" (I.iv.58), his sweat of "wrath" (I.iv.27), and the "thunder-like percussion" of his sounds (I.iv.59), Martius appears in these scenes as a figure of Mars, the god he invokes in battle. Splendid in his relentless fury and terrible in his destruction, Martius is the spirit of war incarnate in Roman armor. Like other epic heroes – Achilles, Hector, Ajax, Diomedes, Aeneas, and Turnus – Martius proves his *vertu* on the battlefield, that testing ground for the rewards of honor and fame. As do Homer and Vergil, Shakespeare defines the epic world by deft contrast with the pastoral and lyric worlds. We recall Cominius's strange simile:

> The shepherd knows not thunder from a tabor
> More than I know the sound of Martius' tongue
> From every meaner man.
>
> (I.vi.25–7)

The allusion to the shepherd, evoking the peaceful world of *otium* and pastoral song, demarcates by implicit contrast the bloody battlefield of epic heroism. We remember also Martius's greeting:

> O! let me clip ye
> In arms as sound as when I woo'd, in heart
> As merry as when our nuptial day was done
> And tapers burnt to bedward!
>
> (I.vi.29–32)

Martius's comparison of the soldierly and the amorous embrace is a violent yoking that emphasizes not the similarities in the two activities but the differences.

Besides illuminating the nature of the epic struggle, Martius's amorous greeting also implies certain criticisms of it. The energies of *eros,* normally occupied in courtship, marriage, and procreation, are here subverted to the purposes of *thumos,* "public spiritedness," and destruction.[20] The tension implicit in Act I, Scene iii between Roman honor and Virgilia's hearth and home surfaces briefly, only to be lost in the ensuing melee. Gradually, however, the audience comes to realize that the Roman fanfare on stage is disturbingly antifamilial. Martius's earlier battlecry, "we'll beat them to their wives" (I.iv.41), suggests the irreconcilable differences between battlefield and home; and Cominius's later oath regarding the sparing of an enemy citizen evokes a dark image of *impietas:* "Were he the butcher of my son, he should / Be free as is the wind" (I.ix.88–9).

Martius's desire to return his enemies to domesticity, Philip Brockbank observes, compares to Antony's boast, "We have beat them to their beds" (*Ant.* IV.viii.19; cf. IV.vii.5, 9).[21] What is more, the spectacle of the triumphant, blood-boltered Scarus of Act IV, Scene vii resembles the similar spectacle of Coriolanus in Act I, Scenes iv–vi of this play. Scarus jests about the shape of his own cuts and cries, "I have yet / Room for six scotches more" (*Ant.* IV.vii.9–10). Coriolanus, likewise bloody, also dismisses his wounds with lighthearted bravado and yearns for more combat:

> Sir, praise me not;
> My work hath yet not warm'd me. Fare you well.
> The blood I drop is rather physical
> Than dangerous to me. To Aufidius thus
> I will appear, and fight.
>
> (I.v.16–20)

For these Romans the spilling of human blood in battle is a rite of sanctification, a quasi-religious ritual that gives meaning to action, confers identity, and creates new life. For the audience, however, the sight of so much blood repels as well as fascinates. We balk at the appearance of Martius "flea'd" (I.vi.22), rendered unrecognizable by the blood on his arms, cloak, and face, and we wonder what kind of life must needs issue from such loathly birth.

[20]See Cantor's application of these terms to the play (pp. 55–124).
[21]Brockbank, *Coriolanus,* p. 129.

After the battle scenes, Lartius and Cominius marvel at Martius's valor and the troops grant noisy acclaim: *"They all shout and wave their swords, take him up in their arms, and cast up their caps"* (s.d. I.vi.75). After Cominius bestows upon him "war's garland" (I.ix.60) and a new title, "Coriolanus," Martius expresses gratitude:

> I thank you.
> I mean to stride your steed, and at all times
> To undercrest your good addition
> To th' fairness of my power.
>
> (I.ix.70–3)

For him, as for Tarquin (*Luc.* 204–10), honor is a heraldic crest on public display. As such, it becomes increasingly problematic. When the soldiers noisily acclaim Martius again and *"cast up their caps and lances"* (s.d. I.ix.40), he becomes angry and abusive:

> May these same instruments, which you profane,
> Never sound more! When drums and trumpets shall
> I' th' field prove flatterers, let courts and cities be
> Made all of false-fac'd soothing!
>
> (I.ix.41–4)

The rebuke of the false-faced populace recalls Martius's opening tirade in which he scorned the giving of garlands and the throwing of caps. He who strives for honor and fame, Coriolanus begins to discover, must serve the fickle and foul-mouthed god of popular opinion. Coriolanus's dawning perception of this paradox, "The gods begin to mock me. I, that now / Refus'd most princely gifts, am bound to beg / Of my lord general" (I.ix.79–81), will come to full understanding in the city that awaits his return.

Coriolanus's entry into Rome is a formal pageant of triumph, complete with crowds, trumpets, a procession, and a herald's introduction:[22]

[22]See Alice S. Venezky, *Pageantry on the Shakespearean Stage* (New York: Twayne, 1951), p. 36.

> *Herald:* Know, Rome, that all alone Martius did fight
> Within Corioles gates; where he hath won,
> With fame, a name to Martius Caius; these
> In honor follows Coriolanus.
> Welcome to Rome, renowned Coriolanus!
> *Sound. Flourish.*
> *All:* Welcome to Rome, renowned Coriolanus!
>
> (II.i.162–7)

The communal repetition of the greeting lends to the entry the air of religious ceremony: The *urbs* reaccepts its illustrious member, ratifies his new identity, transforms his personal success into public victory. As in the triumphal pageant that begins *Titus Andronicus,* discordant notes sound amid the general exultation. There the presence of the doomed Alarbus and the Goths suggests the barbarity of Roman conquest; here Coriolanus's gentle teasing of Virgilia, silent and weeping, likewise creates an ironic perspective on Roman action:

> My gracious silence, hail!
> Wouldst thou have laugh'd had I come coffin'd home,
> That weep'st to see me triumph? Ah, my dear,
> Such eyes the widows in Corioles wear,
> And mothers that lack sons.
>
> (II.i.175–9)

For one brief moment, we glimpse the Roman victory from the other side, that of the defeated. Every gash on Martius's body is indeed an enemy's grave, and every enemy a husband, father, or brother.

Shakespeare allows little time here for reflection on the *impietas* of war, but instead moves the entourage *"in state"* (s.d. II.i.204) to the Capitol. After sweeping past, the procession leaves Brutus and Sicinius behind to conspire against Coriolanus. The action on stage resembles that of *Julius Caesar,* Act I, Scene ii, where Caesar's procession leaves behind the conspiring Cassius and Brutus. Both sets of conspirators note with alarm the victorious soldier's popularity and both anticipate with fear his rise to power. The tribunes' mocking review of the enthusiastic crowd – the "prattling nurse" in rapture, the "kitchen malkin" with "richest lockram 'bout her reechy neck," the "seld-shown flamens" pressing

"among the popular throngs" (II.i.206ff.) – generally resembles
Casca's disgusted review of the hooting, clapping "rabblement"
(*J.C.* I.ii.235ff.). More specifically, Brutus the tribune echoes Cassius's scorn for Caesar, the man "now become a god" (*J.C.*
I.ii.116):

> Such a poother
> As if that whatsoever god who leads him
> Were slily crept into his human powers,
> And gave him graceful posture.
>
> (II.i.218–21)

Julius Caesar functions as a deep source for *Coriolanus*, Shakespeare's later exploration of the city divided against itself. In addition to the parallel conspiracies, both plays feature a formal
showing of wounds, an extension of the various blood rituals in
the Roman works. Caesar's wounds excite sympathy for him and
hatred for Brutus, Cassius, and the conspirators. Similarly, Coriolanus's wounds win the people's sympathy and their voices.[23] In
both scenes the mutilated body of a Roman military hero establishes reputation and effects political change. There is "a tongue /
In every wound of Caesar" (III.ii.228–9), just as there are
"tongues" in Coriolanus's wounds (II.iii.6–8), each speaking on
his behalf.

It should be observed, of course, that there is some difference
between the sensational ploy of a wily rhetorician and the official
ceremony of Roman election. Yet, Shakespeare carefully demonstrates that the difference is not substantive, but superficial. Both
showings of wounds occur in the marketplace, the scene of buying
and selling, of cajoling and persuading.[24] Both occur before a
crowd, portrayed previously as diversely witted, unreasoning, volatile, and inconstant. The showing of Caesar's wounds secures
honor and gains fame. The showing of Coriolanus's, ostensibly for
a specific political purpose, actually works to these same ends. The

---

[23]Whether or not Coriolanus actually disrobes in the marketplace, his appearance there in the gown of humility is clearly intended to remind the people
of his military service and personal sacrifices.

[24]According to Macrobius, the standing of candidates in the marketplace allowed
exposure to Roman city dwellers and country folks, all of whom convened on
market days. *The Saturnalia,* trans. Percival Vaughan Davies (New York: Columbia University Press, 1969), pp. 110–11.

Latin word *honos* and the Greek *timē*, as Ernest Barker points out, mean "office" as well as "honor"; the two concepts are inextricable in antiquity as well as in Shakespeare's conception.[25] Thus, as D. J. Gordon argues, Coriolanus's quest for *voces*, the voices or votes of the people, is inseparably part of his quest for *fama, laus, opinio, gloria, honor,* and *nomen.*[26] Paradoxically, honor in Rome means both personal integrity and public reputation. Coriolanus's oft-expressed revulsion from the stinking breath of the mob succinctly expresses the tension of this paradox, the irony implicit in the Roman quest for mob approval, for honor and fame.

Acts II and III in *Coriolanus* are located inside the *urbs*, within the walls of Rome. The change from the terse remarks of Aufidius in camp (I.x) to the leisurely conversation of Menenius and the tribunes (II.i) marks the entrance into Rome, just as Martius's banishment will emphatically mark the exit (IV.i). Departing from his usual practice, Shakespeare imbues the intervening scenes (rather than the opening ones) with local color, painting a full picture of the Roman background. Various elements of the Roman population – plebs, tribunes, patricians – jostle each other for power, as lictors and aediles appear on stage. Featured in these scenes are a Roman procession, the Roman custom of requests, Roman garboils in the streets, a Roman hearing and banishment. While the political issues aired on stage are timeless, as relevant to Jacobean audiences as to ancient Roman ones,[27] they are placed in Roman context by frequent reference to Roman institutions and

[25] *The Politics of Aristole*, ed. and trans. Ernest Barker (1946; rpt. New York: Oxford University Press, Galaxy, 1962), p. 109, note 1. In *Shakespeare and the Renaissance Concept of Honor* (Princeton: Princeton University Press, 1960), Curtis Brown Watson discusses more generally Shakespeare's view of honor as "Public Esteem" (pp. 367–447).

[26] "Name and Fame: Shakespeare's *Coriolanus*," reprinted from *Papers Mainly Shakespearian* (Edinburgh, 1964) in *The Renaissance Imagination*, ed. Stephen Orgel (Berkeley and Los Angeles: University of California Press, 1975), pp. 203–19.

[27] Several studies have treated the relevance of the play to the Jacobean political scene: E. C. Pettet, "*Coriolanus* and the Midlands Insurrection of 1607," *ShS*, 3 (1950), 34–42; W. Gordon Zeeveld, " 'Coriolanus' and Jacobean Politics," *MLR*, 57 (1962), 321–34; Clifford Chalmers Huffman, "*Coriolanus*" in *Context* (Lewisburg, Pa.: Bucknell University Press, 1971). Pettet focuses on a contemporary uprising, Zeeveld on the debate surrounding the rise of the Commons, and Huffman on the theory of mixed government.

localities – the bench, forum, Capitol, Tarpeian rock, city walls, and gates.

In the city so meticulously portrayed here Romans constantly practice rhetoric, the art of persuading by speech. Virtually all the characters seek to move each other by the spoken word, be it by formal oration or informal argument, outright insult or sly innuendo, boldly asserted truth or whispered lie. For Shakespeare, apparently, a Roman exercised his citizenship in deeds on the battlefields, in words within city walls. Oratory was the means by which the individual partook in the life of the city, resolved its problems, and shaped its future. Nor should this view of Roman oratory be surprising. The humanistic curriculum of Elizabethan grammar schools placed heavy emphasis on the theory and practice of rhetoric, and Shakespeare knew well the standard authors on the subject: Erasmus, Susenbrotus, Cicero, and Quintilian.[28] From the last two, especially from Cicero, Shakespeare learned of a Rome wherein discourse was the primary mode of public and personal interaction, and *eloquentia* the highest personal, civic, and moral achievement.

Familiarity with the work of Roman rhetoricians affords a coign of vantage on the urban sections of *Coriolanus*.[29] Cicero, we recall, defined the duty of an orator succinctly, *dicere ad persuadendum accommodate*, "to speak in a style fitted to convince."[30] Elsewhere he wrote:

> Optimus est enim orator qui dicendo animos
> audientium et docet et delectat et permovet.

[28]Baldwin, Vol. II, pp. 1–238.

[29]That Livy's relatively brief retelling of Coriolanus's history supplies two entries (Martius on corn, Veturia [Volumnia] on mercy) for the table of orations in the back of Philemon Holland's translation, *The Romane Historie* (1600), suggests the importance of rhetoric to the story. Among those who have made use of Cicero in the explication of the play are Simmons, pp. 18–64; Milton Boone Kennedy, *The Oration in Shakespeare* (Chapel Hill: University of North Carolina Press, 1942), passim; and, in passing, John W. Velz, "Cracking Strong Curbs Asunder." It will be evident that I follow the line of inquiry suggested by Velz to conclusions quite different from those of Kennedy and Simmons.

[30]*Cicero, De Oratore*, trans. E. W. Sutton and H. Rackham, The Loeb Classical Library, 2 vols. (1942), Vol. I, pp. 96–7. All further references are cited to this edition.

Docere debitum est, delectare honorarium,
permovere necessarium.

The supreme orator, then, is the one whose speech instructs, delights and moves the minds of his audience. The
orator is in duty bound to instruct; giving pleasure is a free
gift to the audience, to move them is indispensable.[31]

According to this definition, Menenius time and again proves himself a successful Ciceronian orator. Early on, his fable persuades
the plebs to halt (at least temporarily) their march to the Capitol.
The fable is, of course, a well-known rhetorical device, especially
recommended by Erasmus for "uneducated and unsophisticated"
audiences. Menenius delivers his in the three separate parts –
introduction, narration, moral – that Erasmus prescribes.[32] Further, Menenius's sense of humor, evident in the telling of the fable
and elsewhere, is a valuable rhetorical asset. Cicero, for example,
avers that *est plane oratoris movere risum*, "it clearly becomes an
orator to raise laughter," so long as *ratio temporis*, "regard to
occasions," *moderatio*, "control," *temperantia*, "restraint," and
raritas dictorum, "economy in bon-mots," govern the humor
(*D.O.* II.lviii.236; II.lx.247). Menenius plainly knows when to jest
and when not, as his sober and serious exhortations to the angry
mob in Act III, Scene i testify. And once again, Menenius is successful at persuasion, this time persuading the mob to "proceed by
process" (312) and "lawful form" (323), to lay down their weapons and adjourn to the marketplace for a hearing. Throughout the
play Menenius's speech manifests *urbanitas*, that unique mixture
of sophisticated wit and decorousness lauded by Quintilian:

Nam meo quidem iudicio illa est urbanitas,
in qua nihil absonum, nihil agreste, nihil inconditum,
nihil peregrinum neque sensu neque verbis neque ore
gestuve possit deprehendi; ut non tam sit in
singulis dictis quam in toto colore dicendi.

[31] *De Optimo Genere Oratorum* in Cicero, *De Inventione, De Optimo Genere
Oratorum, Topica, with an English Translation by H. M. Hubbell*, The Loeb
Classical Library (1949), pp. 356, 357.
[32] *Collected Works of Erasmus: Literary and Educational Writings 2, De Copia /
De Ratione Studii*, ed. Craig R. Thompson (Toronto: University of Toronto
Press, 1978), Vol. XXIV, pp. 631–3.

For to my thinking *urbanity* involves the total absence of
all that is incongruous, coarse, unpolished and exotic
whether in thought, language, voice or gesture, and resides
not so much in isolated sayings as in the whole complexion
of our language.[33]

As its name implies, *urbanitas* is manifestly an urban virtue peculiar to city dwellers like Menenius. It is not surprising, therefore,
that Menenius's oratory fails outside Roman walls, when in the
enemy camp he tries to persuade Coriolanus to spare Rome from
destruction.

Rome, of course, offers more than one example of successful
oratory. In the marketplace Cominius delivers a brilliant panegyric
for Coriolanus, one that follows closely the general guidelines for
epideictic oratory.[34] The author of *Ad Herennium,* for example,
writes of the Introduction:

Ab eius persona de quo loquemur, si laudabimus:
vereri nos ut illius facta verbis consequi
possimus: omnes homines illius virtutes praedicare
oportere; ipso facta omnium laudatorum
eloquentiam anteire.

When we draw our Introduction from the person being
discussed: if we speak in praise, we shall say that we fear
our inability to match his deeds with words; all men ought
to proclaim his virtues; his very deeds transcend the eloquence of all eulogists.[35]

So Cominius begins: "I shall lack voice: the deeds of Coriolanus /
Should not be utter'd feebly" (II.ii.82–3). The author of *Ad
Herennium* continues:

quoniam in eodem virtutis studio sint apud
quos laudemus atque ille qui laudatur fuerit

---

[33]*The Institutio Oratoria of Quintilian with an English Translation by H. E.
Butler,* The Loeb Classical Library, 4 vols. (1921–2), Vol. II, pp. 498, 499. All
further references are cited to this edition.

[34]Kennedy, *Oration in Shakespeare,* writes that "commendatory rhetoric reaches
a high-water mark in the oration of Cominius," but he does not analyze the
speech (p. 108).

[35][Cicero?] *Ad C. Herennium, De Ratione Dicendi (Rhetorica Ad Herennium)
with an English Translation by Harry Caplan,* The Loeb Classical Library
(1954), pp. 176–7. All further references are cited to this edition.

aut sit, sperare nos facile iis quibus velimus
huius facta probaturos.

Since the hearers of our eulogy have the same zeal for
virtue as the subject of the eulogy had or now has, we hope
easily to win the approval of his deeds from those whose
approval we desire.

(III.vi.12)

And so Cominius moves to a brief discussion of "valor," the
"chiefest virtue," in which Coriolanus "cannot in the world / Be
singly counterpois'd" (84–7).

After the Introduction, the epideictic orator delivers the Statement of Facts, a brief summary of pertinent deeds and events in
chronological order: *deinde ut quaeque quove tempore res erit
gesta ordine dicemus, ut quid quamque tute cauteque egerit intel-
legatur* (*A.H.* III.vii.13), "then [we shall] recount the events, observing their precise sequence and chronology, so that one may
understand what the person under discussion did and with what
prudence and caution." Accordingly, Cominius recounts Coriolanus's deeds beginning with the repulse of the Tarquin and
ending with the recent victory of Corioles. In the remembrance of
the earlier events Cominius stresses Coriolanus's youth – "at six-
teen years" (87), "with his Amazonian chin" (91), in his "pupil
age" (98) – thus following the general recommendation that natural disadvantages be emphasized so as to magnify achievements.
Quintilian enunciates the principle and provides a pertinent illustration: *et interim confert admirationi multum etiam infirmitas,
ut cum idem Tydea parvum sed bellatorem dicit fuisse,* (*I.O.*
III.vii.12), "at times again weakness may contribute largely to our
admiration, as when Homer says that Tydeus was small of stature
but a good fighter." Cominius's insistence on the singularity of
Coriolanus's achievements – he cannot be "singly counterpois'd"
(87), he stops the fliers by "rare example" (104), "alone" he
enters the city (110) – is also rhetorically appropriate. Quintilian
advises:

dum sciamus gratiora esse audientibus, quae
solus quis aut primus aut certe cum paucis
fecisse dicetur, si quid praeterea supra spem aut
exspectationem, praecipue quod aliena potius
causa quam sua.

184

But we must bear in mind the fact that what most pleases
an audience is the celebration of deeds which our hero was
the first or only man or at any rate one of the very few to
perform: and to these we must add any other achievements
which surpassed hope or expectation, emphasising what
was done for the sake of others rather than what he
performed on his own behalf.

(I.O. III.vii.16–17)

The selflessness of the hero, of course, is the dominant theme of
Cominius's close:

> Our spoils he kick'd at,
> And look'd upon things precious as they were
> The common muck of the world. He covets less
> Than misery itself would give, rewards
> His deeds with doing them, and is content
> To spend the time to end it.

(124–9)

In contradistinction to these eloquent Romans, Coriolanus continually demonstrates his inadequacy as an orator and, in so
doing, his inability to fulfill the primary social and civic duty of a
Roman citizen. Differing sharply from Plutarch's Coriolanus of
"eloquent tongue"[36] and Livy's politic young gentleman, the inarticulate Coriolanus on stage is Shakespeare's own creation. In Act
II, Scene ii Coriolanus declares his distrust of speech: "yet oft, /
When blows have made me stay, I fled from words" (71–2), and
leaves the stage, retreating into silence. After putting on the garb
of humility, Coriolanus sputters in confusion about what he
should say:

> What must I say?
> "I pray, sir" – Plague upon't! I cannot bring
> My tongue to such a pace.

(II.iii.49–51)

Instead of adopting the "wholesome manner" (60) Menenius rec-
ommends, Shakespeare's Coriolanus, unlike Plutarch's, employs
sarcasm and thinly veiled contempt. He cannot act the part of
Lucius in *Titus Andronicus,* who uses his scars and his speech to

---

[36]Plutarch, Vol. II, p. 189.

demonstrate fitness for office (V.iii.96ff.). To Coriolanus the required use of language in the custom of requests is nothing more than illegitimate speech – bragging, begging, flattering, counterfeiting. The flat prose of his conversation with the citizens modulates into the awkward verse and clumsy rhyme of his first soliloquy (112–24). While we may not agree with Carol M. Sicherman, who declares that such couplets "evince the strange, hobbled quality of Coriolanus's most private self," we must recognize their rigidity and the speaker's ineloquence.[37]

The ensuing encounter between Coriolanus and the tribunes also demonstrates the warrior's rhetorical deficiencies. Coriolanus disregards the classical prescriptions concerning orderly arrangement (*dispositio*), suitable style (*elocutio*), and graceful delivery (*actio*). He delivers a rodomontade, directing his virulence first at the tribunes, then at the plebs, then at the Senate for their earlier corn distribution. Despite Menenius's efforts to calm the speaker and dam up the verbal flood, Coriolanus rushes on, repeating the tribune's words in shocked disbelief and rising to greater heights of fury and indignation. He calls Sicinius "Triton of the minnows" (III.i.89) and the people "the mutable, rank-scented meiny" (66), the "Hydra" (93), the "rabble" (136), the "crows" that peck at eagles (139). Quintilian supplies appropriate glosses to this hollow thundering:

> Impudens, tumultuosa, iracunda actio omnibus
> indecora, sed ut quisque aetate, dignitate,
> usu praecedit, magis in ea reprehendendus.

> An impudent, disorderly, or angry tone is always unseemly,
> no matter who it be that assumes it; and it becomes all the
> more reprehensible in proportion to the age, rank, and
> experience of the speaker.
>
> (*I.O.* XI.i.29)

[37]"*Coriolanus:* The Failure of Words," *ELH*, 39 (1972), 189–207 (202). Others who have written on Coriolanus's problems with language are Leonard F. Dean, "Voice and Deed in *Coriolanus*," *University of Kansas City Review*, 21 (1955), 177–84; James L. Calderwood, "*Coriolanus:* Wordless Meanings and Meaningless Words," *SEL*, 6 (1966), 211–24; Lawrence N. Danson, "Metonomy and *Coriolanus*," *PQ*, 52 (1973), 30–42; and Joyce Van Dyke, "Making a Scene: Language and Gesture in 'Coriolanus,'" *ShS*, 30 (1977), 135–46.

> Male etiam dicitur, quod in plures convenit,
> si aut nationes totae incessantur aut ordines
> aut condicio aut studia multorum. Ea quae
> dicet vir bonus omnia salva dignitate ac
> verecundia dicet.

Sarcasm that applies to a number of persons is injudicious: I refer to cases where it is directed against whole nations or classes of society, or against rank and pursuits which are common to many. A good man will see that everything he says is consistent with his dignity and the respectability of his character.

(I.O. VI.iii.34–5)

Whatever the excitement generated by Coriolanus's tirade, such speech (*pace* Kennedy)[38] cannot be considered successful classical oratory. Cicero avers repeatedly that the purpose of oratory is to persuade through skillful use of language, and Coriolanus persuades no one. Crassus's [Cicero's] remarks in *De Oratore* gloss Coriolanus's outbursts incisively and conclusively:

> Ac, ne plura, quae sunt paene innumerabilia,
> consecter, comprehendam brevi; sic enim statuo,
> perfecti oratoris moderatione et sapientia non
> solum ipsius dignitatem, sed et privatorum
> plurimorum, et universae reipublicae salutem
> maxime contineri.

And not to pursue any further instances – wellnigh countless as they are – I will conclude the whole matter in a few words, for my assertion is this: that the wise control of the complete orator is that which chiefly upholds not only his own dignity, but the safety of countless individuals and of the entire state.

(I.viii.34)

---

[38]Kennedy's analysis of this speech (III.i.64–161) as a "model of deliberative rhetoric" (*Oration in Shakespeare*, pp. 108, 138) is unconvincing. Angry and sarcastic in tone, the speech actually has two subjects, changing in focus from the Senate's distribution of corn to the creation of the tribunes and back again. As the distribution of corn is a *fait accompli* (not a future option as in Plutarch), Coriolanus's deliberation seems to illustrate his stubborness rather than his capacity for rational discourse.

Far from upholding the safety of the state, Coriolanus's speech turns the civilized *urbs* into a bloody battlefield. As in *Titus Andronicus* and *Julius Caesar,* Rome resounds with the clash of brother arms and the *Furor impius* of civil war. The citizens become "barbarians . . . though in Rome litter'd" (237–8), as does Coriolanus, himself. The impious antifamilial barbarity manifest in the killing of Mutius, the assassination of Caesar, and the Proscription rages in this Rome also. Menenius observes:

> Now the good gods forbid
> That our renowned Rome, whose gratitude
> Towards her deserved children is enroll'd
> In Jove's own book, like an unnatural dam
> Should now eat up her own!
>
> (III.i.288–92)

Significantly, echoes of *Julius Caesar* abound in this scene. Menenius's remarks on the treatment of a diseased limb (294ff.) recall Brutus on Antony (II.i.162ff.) and suggest the present sickness of the body politic. The confused sequence of directions – to leave, to stand fast, to conciliate – appears here (III.i.229ff.) as it does after Caesar's assassination (III.i.86ff.), signaling the same lack of authority, the same dangerous disorder. And finally, Menenius's injunction, "Do not cry havoc where you should but hunt / With modest warrant" (III.i.273–4), recalls the important strain of hunting imagery in *Julius Caesar* and the apocalyptic havoc of Antony's prophecy. To depict the moral and political chaos of this civil war, the poet reverts to tested Roman images and themes.

Because his oratory leads to armed dissension rather than to rational concord, Coriolanus is the antitype of the Ciceronian orator. For according to Cicero, eloquence creates and sustains civilization:

> Ut vero iam ad illa summa veniamus; quae
> vis alia potuit aut dispersos homines unum
> in locum congregare, aut a fera agrestique
> vita ad hunc humanum cultum civilemque deducere,
> aut, iam constitutis civitatibus, leges, iudicia,
> iur a describere?

> To come, however, at length to the highest achievements of eloquence, what other power could have been strong

enough either to gather scattered humanity into one place,
or to lead it out of its brutish existence in the wilderness up
to our present condition of civilization as men and as
citizens, or, after the establishment of social communities,
to give shape to laws, tribunals, and civic rights?

(D.O. I.viii.33–4)

Coriolanus's failure to master and apply the art of reasonable
discourse in the city leads to its destruction. His ineloquence reverses man's evolution from savagery to civilization and plunges
the *urbs* into a wilderness of primitive violence where the din of
inarticulate passion drowns out the sound of intelligible speech.

While demonstrating the consequences of Coriolanus's un-
civilized speech, Shakespeare qualifies our criticisms and balances
our sympathies. Through his portrait of Volumnia he reveals the
corruption in Rome and the current debasement of Roman oratory. Volumnia endeavors to instruct her son in the acts of persuasion. After incongruously yoking the ideal of honor with the sordid practice of policy (III.ii.39ff.), she gives him an impromptu
lesson in *actio:*

> I prithee now, my son,
> Go to them, with this bonnet in thy hand,
> And thus far having stretch'd it (here be with them),
> Thy knee bussing the stones (for in such business
> Action is eloquence, and the eyes of th' ignorant
> More learned than the ears), waving thy head,
> Which often thus correcting thy stout heart,
> Now humble as the ripest mulberry
> That will not hold the handling.

(72–80)

Volumnia's assertion that action is eloquence closely parallels the
Ciceronian dictum, *Est enim actio quasi sermo corporis, quo*
magis menti congruens esse debet, (D.O. III.lix.222–3), "For by
action the body talks, so it is all the more necessary to make it
agree with the thought." Her emphasis on the importance of delivery to the ignorant auditors is also Ciceronian:

> Atque in eis omnibus quae sunt actionis
> inest quadedam vis a natura data; quare etiam
> hac imperiti, hac vulgus, hac denique barbari
> maxime commoventur.

And all the factors of delivery contain a certain force
bestowed by nature; which moreover is the reason why it is
delivery that has most effect on the ignorant and the mob
and lastly on barbarians.

(D.O. I.viii.223)

Volumnia's instructions are unequivocal: She would have her son
be "milder" (III.ii.14), as he fears. In other words, she wants him
to practice the *lenitas,* "mildness," that is the hallmark of Cicero's
conciliatory style (*D.O.* II.lii.211–12). The conversation that
closes the scene, wherein "mildly" sounds five times in seven lines,
drives the point of her rhetorical lesson home to the reluctant
student and to the audience.[39]

That Volumnia presses Ciceronian principles into the service of
hypocrisy, flattery, and self-aggrandizement discredits the art of
oratory in Rome. Successful orators advance themselves and their
arguments, it seems, by compromising their integrity and by acting
degrading parts. In this light, Coriolanus's failure as an orator
appears less disgraceful and more honorable. Unlike the facile
tribunes, for example, who skillfully use rhetoric, Coriolanus is
neither scheming nor self-serving. Menenius and Cominius may be
better orators, but they are certainly lesser men. In a city where
voices often tell lies to gain power, the man who courageously
speaks truth, whose "heart's his mouth" and whose "tongue must
vent" whatever his "breast forges" (III.i.256–7), gains respect. If
his choleric speech is disruptive and fundamentally antisocial, it is
also dramatically exciting and moving, a fiery jeremiad for the
corrupt city.

In his final encounter with the tribunes and the people Coriolanus's angry integrity wins our admiration. Amid the trumped-
up charges of treason and the roar of the rabble, his defiant voice
rings out:

> Within thine eyes sate twenty thousand deaths,
> In thy hands clutch'd as many millions, in
> Thy lying tongue both numbers, I would say
> "Thou liest" unto thee with a voice as free
> As I do pray the gods.

(III.iii.70–4)

[39]The word "mildly" may also echo current parliamentary debates. See Zeeveld,
"'Coriolanus' and Jacobean Politics," p. 333.

Because the voices of civilized men lie, Coriolanus expresses himself in the language of prayer – free, spontaneous, heartfelt, and truthful.[40] He abjures the corrupted language of civic intercourse:

> I would not buy
> Their mercy at the price of one fair word,
> Nor check my courage for what they can give,
> To have't with saying "Good morrow."
>
> (90–3)

To him such speech is merely the expression of ignoble weakness – the prating of fools and the crying of curs. Where such cacophony rules, life cannot be worth the living. Consequently, Coriolanus banishes Rome, its mendacious citizens, its noisy forums. Asserting the sacred primacy of self over city, he seeks a world elsewhere.

Coriolanus's exit from Rome, like his entrance, is a complex symbol of his ambivalent relationship with the city. Coriolanus's inability to live in Rome, like Antony's, measures his virtues and vices as well as those of the city. In so far as Rome is corrupt, a place of inconstant commoners, selfish tribunes, and weak patricians, Coriolanus's exit demonstrates integrity and courage. Refusing to dress himself in humility to pluck allegiance from men's hearts, Coriolanus is again an epic figure who values personal honor more than comfortable life. In exile Coriolanus joins the ranks of all those other worthy men – Roman and Greek – who suffered banishment from their ungrateful cities. The similar fates of Cicero, Metellus, Scipio Africanus, Alcibiades, Aristides, Themistocles, and Cimon, for example, were well known in the Renaissance. Shakespeare uses the literary tradition here, as he does in the closely contemporary *Timon of Athens,* to emphasize the independent virtue of the individual and to deepen the moral complexity of the play.[41]

Insofar as Rome is the city of man, however, Coriolanus's exit is

---

[40]Concerning Coriolanus's penchant for praying and cursing, Joyce Van Dyke explains that prayers and curses are "verbal expressions of a desired action which it is beyond the power of the speaker to accomplish" ("Making a Scene," p. 138). Coriolanus uses speech, then, only when direct action or gesture is impossible.

[41]See my "Timon in Shakespeare's Athens," *SQ,* 31 (1980), 21–30 (26–9). For a different reading of the ostracism see *Discorsi* I.7.29, where Machiavelli argues that the movement against Coriolanus was healthy and partially justified.

a symbol of his antisocial rigidity and absoluteness. Civilization, Cicero explains in *De Officiis*, always requires the sympathetic cooperation of men. Virtue cannot exist apart from civilization but must be manifest in it. The self must define goals in terms of the city, not in defiance of it:

> Ergo unum debet esse omnibus propositum,
> ut eadem sit utilitas unius cuiusque et
> universorum; quam si ad se quisque rapiet,
> dissolvetur omnis humana consortio.

> This, then, ought to be the chief end of all men, to make
> the interest of each individual and of the whole body politic
> identical. For if the individual appropriates to selfish ends
> what should be devoted to the common good, all human
> fellowship will be destroyed.[42]

To value self over city, as Coriolanus does, is to undermine the foundations of society. Banishing the city, Coriolanus renounces his identity as a Roman and his role in a community of speaking men. So doing, he renounces his identity as a civilized human being. Aristotle's comment on such a man is incisive:

> But he that can not abide to liue in companie,
> or through sufficiencie hath need of nothing
> is not esteemed a part or member of a Cittie,
> but is either a beast or a god.[43]

<hr>

Despite Coriolanus's promise, "While I remain above the ground, you shall / Hear from me still, and never of me aught / But what is like me formerly" (IV.i.51–3), he undergoes a series of transformations in exile. At his departure Coriolanus is calm and constant, grateful to family and "friends of noble touch" (49), brave in

---

[42]*Cicero, De Officiis, with an English Translation by Walter Miller*, The Loeb Classical Library (1913), pp. 292, 293. All further references are cited to this edition.

[43]*Aristotles Politiqves*, p. 15.

misfortune.[44] He takes the hand of Menenius in a gesture of warmth and human solidarity, and exits a noble Roman, especially admirable in contrast with Nicanor, the Roman who works as a spy for the Volscians (IV.iii). The next time Coriolanus appears however, he is outside Antium *"in mean apparel, disguis'd and muffled"* (s.d. IV.iv). So garbed and situated, Plutarch notes, Coriolanus resembles Ulysses before his undercover invasion of Troy (*Od.* IV.244ff.).[45] More important, Coriolanus's entrance into Antium reenacts Ulysses's disguised return to Ithaca (*Od.* XVII).[46] Just as the insolent guests try to repel Ulysses from the banquet within, so the insolent servingmen, in a revealing divergence from Plutarch, try to repel Coriolanus from Aufidius's feast (IV.v.7ff.). Unlike Ulysses, however, Coriolanus seeks to enter an enemy town, not his native city. His subsequent unmasking leads not to the reestablishment of order, but to betrayal of Rome and to his own death.

Receiving Coriolanus, Antium receives its scourge, the impious invader. As Coriolanus reflects before entering:

> A goodly city is this Antium. City,
> 'Tis I that made thy widows; many an heir
> Of these fair edifices 'fore my wars
> Have I heard groan and drop. Then know me not,
> Lest that thy wives with spits and boys with stones
> In puny battle slay me.

> (IV.iv.1–6)

The fervid declaration of Aufidius reveals the alliance between Coriolanus and Antium to be perverse, unnatural, and ultimately impious:

> Know thou first,
> I lov'd the maid I married; never man
> Sigh'd truer breath; but that I see thee here,
> Thou noble thing, more dances my rapt heart

[44]Behind this scene may be recollection of Seneca's *Ad Helviam*. See John L. Tison, Jr., "Shakespeare's *Consolatio* for Exile," *MLQ*, 21 (1960), 142–57 (150–2).

[45]Plutarch, Vol. II, p. 169.

[46]The similarity is also noticed by Emrys Jones, *The Origins of Shakespeare* (Oxford: Clarendon Press, 1977), p. 64.

Than when I first my wedded mistress saw
Bestride my threshold.

(IV.v.113–18)

Here as in Martius's earlier protestation (I.vi.29–32) the joy of military fraternity exceeds that of *eros* in its most intense moment. The normal sexual urge, seeking expression in marriage and the creation of a family, serves the exclusively male activity of war and war preparation. Aufidius's dream strongly suggests the sublimation of erotic impulse by martial combat:[47]

I have nightly since
Dreamt of encounters 'twixt thyself and me;
We have been down together in my sleep,
Unbuckling helms, fisting each other's throat,
And wak'd half dead with nothing.

(IV.v.122–6)

Such subordination of *eros* to *thumos* is, of course, unhealthy. It suppresses the most basic social instinct in man, the urge to mate. Aristotle's historical and philosophical account of the *polis* began with consideration of the natural impulse that leads to sexual pairing and procreation:

First it is requisite to ioyne these partes togither, which can not be one without the other, as the man and the woman for procrcation [*sic*]: and that not by way of choice, but in such sort as that there is a certaine naturall desire in all other liuing wights, and euen in the verie plants, to leaue a like of their owne kinde behind them.[48]

In *De Officiis* Cicero concurs:

Nam cum sit hac natura commune animantium,
ut habeant lubidinem procreandi, prima societas
in ipso coniugio est, proxima in liberis, deinde
una domus, communia omnia; id autem est principium
urbis et quasi seminarium rei publicae.

[47]On the relationship between sex and war in this play, see Ralph Berry, "Sexual Imagery in *Coriolanus*," *SEL*, 13 (1973), 301–16.

[48]*Aristotles Politiqves*, p. 4. Cf. Jean Bodin, *The Six Bookes of a Commonweale*, trans. Richard Knolles (London, 1606), reprinted in facsimile, Harvard Political Classics (Cambridge, Mass.: Harvard University Press, 1962), p. 363. Simmons discusses *eros* in the play from a different perspective (pp. 6off.).

For since the reproductive instinct is by nature's gift the common possession of all living creatures, the first bond of union is that between husband and wife; the next, that between parents and children; then we find one home, with everything in common. And this is the foundation of civil government, the nursery, as it were, of the state.

(I.xvii.54)

Perversion of the sexual impulse, then, can only stifle the life of the city. Striving to be men as Lady Macbeth defines the term, Romans like Coriolanus depreciate *eros* and fall into a compulsive and unhealthy misogyny (e.g., I.iii.15–17; II.ii.96–7; V.vi.45–6). Shakespeare's Rome, like any other society founded on the ideal of military honor, is potentially inhuman and self-destructive.

The Rome Coriolanus leaves behind is a divided and diminished thing. Volumnia's Junoesque anger draws only weak replies from the tribunes, current victors in the ongoing struggle for power (IV.ii). The report of Coriolanus's advance soon shatters the illusion of peaceful order, of "tradesmen singing in their shops, and going / About their functions friendly" (IV.vi.8–9). Cominius, half-anxious and half-triumphant, accuses the tribunes of bringing Rome to destruction:

> You have holp to ravish your own daughters, and
> To melt the city leads upon your pates,
> To see your wives dishonor'd to your noses.
>
> (IV.vi.81–3)

The vision of familial violation is strangely familiar; this time, however, Coriolanus threatens to lay impious siege to his own city, not to Corioles or Antium. Consequently, the "thing of blood" does not appear to be praiseworthy as before, but appalling and inhuman, "Made by some other deity than Nature, / That shapes man better" (IV.vi.91–2). According to Cominius, this demigod of destruction sits enthroned in gold, "his eye / Red as 'twould burn Rome" (V.i.63–4). He dismisses entreaties with a "speechless hand" (67), a gesture all the more ominous and terrifying for the poignant handclaspings preceding (IV.i.57; IV.v.147).[49]

[49]The motif of handclasping, like that of kneeling, recurs throughout Shakespeare's Roman canon. In *Coriolanus* both represent civilized rituals of interaction that contrast sharply with the Roman business of war making.

As he does in the beginning of the play, Shakespeare strives in the end to create a figure of epic proportions. Like a Homeric hero, Coriolanus in exile is part deity, "son and heir to Mars" (IV.v.192), and part dragon. His epic character appears not so much in specific details, but in general affinities. The description of the enthroned Coriolanus outside Rome, for example, resembles in imagery and tone Vergil's description of Aeneas outside the Rutulian stronghold:

> ardet apex capiti cristisque a vertice flamma
> funditur et vastos umbo vomit aureus ignis:
> non secus ac liquida si quando nocte cometae
> sanguinei lugubre rubent, aut Sirius ardor
> ille, sitim morbosque ferens mortalibus aegris,
> nascitur et laevo contristat lumine caelum.
>
> (X.270–5)

> On the hero's head blazes the helmet-peak, flame streams
> from the crest aloft, and the shield's golden boss spouts
> floods of fire – even as when in the clear night comets glow
> blood-red in baneful wise: or even as fiery Sirius, that
> bearer of drought and pestilence to feeble mortals, rises and
> saddens the sky with baleful light.

Few would argue that Shakespeare had this passage in hand or conscious mind when writing *Coriolanus;* yet few will deny the general consonance of effect created by the colors gold and red – that striking combination of metallic richness and splendor and that ominously prophetic conjunction of blood and fire. Like Aeneas, Coriolanus is a cosmic force, a malignant planet about to strike feeble mortals. Just as Vergil combines elements of Apollonius and Homer with his own sense of doom to forge the striking passage above, so Shakespeare combines elements of Homer, Vergil, and Plutarch throughout his play.[50]

[50]For the sources of Vergil's imagery I rely on Brooks Otis, *Virgil: A Study in Civilized Poetry* (Oxford: Clarendon Press, 1963), p. 355. Also epic is the image of Coriolanus as tiger (V.iv.28), which invites comparison with Vergil's description of Turnus as *"immanem tigrim"* (IX.730). Compare also the Second Watchman's description of Coriolanus as "the rock, the oak not to be wind-shaken" (V.ii.111), with *Iliad* XXII.126, *Odyssey* XIX.163, and with Vergil's description of Aeneas as oak (IV.441ff.) and as rocky mountain (XII.701ff.). The Homeric linking of oak and rock makes use of an old folktale concerning the origin of mankind (see notes to the Loeb editions).

Plutarch, in fact, provides Shakespeare with a precedent for casting Coriolanus in the epic mold. He alludes to Homer several times in "The Life of Caius Martius Coriolanus" and even recalls a pertinent passage on Achilles's anger:

> Achilles angrie was, and sorie for to heare him so to say,
> his heavy brest was fraught with pensive feare.[51]

Perceptively, Reuben A. Brower discusses Coriolanus as "Achilles in the Forum":

> Perhaps Coriolanus is most like Achilles in his passionate pride, in his "choler," in his shifting from "rage to sorrow," emotions that lie very close together, as Plutarch had noted. But he comes nearest to the essence of Homer's hero in his absoluteness, in his determination to imitate the "graces of the gods," in his will to push the heroic to the limit until he destroys his own society along with his enemy's. In reducing all virtues to *virtus,* he is the Greek hero Romanized, while in appealing to "Great Nature" and at the same time asserting the greatness of his own nature, he betrays the Stoic ancestry of the Elizabethan tragic hero.
>
> But there is no moment when, like Achilles, he sees his anger and curses it, nothing to correspond to the scene with Priam, no vision of himself and a higher order within which his action and suffering are placed and made more comprehensible. His last gesture is like his first, to "use his lawful sword." He knows little of what Chapman calls the soul's "sovereignty in fit reflection," not to mention "subduing his earthly part for heaven." He is the most Roman, the least "gentle" and the least Christian, of Shakespeare's major heroes.[52]

To this fine interpretation it need only be added that likeness to Achilles means admittance to a whole family of epic figures including Achilles' son, Pyrrhus; his chief enemy, Hector; and his Vergilian descendant, Turnus. As synthesizer and transformer of epic traditions, Vergil exploits the essential kinship between various incarnations of heroic character to great ironic and tragic effect in the *Aeneid.* Aeneas becomes the dreaded other, Pyrrhus, slaying

[51]Plutarch, Vol. II, p. 181.
[52]Brower, p. 372.

the son (Lausus) before the father (Mezentius) and then the father (X.794ff.; cf. X.510ff.). After, he becomes a newer and sadder Achilles, the destined conqueror. Though Turnus constantly boasts of himself as a new Achilles, he, like Coriolanus, meets his end in the role of Hector, dying a lone and tragic death outside the walls of a city no longer his.[53]

Shakespeare's use of the dragon metaphor (IV.i.30; IV.vii.23; V.iv.13) shows him fusing various epic images into rich and resonant symbols. In addition to pertinent analogs in the *Faerie Queene* and the Bible,[54] memorable dragons appear in Homer and Vergil. In Book II of the *Seaven Bookes of the Iliades* (1598), a source for *Troilus and Cressida,* Chapman relates Homer's horrible portent:

> A Dragon with a bloodie backe most horrible to sight,
> Which great Olympius himselfe did send into the light:
> This, tumbling from the Altar's foote, did to the
>   Plantane creepe,
> Where, nestling in an utter Bow and under shade, did sleepe
> The russet sparrowe's little young, which eight in number were,
> The dam the ninth that brought them forth, with which the
>   beast did smere
> His ruthles jawes and crasht their bones: the mother
>   round about
> Fled mourning her beloved birth, who by her wing stretcht out
> The dragon caught and, crying, eate as he her young had done.[55]

According to Calchas, the impious feeding signifies the fall of Troy in the tenth year of siege. Hideous *dracones* also appear in *Aeneid* II and devour Laocoon and his sons. Their blazing eyes suffused with blood and fire (note again the red–gold recurrence), *ardentis*

---

[53]For specific parallels, see Anderson, "Vergil's Second *Iliad*," and *Art of the Aeneid,* pp. 87–9, 92–3.

[54]See Furness, *Tragedie of Coriolanus,* p. 403; Brockbank, *Coriolanus,* p. 239. Clifford Davidson notes the association of the dragon with the devil in medieval iconography. "*Coriolanus:* A Study in Political Dislocation," *ShakS,* 4 (1969 for 1968), 263—74 (269—70). Baldwin discusses Susenbrotus's use of the dragon as the stock figure for "hominem rapacem ac uirulentum" (Vol. II, p. 173).

[55]*Chapman's Homer: The Iliad, The Odyssey and The Lesser Homerica,* ed. Allardyce Nicoll, Bollingen Series, No. 41, 2nd ed., 2 vols. (Princeton: Princeton University Press, 1967), Vol. I, p. 534.

que oculos suffecti sanguine et igni (210), these creatures likewise portend the horrifying invasion. As Donatus comments:

> Potuimus hoc signo preuidere manifestā imminere
> perniciē, significabāt.n. hostes vēturos a Tenedo,
> & maximos duces & geminos.[56]

> We are able to see by this sign the imminent destruction;
> they [the snakes] signify the enemy about to come from
> Tenedos, and more specifically, the great twin leaders
> [Agamemnon and Menelaus].

There is also the striking image (important to Shakespeare in *Julius Caesar*) of Pyrrhus as a snake, emerging from the once-frozen ground, glistening in sunlight, and darting his forked tongue (II.469–75). The thrice-repeated identification of Coriolanus and the dragon suggests his Turnus-like transformation from brave warrior to inhuman avatar of destruction. Like these dragons in Homer and Vergil, Coriolanus becomes a vision of invading *impietas,* a merciless, bloody-jawed devourer of parents and children.

Cominius's report of the failed embassy prepares the audience for the transformation of Coriolanus's character:

> Yet one time he did call me by my name.
> I urg'd our old acquaintance, and the drops
> That we have bled together. Coriolanus
> He would not answer to; forbade all names;
> He was a kind of nothing, titleless,
> Till he had forg'd himself a name a' th' fire
> Of burning Rome.
>
> (V.i.9–15)

Ironically, Cominius recoils from the savagery of the warrior hero whom he lauded earlier for forging a name in burning Corioles. When turned against Rome itself, the Roman ethos inspires not

---

[56]Virgil, *Opera* (Venice, 1544), reprinted in *The Renaissance and the Gods*, No. 7, 2 vols. (New York: 1976), Vol. I, fol. 210ᵛ.

praise but fear and horror. Coriolanus appears as a new unnamed creation, "titleless," seeking to establish his identity through new deeds. Beyond the walls he looms, a perverse apocalyptic judge, an angry god who will not separate the wheat from the chaff on the day of judgment, but burn all alike. Menenius can only respond, almost ludicrously, by insisting that Coriolanus eat before the next embassy. Thus he nervously attempts to assure himself and his fellow citizens that Coriolanus is still human.

Shrewdly, Menenius takes a similar tack in his confrontation with Coriolanus. Seeking to identify Coriolanus as flesh and blood, he regales the sullen, silent warrior with the greeting "O my / son, my son!" (V.ii.70–1), and pointedly refers to himself as "thy old father Menenius" (70). Obviously understanding Menenius's intentions, Coriolanus cuts off the familial appeal to his humanity:

> *Coriolanus:* Away!
> *Menenius:* How? Away?
> *Coriolanus:* Wife, mother, child I know not.
>
> (V.ii.80–2)

Later he resolves to stand "As if a man were author of himself, / And knew no other kin" (V.iii.36–7). There is more than a touch of the "northern star" complex in such haughty claims of self-subsistence. Like Caesar, Coriolanus seems inordinately proud of his independence and constancy just before he is shown to be most mortal indeed.

The entrance of Volumnia, Virgilia, Valeria, and Young Martius exposes the conflict between natural impulse and unnatural constancy within Coriolanus. Even as he cries, "But out, affection, / All bond and privilege of nature, break!" (V.iii.24–5), he begins to weaken: "I melt, and am not / Of stronger earth than others" (V.iii.28–9).[57] The forces of *pietas* stir in Coriolanus, showing his

[57] J. L. Simmons calls attention to the similarity between these lines and Antony's "melting" (IV.xiv.13–14): "'Antony and Cleopatra' and 'Coriolanus,' Shakespeare's Heroic Tragedies: A Jacobean Adjustment," *ShS*, 26 (1973), 95–101 (99). Hermann Heuer argues persuasively that North's idiom provided cues for Shakespeare's emphasis on the natural and unnatural in this scene: "From Plutarch to Shakespeare: A Study of Coriolanus," *ShS*, 10 (1957), 50–9. See also Valerius Maximus, *Dictorvm Factorvmque Memorabilivm Libri IX* (Antwerp, 1567), pp. 230–1, where Coriolanus's refusal to burn Rome is discussed under "De pietate in parentes."

heart to be of penetrable stuff; he realizes that he is a human being playing a tyrannic part (40–3), not an inhuman tyrant. Effectively Volumnia harps on the unnaturalness of the imminent invasion, of the spectacle of "The son, the husband, and the father tearing / His country's bowels out" (102–3). She also threatens Coriolanus with the fate most dreaded by Romans – disgrace and loss of honor. Should Coriolanus be defeated, he will suffer the ignominy feared by Brutus, Antony, and Cleopatra, the triumphal march, the shame of being led in manacles through Roman streets. Should he be victorious, Coriolanus, like Tarquin, will win for himself only eternal infamy, "a name / Whose repetition will be dogg'd with curses" (143–4).

Coriolanus finds himself in an impossible dilemma: To be Roman is to act and not to act, to conquer and to surrender. Finally, he yields to his mother's argument and to the promptings of his own natural compassion. The most eloquent action for this Roman is not the thunder of retribution, but the silent poetry of acceptance: *"Coriolanus holds her by the hand, silent"* (s.d. V.iii.182). Like the emotional Brutus in the quarrel scene and the grieving Antony at the news of Cleopatra's death, the heart-shaked Coriolanus gains the audience's sympathetic attention before facing his own end.

The scenes preceding Coriolanus's death are resonant with epic overtones. Surrounded by his pleading mother, wife, and child, Coriolanus appears once again a Hector. Coriolanus's affectionate pride in Young Martius, the son who will keep his "name / Living to time" (V.iii.126–7), recalls Hector's feelings toward Astyanax.[58] What is more, Shakespeare's portrayal of Hector and his family in Act V, Scene iii of *Troilus and Cressida* functions as a deep source for the pleading scene in *Coriolanus*. In Shakespeare's version, Andromache and Cassandra beg Hector to unarm and to avoid the field. Priam enters to add his voice to the chorus of dissuasion and that of Hecuba: "Thy mother hath had visions" (63). Hector, however, does not heed familial pleas: "Hold you still, I say; / Mine honor keeps the weather of my fate" (25–6). Of course, his dilemma is much simpler than that of Coriolanus, who stands outside his own city and who faces dishonor at every turn.

[58] I owe the point to Brower, p. 368.

Yet, Shakespeare's habit of quoting himself, of reworking successful scenes, of creating richly allusive visual tableaux – all combine here to shift our sympathies to Coriolanus and to enlarge his stature.

Coriolanus's death likewise recalls Hector's tragedy. Here (as elsewhere) Shakespeare greatly expands Plutarch's account of Aufidius, adding in particular the gratuitous dishonoring of Coriolanus's body: *"Draw the Conspirators, and kills Martius, who falls; Aufidius stands on him"* (s.d. V.vi.130). These changes create a scenario that recalls visually the climactic struggle of Achilles and Hector. In *Troilus and Cressida*, of course, Shakespeare portrays Hector's death (V.viii) by conflating Caxton's account of it with his and Lydgate's account of Troilus's murder.[59] In Shakespeare's play Achilles and the Myrmidons surprise and murder the unarmed Hector; Achilles then orders that the body be tied to his horse's tail. Similarly, Aufidius surprises Coriolanus, overwhelms him with numbers, and foully dishonors his body. Like the noble Trojan, Coriolanus cannot vanquish his enemies, control his fate, or participate in the new and emerging order; he can only meet his end with constancy and courage.

It is Coriolanus's tragedy to die not on the battlefield, but in an alien marketplace, defeated finally by the ignoble forces of craft, conspiracy, and mob action.[60] The marketplace, of course, suggests all his shortcomings: his ineloquence, choler, pride, and impatience. It also suggests, however, his virtues: his uncompromising integrity and personal excellence. Alone against the enemy, Coriolanus becomes again for the one last time the brave warrior

---

[59]See Bullough, Vol. VI, p. 107; Kenneth Muir, *The Sources of Shakespeare's Plays* (New Haven: Yale University Press, 1978), pp. 146–7.

[60]There has been much debate about whether or not the play is a tragedy. Some of the critical positions are summarized by Patricia K. Meszaros, "'There is a world elsewhere': Tragedy and History in *Coriolanus*," SEL, 16 (1976), 273–85 (273). For examples of different generic approaches, see Oscar James Campbell, *Shakespeare's Satire* (London: Oxford University Press, 1943), pp. 198–217; D. J. Enright, "*Coriolanus*: Tragedy or Debate?" in *The Apothecary's Shop* (1957; rpt. Westport, Conn.: Greenwood Press, 1975), pp. 32–53; H. J. Oliver, "Coriolanus as Tragic Hero," SQ, 10 (1959), 53–60; Jay L. Halio, "*Coriolanus*: Shakespeare's 'Drama of Reconciliation,'" ShakS, 6 (1972 for 1970), 289–303; Leigh Holt, *From Man to Dragon: A Study of Shakespeare's 'Coriolanus,'* Salzburg Studies in English Literature, JDS, No. 61 (Salzburg: Institut für Englische Sprache und Literatur, 1976), pp. 179–235.

who entered Corioles and took the town. Coriolanus dies as he lived, the "eagle in a dove-cote" (V.vi.114), surrounded by a swarm of lesser beings.[61]

⫤⫥

Shakespeare's last Plutarchan tragedy, *Coriolanus*, occupies an important place in the Roman canon. The play evinces a hard-won mastery of *Romanitas:* It exhibits a complex interweaving of previously explored themes and a sophisticated rhetoric of gesture and metaphor. Recurring here in the clearly portrayed city are the familiar conflicts arising from the clash between private and public responsibility, from the paradoxes of "reflection" (cf. *J.C.* I.ii.66ff.; *Tro.* III.iii.95ff.), from the Roman code of honor, from the human needs for love, family, and society. Furthermore, the play features in close juxtaposition the two models by which Shakespeare explores the inner workings of the city: invasion and rebellion. Characterized throughout by a compact intensity of language, the play is clearly the work of a practiced hand.[62]

As in *Julius Caesar* and *Antony and Cleopatra*, Shakespeare here chooses a controversial (though lesser known) Roman figure who drew contemporary attention for his virtues and his vices. Livy and Plutarch supplied ample material for a mixed view of Coriolanus, and Renaissance humanists did not hesitate to emphasize that which suited their purposes. Jaques Hurault, for example,

---

[61]The animal imagery in the play is more interesting and ambivalent than is usually recognized. Coriolanus's identification with the Roman eagle, for example, should be considered in light of Erasmus's "Scarabeus aquilam quaerit," *Omnia Opera*, Vol. II (Basel, 1536), pp. 777–89. Possible sources and analogs for the doves in the play have been found in *Canticles* (Furness, *Tragedie of Coriolanus*, p. 531) and Camerarius's *Fabulae Aesopicae* (1573) (Baldwin, Vol. I, pp. 627–8). Also significant, perhaps, are Vergil's *Eclogues* IX.12–13, which pits an eagle against a dove, and *Aeneid* II.515–16; XI.721–4. Students of the animal imagery include Knight, pp. 163ff.; J. C. Maxwell, "Animal Imagery in 'Coriolanus'" *MLR*, 42 (1947), 417–21; Wolfgang H. Clemen, *The Development of Shakespeare's Imagery* (Cambridge, Mass.: Harvard University Press, 1951), pp. 155–6; Charney, pp. 163–9; and Paster, "To Starve with Feeding," pp. 135ff.

[62]See Brockbank, *Coriolanus*, pp. 68–71.

remembered Coriolanus as an example of pride; Lodowick Lloid, for another, recalled his rare exploits and his compassionate yielding to his mother.[63] From the various traditions Shakespeare creates a hero at odds with himself as well as with his city.

The imaginative process behind this creation is also familiar. Shakespeare ranges widely to bring the ancient city to life. Cicero and Quintilian provide material and perspective for the events occurring in the street and forum; Homer and Vergil, for those that take place outside city walls. Shakespeare's adaptation of epic characters, incidents, and images is subtle and synthetic. Like Vergil, he combines, reshapes, and molds epic traditions to ironic and tragic effect. Shakespeare's memory of Achilles, for example, vibrates sympathetically with his memories of Ulysses, Pyrrhus, Turnus, and Hector, and serves to chart the changes in Coriolanus's development. His tacit dialogue with Vergil leads him in this play to the last six books of the *Aeneid* rather than to the first six. The central issues in that half of the epic are the same as those in *Coriolanus*. There Vergil depicts the agony and sacrifice necessary to bring a city into being. There, through the character of Turnus, he explores the tension between the heroic self and the city. The frequent shifting between the wide fields of battle and the walled cities and encampments, between the open primitive spaces and the enclosures of civilization, dramatizes these issues in both the epic and the play.

Despite its sophistication, *Coriolanus* is in some ways a return to the beginning, specifically to *Titus Andronicus*.[64] The titular heroes resemble each other. Both are famous warriors who live strictly by a military code of honor. Both lose control of language amid the treachery of the city, and both seek revenge on Rome. Moreover, both Titus Andronicus and Coriolanus prove manifestly unfit for life in the city. They are men of iron, hard, unyielding types, not given to reflection, whose hearts and minds often lie hidden behind extraordinary exploits and ranting speeches. John

---

[63]Hurault, *Politicke, Moral, and Martial Discourses*, trans. Arthur Golding (1595), p. 271; Lloid, *The Consent of Time* (1590), pp. 496–7.

[64]It is no accident that Coriolanus is recalled in *Titus Andronicus* (IV.iv.63–8). As Bullough observes, Plutarch's "Life of Coriolanus" contributed directly to Shakespeare's first Roman tragedy (Vol. VI, p. 24).

Palmer's remarks on *Coriolanus* as statuary apply equally well to both heroes:

> *Coriolanus* has all the qualities of the finest statuary. It has the boldness and simplicity of a classical monument. It commands respect for its weight and substance, for the impression it gives of being determined in its form by the material of which it is wrought, for an ascetism which rejects all superfluous ornament. It is a composition without light or shade. It stands, as it were, in the public square.[65]

Both Titus and Coriolanus excite wonder, but they do not inspire sympathy. In this last Plutarchan tragedy, Shakespeare has done with such coldly standing figures. The Romans in *Cymbeline,* we shall see, are quick with life and warm of breath.

[65]*Political and Comic Characters of Shakespeare* (1945; rpt. London: Macmillan, 1965), p. 307.

VII

CYMBELINE
BEYOND ROME

Generally regarded as a tragicomedy or romance (each genre defined differently by different critics) and studied in the context of
Shakespeare's last plays, *Cymbeline* has attracted little attention as
Shakespeare's final Roman work.[1] Tacitly most assume that the
incarnation of Rome in *Cymbeline* is insignificant next to that in
Lucrece, Titus Andronicus, and the Plutarchan tragedies. After all,
the titular figure is a British king ruling in Britain, and Rome is
merely the other place in opposition, domain of an Emperor we
never see and of characters who seem more like Renaissance Italians than classical Romans. The play affords only the briefest
glimpse of the ancient city, that strangely unmoored scene (III.vii)
in which the senators serve the tribunes a commission to levy
soldiers for the upcoming war. The Capitol is mentioned only once
in a blatant lie (I.vi.106), and no other familiar landmarks create
atmosphere or establish place. Physical detail is kept to a mini-
mum, and only one character, Caius Lucius, embodies anything
like the stalwart *Romanitas* we observe in Lucrece, Titus, Brutus,
Antony, Caesar, and Coriolanus. The seriousness of Shakespeare's
previous Roman efforts, resulting from an abiding interest in character and politics, here yields to a cavalier nonchalance that toler-
ates inconsistencies, eschews political analysis, and trumpets its
own artifices.[2] *Cymbeline*'s liberal mixing of incompatible charac-

[1]The exceptions are Hugh M. Richmond, "Shakespeare's Roman Trilogy: The
Climax in *Cymbeline*," *SLitI*, 5 (1972), 129–39; and David M. Bergeron,
"*Cymbeline:* Shakespeare's Last Roman Play," *SQ*, 31 (1980), 31–41. Some
have made in passing interesting comments on *Cymbeline* as a Roman play: Roy
Walker, "The Northern Star: An Essay on the Roman Plays," *SQ*, 2 (1951),
287–93; A. P. Rossiter, *Angel with Horns* (London: Longmans, 1961), p. 252;
Simmons, pp. 10, 165–6. Walker speaks of Shakespeare's Rome as devolving to
degenerate Italian brilliance; Rossiter, of *Cymbeline* as an escape from the darkness of history evident in *Coriolanus;* and Simmons, of the providential Roman
peace with which the play ends.
[2]On the self-conscious theatricality of the play, see R. A. Foakes, *Shakespeare:
The Dark Comedies to the Last Plays: From Satire to Celebration* (Charlottes-

ters, plots, themes, conventions, and styles has largely disqualified it as successor to the masterful *Antony and Cleopatra* and the carefully wrought *Coriolanus*.

Yet, Rome is undeniably present in *Cymbeline*. The city is a major locality in the play, and its historical skirmishes with Britain make up a good part of the action. What is more, *Cymbeline* incorporates and transforms (sometimes almost beyond recognition) many of the scenes, characters, images, and allusions from previous Roman works. By so doing, the play dramatizes the liberation of Britain from Roman domination, from the hazy past of Sicilius's Roman service, Cymbeline's knighting by Caesar, Caesar's invasion, and Cassibelan's promise of tribute. It celebrates an assertion of British independence as well as the creation of a new alliance with Rome, one in which Britain will be ascendant.[3]

The Roman elements in *Cymbeline* color the entire play and appear unexpectedly at various places. Analysis of these elements illuminates the drama and, in addition, reveals the conclusion of Shakespeare's Roman vision. *Cymbeline* demonstrates that Britons can meet Romans on Roman terms – on the battlefield. The play acknowledges the grandeur that was Rome, but suggests that such grandeur is past, superseded by that of a young nation, awakening to its strength and potential. In some ways Britons live like Romans, but in some ways they are quite different. In the best of them Roman pride is balanced by humility, Roman courage by the qualities of mercy and forgiveness, Roman constancy by a capacity for flexibility, growth, and change.

The play opens with a curious mixture of elements – comic and tragic, Roman and non-Roman. As often in Shakespearean come-

---

ville: University Press of Virginia, 1971), pp. 98–118; Barbara A. Mowat, *The Dramaturgy of Shakespeare's Romances* (Athens: University of Georgia Press, 1976), pp. 51ff.

[3]In taking this approach I follow the leads of G. Wilson Knight, *The Crown of Life* (1947; rpt. London: Methuen, 1961), pp. 129–67; and J. P. Brockbank, "History and Histrionics in *Cymbeline*," *ShS*, 11 (1958), 42–9.

dy, an angry father blights his daughter's budding romance by separating her from her beloved and by championing the suit of another. Cymbeline, however, is no mere *senex iratus,* but the king of Britain. His actions create in himself and the court a potentially tragic rift between form and feeling, between external appearance and internal reality. Though outwardly he shows only grief and rage, he still loves and pities Imogen: He is "touch'd at very heart" (I.i.10), as the First Gentleman puts it. Though outwardly the courtiers follow the king and frown, all are really "glad at the thing they scowl at" (15). This early emphasis on heart mysteries, implicit as well in the story of Imogen's secret marriage to Posthumus, is proleptic. *Cymbeline* will attempt to explore these mysteries as it reconciles internal feeling with external form by transforming both.

Various Roman analogs underlie the situation in the British court and greatly sharpen its tragic potential. Recently, David M. Bergeron has discussed the ways in which Roman history influences Shakespeare's conception of British characters in this play.[4] He notes the parallels between Augustus and Cymbeline, both lacking male heirs and angry with their daughters; between Posthumus and Agrippa, both possessed of two older brothers, both banished, and both ultimately reconciled with the king; between Posthumus and Germanicus, two valorous men who are respected by the people. Cloten, he observes, has much in common with Tiberius, the lusty, vengeful, and cruel stepson to the ruler. And the Queen resembles remarkably the infamous Livia – ambitious, cruel, and dissimulating dealer in poisons.

Shakespeare also recalls in *Cymbeline* his earlier depiction of a troubled Roman court in *Titus Andronicus.*[5] Both Saturninus and Cymbeline appear initially as colorless dupes, deceived by ambitious queens who marry for power. Both the "high-witted" Tamora and the Queen are outsiders who attempt to manipulate others and who enact elaborate charades. Both women on occasion give patriotic speeches that defy the power of coming invaders

---

[4]"*Cymbeline:* Shakespeare's Last Roman Play."
[5]Some of the parallels between the two plays have been noted by George Lyman Kittredge, ed., *The Complete Works of Shakespeare* (Boston: Ginn, 1936), p. 1332; and Norman Rabkin, *Shakespeare and the Common Understanding* (New York: Free Press, 1967), pp. 206–7.

(*T.A.* IV.iv.78ff.; *Cym.* III.i.14ff.). Both show concern for the success of worthless sons; both conspire with their offspring against innocent heroines. The sons of these queens also are similar. Demetrius, Chiron, and Cloten are all vainglorious princes who have had their greatness thrust upon them by the marriage of a mother. Violent, lecherous, and vengeful, they all suffer from a woman's rejection and turn to rape. Cloten's plan to kill Posthumus and to rape Imogen near her husband's body (III.v.137– 45) recalls the murder of Bassianus and Chiron's proposal to make the "dead trunk pillow" to his and his brother's lust (*T.A.* II.iii.130). All the evil princes meet similarly hideous ends: Titus cuts the throats of Demetrius and Chiron in full view of the audience; Guiderius cuts off Cloten's head and carries it on stage.

Like the others, Posthumus is also recognizably Roman, resembling in some ways Lucius of *Titus Andronicus*. Both men suffer banishment and both return home with an invading army. Like Lucius, Posthumus is the son of a famous warrior:

> His father
> Was call'd Sicilius, who did join his honor
> Against the Romans with Cassibelan,
> But had his titles by Tenantius, whom
> He serv'd with glory and admir'd success:
> So gain'd the sur-addition Leonatus.
>
> (I.i.28–33)

The First Gentleman's account of the Leonatus genealogy strikes other familiar Roman notes. We hear the Latinate names, Sicilius, Tenantius, and Leonatus, the last an agnomen like "Coriolanus." The name "Posthumus" obviously derives from unhappy circumstances of birth, but it may owe something as well to Raphael Holinshed's mention of Posthumus, son of the first Roman, Aeneas, and Lavinia.[6] There is also here the characteristically Roman emphasis on fame achieved by military exploits, on "honor" (29), "titles" (31), "glory and admir'd success" (32).

Like many of Shakespeare's Romans, Posthumus is heir to a tradition of honor and military excellence. Demonstrating his met-

---

[6]"The First Booke of the Historie of England," in *The First and Second Volumes of Chronicles* (1587), p. 7. There is also a Posthumus in Ben Jonson's *Sejanus* (1603).

tle early, he confronts Cloten and advances "forward still" (I.ii.15) toward the enemy's face. Imogen refers to Posthumus as an "eagle" (I.i.139), a metaphor here as in *Coriolanus* associated with the Roman eagle, symbol of the city's strength, courage, and superiority. Confident in Posthumus's martial skill and courage, Imogen wishes that he and Cloten could fight it out in "Afric" (I.i.166–9). Volumnia, of course, expresses similar confidence in Coriolanus against the tribunes: "I would my son / Were in Arabia, and thy tribe before him, / His good sword in his hand" (IV.ii.23–5).

As parts of a larger, more complex whole, Roman elements in *Cymbeline* appear with a difference: They are continually balanced and modified by non-Roman elements. Although Sicilius certainly lives like a Roman patriarch, he dies in a distinctly non-Roman manner. After his sons died "with their swords in hand ... their father, / Then old and fond of issue, took such sorrow / That he quit being" (I.i.36–8). Sicilius's response to the death of his sons pointedly contrasts with the response of a Roman parent such as Titus, who proudly contemplates his sons' honorable burial. Valuing his sons' lives as much as their honor, Sicilius Anglicizes Roman *pietas*. This transformed virtue manifests itself throughout the play, often in the form of intuitive and powerful familial sympathy.

Son of such a father and a "gentle" mother (38) (unlike Volumnia), Posthumus has a non-Roman capacity for romantic affection. We first encounter him many fathoms deep in love with Imogen. Their tender parting differs sharply from the leave-takings of Brutus and Portia, Caesar and Calphurnia, Coriolanus and Virgilia, wherein the men sternly subordinate private emotion to public duty. Nor does Posthumus recall here Bassianus or Antony, who valiantly assert their right to love with their swords. Instead, he appears a Lysander or Romeo – naive, innocent, fervent, amorous, fallible, and young. What Shakespearean Roman could emphatically declare that the exchange of his "poor self" for his beloved works to her "so infinite loss" (I.i.119–20)?

When in Rome Posthumus appears as a Roman and does as Romans do. At Philario's house, the Frenchman describes him as an eagle, as one who can behold the sun with firm eyes (I.iv.12). Before refusing to "story him" further (33), Philario remembers serving with Posthumus's father, Sicilius, when Britons and Romans fought side by side. After Posthumus enters, he defends the honor of his lady against Iachimo's verbal attacks. The resulting wager on stage strongly resembles the contest in the Argument of *The Rape of Lucrece*. In this early Roman work, Collatine praises the "incomparable chastity of his / wife Lucretia" (Arg. 12–13) and disbelieving Romans prove the boast true by a late-night visit. Lucrece is praised as "priceless wealth the heavens" lend (17), Imogen as "only the gift of the gods" (85). The report of stainless chastity arouses both Tarquin and Iachimo. Like *Titus Andronicus*, *Lucrece* serves as a deep source for much of the Roman action in *Cymbeline*.

Superbly paced and dramatically exciting, the wager scene is very complex. The force of literary tradition works to exonerate Posthumus for his part, suggesting that he is a perfect lover and gentleman.[7] According to the conventions of chivalry and medieval romance, Posthumus is a knight who champions his lady's virtue. And yet, Shakespeare does not rest content with received traditions. As Homer Swander argues, Shakespeare's treatment of the traditional wager story puts Posthumus in a bad light.[8] The unique recollection of a past quarrel makes his praise of Imogen seem arrogantly proud, his defense of her chastity contentiously aggressive, especially as he promises to make Iachimo answer with "sword" (163). Shakespeare also adds to the typical wager scene the common sense of Philario, who opposes the bet and tries to stop it. Like Enobarbus, Philario functions to point up the folly of Roman boasting and self-assertion. We note that the words "honor" and "constancy," evoking two central Roman virtues in Shakespeare's conception, sound throughout the scene. As Imogen's ring becomes part of the wager, Posthumus vows:

> If you
> make your voyage upon her and give me directly to
> understand you have prevail'd, I am no further your
> enemy; she is not worth our debate.
>
> (157–60)

---

[7]See William Witherle Lawrence, *Shakespeare's Problem Comedies* (New York: Macmillan, 1931), pp. 174–205.

[8]"*Cymbeline* and the 'Blameless Hero,'" *ELH*, 31 (1964), 259–70. Below, I follow the First Folio and read "Iachimo" for Evans's "Jachimo."

How unlike the perfervid lover a few scenes earlier! Posthumus's inconsistency of character is precisely the problem he must work out in the play. From the disparate parts of his personality he must learn to forge a new, well-integrated identity. In other words, he must learn to reconcile his British heart with his Roman arms.

Iachimo's subsequent encounter with Imogen borrows significant details from Tarquin's encounter with Lucrece. The imagery of siege and invasion defines character and action in both instances. Tarquin appears as a "foul usurper" (412) who makes a "breach" in Lucrece's defenses and enters the "sweet city" (469). Similarly, Iachimo prefaces the attack by bragging that an "easy battery" will lay Imogen's judgment flat and that he can "get ground" of her (I.iv.22, 104). Both women are described as a walled fortress and a sacred temple (*Luc.* 1170–6; *Cym.* II.i.63–4). The sight of the victims astonishes both invaders. "Enchanted Tarquin" gazes in "silent wonder" (83–4); Iachimo exclaims in a breathless aside: "All of her that is out of door most rich! / If she be furnish'd with a mind so rare, / She is alone th' Arabian bird" (I.vi.15–17). Both women admit the invaders for their husbands' sakes. Lucrece explains later: "for thy [Collatine's] honor did I entertain him; / Coming from thee, I could not put him back" (842–3); and Imogen, in a divergence from the traditional plot, follows Posthumus's written instructions to welcome Iachimo and treat him kindly (I.vi.22–5). Both invaders praise the absent husband. Tarquin "stories to her ears her husband's fame" (106); Iachimo, after the initial slander, reports of Posthumus:

> He sits 'mongst men like a descended god;
> He hath a kind of honor sets him off,
> More than a mortal seeming.[9]
>
> (I.vi.169–71)

The actual invasion scene in *Cymbeline* (II.ii) is a palimpsest of Roman elements. The language closely parallels that of *Lucrece*. Images of locks and treasures appear in the poem (16) and in the

---

[9]In his Arden edition (1955; rpt. London: Methuen, 1966), J. M. Nosworthy comments on these lines: "Posthumus is, so to speak, the noblest Roman of them all, and, in order to emphasize his pre-eminence even in a Roman milieu, Shakespeare describes him as he several times describes the heroes of the Roman tragedies." Nosworthy cites *Julius Caesar* I.ii.135–8; *Antony and Cleopatra* V.ii.82–92; *Coriolanus* V.iv.23–6, IV.vi.90–3 (p. 42).

play (41–2), and both sleeping victims are described as flowers (*Luc.* 395–7; *Cym.* 15). The eyes of both victims are "canopied" in darkness (*Luc.* 398; *Cym.* 21); and both have "azure" veins (*Luc.* 419; *Cym.* 22), a characteristic unique to them in all of Shakespeare's canon. Both women have the look of death in their sleep (*Luc.* 402–6; *Cym.* 31). Iachimo's hope that Imogen's sense remains a "monument, / Thus in a chapel lying" (32–3) echoes the description of Lucrece as "virtuous monument" (391). Little wonder that Iachimo, upon emerging from the trunk, declares:

> Our Tarquin thus
> Did softly press the rushes ere he waken'd
> The chastity he wounded.
>
> (12–14)

The possessive pronoun, of course, gives the entire game away. Iachimo fancies himself another Tarquin, and Shakespeare delights in fostering the illusion. All the while, however, the disparity between the brutally tragic rape and the sneakily malicious note taking comes into focus. Iachimo never violates Imogen, but merely plays a cheap trick. His busy quill is a poor substitute for Tarquin's gleaming falchion.

The sophisticated playfulness of allusion here appears also in Shakespeare's subsequent reference to Tereus and Philomela (44–6). This myth, of course, surfaces in *Lucrece* – once in the narrator's description of the victim (1079–80) and again in her own complaint (1128ff.). More important, this myth underlies much of the action in *Titus Andronicus*.[10] Like Lucrece, Lavinia appears as a figure of Philomela; like Tarquin, Demetrius and Chiron appear as figures of Tereus. Iachimo's discovery of the book with the leaf turned down at the tale of Tereus and Philomela in Imogen's chamber unmistakably recalls the incident in Act IV, Scene i of *Titus Andronicus,* where Lavinia opens a copy of Ovid's *Metamorphoses* to the same place. Recollection of Shake-

[10]See Ann Thompson, "Philomel in 'Titus Andronicus' and 'Cymbeline,'" *ShS,* 31 (1978), 23–32, who argues that the symbolic power of the allusion is latent in *Titus Andronicus* and fully realized in *Cymbeline.* I think just the reverse is true (see pp. 59–61). Some of the allusions in *Cymbeline* are ornamental; others, like this one, are mildly ironic. On the ironic ones, see R. J. Schork, "Allusion, Theme, and Characterization in *Cymbeline*," *SP,* 69 (1972), 210–16.

speare's models again illuminates ironically the present scene. For Iachimo is no Tereus, Tarquin, Demetrius, or Chiron; and Imogen, to be sure, will prove no Philomela, Lucrece, or Lavinia.

As in *Titus Andronicus*, remembrance of Ovid in *Cymbeline* combines with remembrance of Vergil, particularly with the tale of Troy. It is surely no accident that the fortress of Imogen's bedroom contains a Helen (II.ii.1) and that the deceitful invader hides himself in a false gift. The visual allusion to the Trojan horse emphasizes the comic disparity between the ancient Greek and modern Italian invasions, thereby helping to shift the scene from tragedy to comic melodrama.[11]

Upon returning to Rome, Iachimo delivers a false account of the escapade. Once again Shakespeare playfully returns to past Roman scenes and mythological allusions:

> *Iachimo:* First, her bedchamber
> (Where I confess I slept not, but profess
> Had that was well worth watching), it was hang'd
> With tapestry of silk and silver; the story
> Proud Cleopatra, when she met her Roman,
> And Cydnus swell'd above the banks, or for
> The press of boats or pride.
>
> (II.iv.66–72)

This tapestry recalls quite clearly Enobarbus's famous description of Cleopatra on Cydnus (II.ii.190ff.), echoing in particular the words "silver" (194), "silken" (209), "swell" (210), and "rare" (205, 218; *Cym.* 75).[12] Cleopatra's "cloth of gold" pavilion (199) inspires Imogen's ceiling, fretted with "golden cherubins" (88).

---

[11] Harley Granville-Barker writes, "no tragically-potent scoundrel, we should be sure, will ever come out of a trunk." *Prefaces to Shakespeare*, Vol. I (Princeton: Princeton University Press, 1946), p. 512. A review of recent stage history confirms this opinion. See Muriel St. Clare Byrne, "The Shakespeare Season at The Old Vic, 1956–57 and Stratford-upon-Avon, 1957," *SQ*, 8 (1957), 461–92 (466); Alexander Leggatt, "The Island of Miracles: An Approach to *Cymbeline*," *ShakS*, 10 (1977), 191–209: "I have seen four productions of *Cymbeline*, and on each occasion Iachimo's emergence from the trunk was greeted with laughter" (p. 195); J. C. Trewin, *Going to Shakespeare* (London: Allen & Unwin, 1978): "Any Iachimo must have to calm the laughter when the lid of his trunk first rises" (p. 253).

[12] J. M. Nosworthy detects the influence of Enobarbus's description elsewhere, in Act IV, Scene ii, Lines 169–81. "The Integrity of Shakespeare Illustrated from *Cymbeline*," *ShS*, 8 (1955), 52–6 (54–5).

Enobarbus's references to the Venus "where we see / The fancy outwork nature" (200–1) and to Cleopatra "breathless" (232) lie behind Iachimo's praise of the chimney carver, "another Nature, dumb; outwent her, / Motion and breath left out" (84–5). The two boys standing beside Cleopatra "like smiling Cupids" (202) reappear as Imogen's andirons, "two winking Cupids / Of silver, each on one foot standing, nicely / Depending on their brands" (89–91).

Like Lucrece's remembrance of Troy, Iachimo's recollection of this scene reveals his own character and state of mind. The tapestry Iachimo describes celebrates the beginning of an illicit passion, the infamous affair between Cleopatra and an extravagant, wheeling Roman, Antony. Smooth, eloquent, and subtle though Iachimo is, the pretension implicit in his self-inflating remembrance of the warrior Antony and the earlier Roman conquest undercuts him and fits him for comic retribution. After all, he confesses to have seen "Chaste Dian bathing" (82), and neither the playwright nor the audience would have needed much prompting to recall Actaeon's fate.[13]

Posthumus's reaction to Iachimo's report modulates from worried skepticism to outraged credence. Hearing of Imogen's mole, he flies into a rage:

> O that I had her here, to tear her limb-meal!
> I will go there and do't, i' th' court, before
> Her father. I'll do something –
>
> (147–9)

Although Posthumus has been played upon most cruelly, it is difficult to accept and forgive such threatening, especially as the murderous intention proves quite real. Posthumus soliloquizes on the vicious nature of women, extending the indictment to include all females, even his own mother. This harangue recalls the recurrent strain of misogyny in the Roman works as well as similar fulminations by Hamlet, Othello, and Troilus. Like the Roman expressions of misogyny, however, this one is ironic because it suggests the faults of the speaker, not the subject.

Iachimo's siege of Imogen's bedchamber is replayed in various

---

[13]The implied reference to Actaeon is also noted by Schork, "Allusion," pp. 212–13.

incidents. Accurately and appropriately, for example, Imogen describes Cloten's love suit as a fearful siege (III.iv.133–4). Cloten, the besieger, is a *miles gloriosus,* a parody of Posthumus's Roman self. We first meet him bragging about the fight with Posthumus (I.ii) – wherein, we recall, Posthumus "rather play'd than fought" (I.i.162). Petulance and volatility wed unhappily in Cloten's boorish temperament: He breaks the pate of a standerby when he loses at bowls (II.i.1–7); he gets "hot and furious" when he wins at cards (II.iii.5–7). After Iachimo's covert invasion of Imogen's bedchamber, Cloten hopes to "penetrate" her with the "fingering" of musicians (II.iii.14–15). The lyrical sweetness of the aubade, "Hark, hark, the lark" (20–6), serves the gross desire of the would-be soldier and lover. Imogen's lively repulse reassures because it testifies to the life-affirming presence of the comic spirit in the play. After enduring Imogen's rankling comparison of him to Posthumus's "mean'st garment" (133), Cloten vows revenge. From this point on he, like Posthumus, will lay a new siege to Imogen, once conceived in hatred and undertaken to destroy her.

Both Iachimo's and Cloten's amatory sieges of Imogen, who is described by G. Wilson Knight as "Britain's soul-integrity,"[14] are parallel to the military siege and invasion of Britain. In the background of this threat looms the past invasion of Britain by Julius Caesar, a Roman victory that Shakespeare in this play takes pains to diminish and finally expunge. The conversation between Philario and Posthumus in Act II, Scene iv prepares the audience for the confrontation between Cymbeline and Caius Lucius in Act III, Scene i. Philario predicts that Cymbeline will concede the tribute because remembrance of Roman conquest is "yet fresh" in British grief (14). Posthumus disagrees, asserting that "not-fearing Britain" (19) will make known "to their approvers they are people such / That mend upon the world" (25–6).

The conflict between the past tyranny of Rome and the present struggle of the British for a new future receives fuller articulation in Act III, Scene i. Caius Lucius begins by invoking the talismanic name of Julius Caesar, "whose remembrance yet / Lives in men's eyes, and will to ears and tongues / Be theme and hearing ever" (2–4). Here Lucius pithily enunciates the familiar Roman view of

[14]*Crown of Life,* p. 148.

history, of the past that Caesar rules and that originates all present and future action. The Britons directly confront and contradict this view of history by supplying their own version of the "kind of conquest / Caesar made" (22–3). According to the Queen, Caesar suffered two shameful defeats at British hands and had his ships cracked "like egg-shells" (28) on British rocks. Were it not for "giglet Fortune" (31), Cassibelan, who made London bright with rejoicing and filled Britons with pride, would have mastered Caesar's sword. The great conqueror was merely a lucky mortal, one, as Cloten reminds us, with a crooked nose.

That the Britons write their own past up as they write the Roman past down is hardly surprising.[15] Revisionist history always accompanies revolution. And like most revolutions, Britain's assertion of independence from Roman domination excites and perplexes onlookers. At a loss to reconcile the Queen's and Cloten's nationalism in Act III, Scene i with the later reunion with Rome, many have judged their outbursts to be self-serving, part of a dishonorable scheme to gain power. According to this view, Jacobean audiences would not have cheered the patriotic sentiments expressed on stage, but instead would have perceived iniquity in the speakers and loathsome uxoriousness in the king.[16] But surely this reading expands some difficulties and introduces many new ones. Cymbeline's refusal to pay tribute (46–61) shows firmness and courtesy, qualities not likely to alienate an audience or indicate moral turpitude. Moreover, the claims for Cloten's patriotism are exaggerated. Boorishly, Cloten insults the dignified Lucius by repeating the puerile joke about Italian noses (14, 37). He inter-

---

[15]Rewriting the story of Julius Caesar's invasion was a common activity in Europe from ancient times onward. See Homer Nearing, Jr., "The Legend of Julius Caesar's British Conquest," *PMLA*, 64 (1949), 889–929.

[16]See variations of this interpretation by Warren D. Smith, "Cloten with Caius Lucius," *SP*, 49 (1952), 185–94; Robin Moffet, "*Cymbeline* and the Nativity," *SQ*, 13 (1962), 207–18 (209–10); D. R. C. Marsh, *The Recurring Miracle: A Study of Cymbeline* (Pietermaritzburg: University of Natal Press, 1962), pp. 51–2; Joan Hartwig, *Shakespeare's Tragicomic Vision* (Baton Rouge: Louisiana State University Press, 1972), pp. 94–5; Howard Felperin, *Shakespearean Romance* (Princeton: Princeton University Press, 1972), pp. 187–8. Cymbeline's later remark that he was "dissuaded" from paying tribute by the "wicked Queen" (V.v.463) simply clears the way for reconciliation; it can hardly be used post facto to discredit the patriotism of Act III, Scene i and the battle scenes.

rupts his mother (34–8), and in pointed contrast to Cymbeline, dismisses Lucius with a jeering threat: "If you fall in the adventure, our crows shall fare the / better for you; and there's an end" (81–2). Finally, this reading of the scene ignores the connection between the imminent Roman siege and the amatory ones. Because the emphasis of the play is on the wager plot, the Roman invasion appears as a reflection of Iachimo's, as another example of Roman pride and arrogance. In both invasions we witness Roman self-assertion, manifested variously in the attempt at military domination and in the degenerate modern Italian try at amorous conquest.

The scene of British defiance is crucial to the play as it outlines the ambivalences in Britain's relationship with Rome. Clearly, Britain is proper heir to Roman civilization and values. Cymbeline says:

> Thou art welcome, Caius.
> Thy Caesar knighted me; my youth I spent
> Much under him; of him I gather'd honor.
>
> (68–70)

And yet, it is equally clear, the time has come for Britain to declare its independence of Rome and Roman values. The play depicts Britain's struggle to come into its own as a strong but gentle nation, seasoned with courtesy, humanity, and a respect for the human heart.

Imogen's journey to "Blessed Milford" removes her from the potentially tragic British court to what Alvin Kernan calls the "second place" of Shakespearean drama, a natural spot of imagination and transformation.[17] Belarius's homily on the virtues of a low

[17]"Place and Plot in Shakespeare," *Yale Review*, NS 67 (1977), 48–56. Leggatt, "Island of Miracles," sees all of Britain as the "second place," not distinguishing between the court and Wales; more perceptive is J. S. Lawry, "'Perishing Root and Increasing Vine' in *Cymbeline*," *ShakS*, 12 (1979), 179–93, who regards Britain and Rome as fixed "in static malevolence" and Milford Haven as "a third direction, place, 'way,' and metaphor" where lies the possibility of

roof (III.iii.1–9) is overpious, but signals our entrance into a world of clean air and simple living where trivial daily business accords harmoniously with divine order. Belarius's preference for the "safer hold" of the "sharded beetle" over the domain of the "full-wing'd eagle" (20–1) suggests pastoral reverence for quietness and humility as well as pastoral aversion to expansive acquisitiveness. The reference to the "eagle" appropriately evokes Rome, about to invade Britain once again.

Belarius's praise of the pastoral life, complete with the usual derogations of courtly vanity and folly, does not stand unqualified and unchallenged. Both Guiderius and Arviragus respond by lamenting their ignorance of the world and the narrowness of their present horizons. Pointedly, Guiderius replies to Belarius's beetle-and-eagle metaphor:

> Out of your proof you speak; we poor unfledg'd
> Have never wing'd from view o' th' nest, nor know not
> What air's from home.
>
> (27–9)

The recurrence of the eagle image suggests that these pastoral princes are really Roman Britons, yet to prove their *Romanitas* by performing valorous deeds. Not surprisingly, Belarius preaches against the toil of war, "A pain that only seems to seek out danger / I' th' name of fame and honor which dies i' th' search, / And hath as oft a sland'rous epitaph / As record of fair act" (50–3). Yet, this sermon rings false. For soon after, Belarius delights in memory of his past achievements, when his body was marked with Roman swords and his report "first with the best of note" (58). And clearly he admires the warlike spirit of the princes, striking proof, he declares in secret, of their genuine nobility (79ff.). The pastoral setting in the play thus presents a curious mixture of conventional and Roman elements.

Such mixing is not new for Shakespeare. His first Roman play,

---

"gainful loss" (p. 183). Recent commentators have made much of the fact that Milford Haven was the landing place of Henry Tudor en route to the throne and was celebrated as such in Jacobean masques. See Emrys Jones, "Stuart Cymbeline," *EIC*, 11 (1961), 84–99; Glynne Wickham, "From Tragedy to Tragi-Comedy: 'King Lear' as Prologue," *ShS*, 26 (1973), 33–48 (44–5); Frances A. Yates, *Shakespeare's Last Plays: A New Approach* (London: Routledge & Kegan Paul, 1975), pp. 41–61.

Titus Andronicus, features a similar Roman pastoral, the central activity of which is also hunting. Titus salutes the bright morning (II.ii.1ff.) and accompanies his sons in search of game. Likewise, Belarius rises shining and hunts venison with his foster sons. In both plays the natural and sociable activity of hunting contrasts sharply with the perverse hunting of an innocent girl. Lavinia appears as a "dainty doe" (*T.A.* II.ii.26) and Imogen as an "elected deer" (*Cym.* III.iv.109). Demetrius and Chiron plan to make the forest a scene for unnatural lust, revenge, and murder; Cloten, in like manner, plans to kill Posthumus and rape Imogen (III.v.137ff.). Posthumus also hunts Imogen through the agency of Pisanio. The pastoral scenes in both plays provide a backdrop that sharply defines the human predator.

Faced with Pisanio's letter from Posthumus and with death, Imogen initially acts the part of Lucrece. Like the chaste Roman matron, she invokes the tale of Troy as an analog to her own desperate situation:

> True honest men being heard, like false Aeneas,
> Were in his time thought false; and Sinon's weeping
> Did scandal many a holy tear.

(III.iv.58–60)

The allusion to false Aeneas makes Imogen a figure of Dido, betrayed by a cruel and faithless lover.[18] The allusion to Sinon suggests that Posthumus is a deceiver who discredits all true misery and suffering. Both Lucrece and Imogen, chaste and guiltless, draw weapons upon themselves for their husbands' sakes. Lucrece seeks to save Collatine from dishonor, Imogen to demonstrate her "obedience" to Posthumus (III.iv.66). Both envision the time when others will look back on their brave deaths (*Luc.* 1201ff.; *Cym.* 92ff.).

The scene recalls as well characters and incidents from the Roman plays. After the revelation of Posthumus's murderous intention, for example, Pisanio evokes Cleopatra in her most Roman moment: He talks of slander, "whose tongue / Outvenoms all the worms of Nile" (III.iv.34–5). And when Imogen, sword at her

---

[18]Interestingly, *The Rare Triumphes of Love and Fortune* (1589), a probable source for *Cymbeline,* features a brief appearance of the betrayed Dido on stage. See Bullough, Vol. VIII, p. 92.

breast, beseeches Pisanio to strike home, we remember the similar scenes enacted by Cassius and Pindarus, Brutus and Strato, Antony and Eros. Imogen here is no weak, pleading, and pitiful girl, but a brave Roman ready to end her life honorably. She orders the servant, "Prithee dispatch" (95), and reminds him several times of his duty to his master. When he whimpers that he hasn't slept a wink since receiving Posthumus's command to kill her, she curtly answers, "Do't, and to bed then" (100).

The expected end to the Roman scene never takes place. Instead of participating in a bloody ritual for honor and fame, Pisanio and Imogen resort to disguise and deception. Instead of boldly asserting her identity by death and consecrating her name for all posterity, Imogen decides to lose both identity and name. She bids easy farewell to the old self, restricted by responsibility, burdened by sorrow, and takes on a new one, Fidele. The conventions of comedy completely reverse the tragic Roman momentum. In so doing, they reveal the brittleness of Roman egotism and the importance of British flexibility. Sometimes one must lose oneself in order to be found.

Significantly, Imogen decides not to return to Britain, but to reside in "other place":

> Hath Britain all the sun that shines? day? night?
> Are they not but in Britain? I' th' world's volume
> Our Britain seems as of it, but not in 't;
> In a great pool a swan's nest. Prithee think
> There's livers out of Britain.
>
> (136–40)

Such an alternative, of course, is unthinkable for Shakespeare's Romans, for whom all roads lead directly home. For them, Rome is the world; they must either live in the city or die. Antony cannot find in all the earth's spaces room enough for him and Cleopatra; he leaves the world and seeks a place with her in another life. Coriolanus vows to find "a world elsewhere" but discovers that there can be no honorable life for him outside Rome. Imogen, however, dons a doublet, hat, and hose, and cheerfully decides to live in Wales. Comedic vivacity and flexibility work to ensure survival and to achieve a resolution. These qualities are fostered by Pisanio, the faithful servant who refuses to play the part of his staunch Roman counterparts. Instead, he exhibits kindness, mercy, and a strong faith that Fortune, as he later puts it, often "brings in some boats that are not steer'd" (IV.iii.46).

When the disguised Imogen comes upon the cave of her long-lost brothers, she has a Roman thought:

> Yet famine,
> Ere clean it o'erthrow nature, makes it valiant.
> Plenty and peace breeds cowards; hardness ever
> Of hardiness is mother.
>
> (III.vi.19–22)

The curious soldierly sentiment, perhaps an echo of *Coriolanus* (IV.v.217ff.), serves to reveal the differences between the British maiden and the Roman warrior, between the cave of Belarius and the battlefield.[19] The ensuing scene illustrates not her capacity for "hardiness," but her (and her brothers') capacity for love – intuitive, overpowering, and familial. Witness the following exchange:

> *Guiderius:* Were you a woman, youth,
>   I should woo hard but be your groom in honesty:
>   I bid for you as I do buy.
> *Arviragus:* I'll make 't my comfort
>   He is a man, I'll love him as my brother:
>   And such a welcome as I'd give to him
>   After long absence, such is yours. Most welcome!
>   Be sprightly, for you fall 'mongst friends.
> *Imogen: Aside.* 'Mongst friends?
>   If brothers: would it had been so, that they
>   Had been my father's sons.
>
> (III.vi.68–76)

The Britons immediately respond to each other and instinctively grasp the hidden truth about their relationship. Later, both princes assert that they love the gentle youth as much as they do their father (IV.ii.16ff.). The repeated expression of such miraculous perception and affection suggests the innate capacities of the Brit-

---

[19]These differences have often been emphasized in performance by Imogen's comical timidity and fear. See Arthur Colby Sprague, *Shakespeare and the Actors: The Stage Business in His Plays (1600–1905)* (Cambridge, Mass.: Harvard University Press, 1944), p. 62.

ish heart; it asserts the sacredness and naturalness of familial love and sympathy.[20]

Shakespeare carefully balances British and Roman elements in the princes as well as in the play. The scenes of family harmony alternate with scenes of military confrontation and battle. Cloten arrives in Wales and insults Guiderius. Guiderius staunchly rebuffs him, finally cutting off his head. Thus he demonstrates his natural nobility in high Roman style, through use of a strong right arm. Arviragus envies his brother the valorous deed while Belarius again ruminates on the innate honor of the princes:

> 'Tis wonder
> That an invisible instinct should frame them
> To royalty unlearn'd, honor untaught,
> Civility not seen from other, valor
> That wildly grows in them but yields a crop
> As if it had been sow'd.
>
> (IV.ii.176–81)

In this play, however, such Roman regard for honor and military prowess is Anglicized in important ways. Guiderius, it is plain, fights Cloten in self-defense, using the aggressor's sword against him (IV.ii.149–51). Not only does Cloten start the trouble, but, we are told, he also threatens to kill Belarius and Arviragus as well (120–3). The implausibility of this threat (how could Cloten know that the others existed?) raises no doubts about Guiderius's veracity, but justifies his actions as self-defense. He is not a Roman, seeking glory and conquest, but a Roman Briton, courageously defending himself, his home, and his family.

The differences between British and Roman warriors are also apparent in the funeral service for Fidele, not really dead but

---

[20]The reunion of Imogen and her brothers in the cave may owe something to Torquato Tasso's story of Erminia and the shepherds, *Jerusalem Delivered*, Book VII. Edwin Greenlaw, "Shakespeare's Pastorals," *SP*, 13 (1916), 122–54 (136–47) notes the connections, and Bullough reprints portions from Edward Fairfax's translation (1600) as an "analogue" to *Cymbeline* (Vol. VIII, pp. 103–11). Renato Poggioli's comment on the Erminia episode, "the natural outcome of the pastoral of innocence is the family situation, or the domestic idyll," is also very apt for the episode in the play. *The Oaten Flute: Essays on Pastoral Poetry and the Pastoral Ideal* (Cambridge, Mass.: Harvard University Press, 1975), p. 12.

drugged. Belarius and the princes decide to inter Cloten with their friend, magnanimously granting the enemy the courtesy of princely burial. Guiderius and Arviragus recite poignant obsequies over Fidele's body. Their exquisite dirge, "Fear no more the heat o' th' sun" (IV.ii.258–81), reflects upon the dangers and difficulties of life and extolls the peace and quiet of death, the inevitable end: "Golden lads and girls all must, / As chimney-sweepers, come to dust" (262–3). The evocative "golden," richly suggestive of health, youth, wealth, and perhaps the lost golden age, combines with the homely detail of "chimney-sweepers" coming to dust to soften grief into bittersweet resignation. Unlike the various Roman funerals previously encountered – those of Lucrece, the Andronici, and Caesar, for example – this service is personal, intimate, and familial. Three times it is iterated that the princes performed the same ritual for Euriphile, their "mother," many years ago (190–1, 223–4, 236–8). There is no recognition here of civic meaning in death, nor is the corpse a spur to political or military action. Instead, the princes quietly consign their beloved to the earth with flowers and song.

The tragic rhythm of the play, tending toward separation and death, yields gradually to the comic rhythm of life and renewal. Imogen wakes from her deathlike sleep only to find Cloten's headless corpse in Posthumus's clothing:

> The garments of Posthumus?
> I know the shape of 's leg; this is his hand,
> His foot Mercurial, his Martial thigh,
> The brawns of Hercules; but his Jovial face –
> Murther in heaven? How? 'Tis gone. Pisanio,
> All curses madded Hecuba gave the Greeks,
> And mine to boot, be darted on thee!
>
> (IV.ii.308–14)

Imogen sees Cloten as a composite of Olympian qualities, a vision all the more amusing in light of her past opinion. The inappropriate allusions measure the gap between what is and what appears to

224

be. Consequently, the audience looks with sympathy upon the befuddled Imogen, cooling the air with sighs, her arms in a sad knot. Comparing herself to Hecuba, mad with sorrow, grief, and rage, Imogen recalls the similar allusions characterizing Lucrece (1445ff.) and Lavinia (*T.A.* IV.i.20ff.). In those early works, of course, the allusions express real anguish and the enormity of the suffering and the losses. Here, however, the reference to Hecuba works to opposite effect. Because the audience knows that Imogen's Posthumus is really Cloten and that Pisanio is blameless, the scene appears as an elaborately ironic confusion, not as a high tragic moment.[21] The allusion to Hecuba is an antiquated, melodramatic costume that Imogen cannot fit or cut to size.

The flight of the heroine's imagination is worth remarking. We have not seen fancy so vie with nature in the creation of strange forms since Cleopatra's glazed remembrance of Antony. As a matter of fact, R. Warwick Bond calls *Cymbeline* a "direct sequel" to *Antony and Cleopatra* and Imogen "the English [*sic*] contrast" to the Egyptian queen.[22] Both Cleopatra and Imogen embrace the corpses of their lovers; both split the air with laments in the approaching shadows of Roman invaders. Whereas Cleopatra's apotheosis of Antony evokes wonder and sorrow, however, Imogen's apotheosis of Cloten evokes laughter and pity. Cleopatra resolves to follow Antony "after the high Roman fashion" (IV.xv.87), but Imogen merely falls on the corpse, "That we the horrider may seem to those / Which chance to find us" (IV.ii.331–2). Cleopatra chooses to die rather than submit to the invading Roman; Imogen quickly agrees to serve the kindly Lucius. Cleopatra responds trag-

[21]See F. D. Hoeniger, "Irony and Romance in *Cymbeline*," *SEL*, 2 (1962), 219–28: "The effect of the mythological comparisons is at first funny, but immediately qualified by Imogen's profound grief. When pathos and grotesque irony combine acutely, as they do here, we move in the sphere neither of tragedy nor of comedy but in the world of a genre different from both" (p. 223).

[22]*Studia Otiosa: Some Attempts in Criticism* (London: Constable, 1938), p. 74. Derek Traversi notices on separate occasions that the poetry of *Cymbeline*, "though more diluted with romantic sentiment," recalls passages from *Antony and Cleopatra. Shakespeare: The Last Phase* (1955; rpt. Stanford: Stanford University Press, 1965), pp. 48, 69. (The quoted phrase appears on p. 48.) Granville-Barker declares that Cleopatra and Imogen are "companion pictures of wantonness and chastity; and, of women, are the fullest and maturest that he drew" (*Prefaces*, Vol. I, p. 530).

ically to a tragic world, wherein Antony's death is final and her own disgrace imminent. Imogen responds comically to a comic world, wherein time and good faith dissolve difficulties, remove illusions, and sometimes bring the living back from the dead.

The comedic process outlined above, here as always in Shakespeare, requires the assistance of the human heart. Imogen's forgiveness of Posthumus's treachery prepares for an important turning point in the play – Posthumus's own repentance and sorrow. In a soliloquy parallel to Imogen's (IV.ii.291ff.), Posthumus comes to his senses:

> *Enter* Posthumus *alone with a bloody handkerchief.*
> *Posthumus:* Yea, bloody cloth, I'll keep thee, for I wish'd
>   Thou shouldst be color'd thus. You married ones,
>   If each of you should take this course, how many
>   Must murther wives much better than themselves
>   For wrying but a little!
>
>   (V.i.1–5)

The various blood rituals of the Roman works contrast sharply with this confession and cherishing of the bloody handkerchief. The closest Roman analog, namely the imagined dipping of napkins in Caesar's sacred blood (III.ii.130ff.), illustrates the uniqueness of Posthumus's ritual. In *Cymbeline* the handkerchief is a martyr's relic that privately mortifies the possessor; the blood ritual permanently indicts the aggressive and destructive impulses instead of glorifying and encouraging them. Imogen's "infidelity," formerly an unforgivable affront to Posthumus's honor, becomes merely "wrying but a little," a slight and all too human deviation into vice. Repenting his "murder" of Imogen, Posthumus wishes that the gods had permitted her to live and struck him down, "more worth" their "vengeance" (V.i.11). Posthumus's unfeigned humility and recognition of his own unworthiness lead to resignation and acceptance of divine will. He prays: "But Imogen is your own, do your best wills, / And make me blest to obey" (16–17). Remarkably, Posthumus repents before he discovers the truth about Imogen, chaste and alive. Shakespeare portrays here a change of heart that is motivated by a sympathetic understanding of human weakness and by an accompanying appreciation for precious love and life.

The resolution to amend life and perform penance perfects Posthumus's contrition.[23] The penance he has in mind, however, is unusual. Posthumus plans to change into the costume of a British peasant and to fight for Imogen:

> Let me make men know
> More valor in me than my habits show.
> Gods, put the strength o' th' Leonati in me!
> To shame the guise o' th' world, I will begin
> The fashion: less without and more within.

> (V.i.29–33)

At first glance, Posthumus's resolution to fight, to live up to his noble ancestry, seems a most Roman way of making reparation, reminiscent, perhaps, of Antony after Actium. Yet, Posthumus is un-Roman in a number of important particulars. Disguised as a British peasant, he does not seek in battle self-aggrandizement, but self-abnegation. Posthumus hopes to die not for country, but for his wife.

Posthumus's intention to "shame the guise o' th' world" by starting a new "fashion" aims directly at overturning the Roman military ethos that encourages destruction of life for fame and glory. The difference between Posthumus and his Roman predecessors, Roman enemies, and former Roman self (who wanted Iachimo, himself, or both killed in combat [II.iv.58–61]) becomes evident in the ensuing battle. After vanquishing and disarming Iachimo, he leaves him unharmed, pointedly refusing to exalt himself over the body of an enemy. Posthumus rejects the Roman vanity of personal honor for the exercise of British mercy and compassion.

Posthumus's expression of Anglicized *Romanitas* is balanced by additional proof of Roman excellence in Britain, that provided by Belarius and the princes. Unable to hide in the mountains and watch their country invaded, this trio helps rescue Cymbeline and rout the Romans. Like Coriolanus, they encourage fleeing companions and inspire them to fight on to honor and victory. Stouthearted Britons thus overcome mighty Romans, a triumph that

[23]Robert Grams Hunter demonstrates in *Shakespeare and the Comedy of Forgiveness* (New York: Columbia University Press, 1965) that Posthumus's repentance and renewal are presented as the pagan equivalent to Christian regeneration (pp. 159ff.).

surely excited original audiences. The young challenger finally breaks the hold of Roman history. The defeat of the Romans on the battlefield, their own proving ground, marks the end of their domination and the beginning of a new regime. Though heir to Roman traditions, this regime, as Posthumus's story intimates, will be different, more merciful and humane, "less without and more within."

The joy of British conquest is not for Posthumus, however, whose search for death leads to further self-denial, penance, and purification. "No more a Britain" (V.iii.75), he withdraws from the victory celebration and puts on Roman clothing. This change from British to Roman appearance covers the opposite internal change from Roman to British. In non-Roman fashion, Posthumus refuses to claim due honor and receive public recognition. Instead of enjoying victory and hard-earned fame, he chooses anonymity, suffers capture, and endures unceremonious imprisonment. In soliloquy Posthumus expresses sincere sorrow and again offers his life in exchange for Imogen's, this time in accents reminiscent of the earlier exchange of his "poor self" to her "so infinite loss" (I.i.119–20): "For Imogen's dear life take mine, and though / 'Tis not so dear, yet 'tis a life" (V.iv.22–3). The Briton who exercised Roman virtue in British costume now, in Roman costume, shows a British capacity for humility and spiritual growth.[24]

After Posthumus's prayer, solemn music plays while the ghosts of his father, mother, and brothers come to accuse Jupiter of harassing Posthumus. As is usual in Shakespeare's last plays, the fantastic and elaborate apparition expresses central themes. The Leonati here, as in the First Gentleman's description, embody Roman elements. The father, "great" Sicilius (V.iv.51), is *attired like a warrior* (s.d. V.iv.29) and the British are described as "a valiant race" (83). The brothers remind Jupiter that they fought for their

---

[24]On the importance of costuming to the play, see John Scott Colley, "Disguise and New Guise in *Cymbeline*," *ShakS*, 7 (1974), 233–52.

country, "Fell bravely and were slain, / Our fealty and Tenantius'
right / With honor to maintain" (72–4). Furthermore, they aver,
in Posthumus (as well as in Coriolanus):

> Great nature, like his ancestry,
>   Moulded the stuff so fair,
> That he deserv'd the praise o' th' world.
>
> (48–50)

Despite the Roman emphasis on martial exploits, honor, and
fame, the apparition is distinctly non-Roman. These ghosts take
Jupiter to task, basing their presumption not only on their past
honor, but also on the sacredness of familial bonds. They stage a
family reunion and repeatedly call attention to the nature and
strength of their relationships. Sicilius refers to Posthumus as "my
poor boy" (35), who attended "nature's law" (38) by staying in
the womb while his father died. The mother remembers birth
throes and the ripping of Posthumus from her. The dead brothers
stand by their living brother and praise his "like hardiment" (75).
Sicilius accuses Jupiter of failing in his fatherly responsibilities to
Posthumus,

> Whose father then (as men report
>   Thou orphans' father art)
> Thou shouldst have been, and shielded him
>   From this earth-vexing smart.
>
> (39–42)

The familial sympathy evident in the earlier scenes with Imogen
and her brothers appears here in more incredible form. In contrast
to Roman families, bound together by tradition and honor, British
families are bound by love. So powerful and so inviolable is this
love that members may return from beyond the grave to defend
their own and to censure the almighty thunderer himself for ne-
glecting paternal duties.

In a spectacular display of thunder and lightning, Jupiter descends on an eagle to answer the Leonati:

> Be not with mortal accidents oppress'd,
> No care of yours it is, you know 'tis ours.
> Whom best I love, I cross; to make my gift,
> The more delay'd, delighted.
>
> (99–102)

Before ascending into the heavens he leaves behind a riddling prophecy that foretells the ending of Posthumus's misery and the flourishing of Britain. The Leonati are satisfied that Jupiter, despite appearances to the contrary, is a loving father who takes care of all his children. The audience, however, may not rest content so easily. The prophecy appears too late to strike up any real dramatic interest or suspense, and the riddle will prove silly rather than wondrous. The assurance of divine providence is not well integrated with the action of the play, the promised end of which depends more directly on human kindness, compassion, and willingness to take risks.[25] At the conclusion we will give thanks not to Jupiter, but to Cornelius for deceiving the Queen with the potion; to Pisanio for disobeying Posthumus's command and retaining faith; to Belarius, Guiderius, and Arviragus for risking their lives in order to save their king and country; to the Leonati for their exemplary courage and concern; to Imogen for her vivacity, resourcefulness, and forgiveness; to Posthumus for exchanging vengeance for the rarer virtues of humility and kindness; to Cymbeline for achieving a peaceful reconciliation with Rome.

After Jupiter's ascent and before the final unraveling of the many knotted threads, the scene between Posthumus and the Jailer intervenes. Their conversation effects a lightening of mood preparatory to the comic conclusion. The Jailer's mundane reflections on the advantages of death – namely, the cessation of tavern reckonings – provides a humorous counterpoint to the poignant dirge for Fidele. As Posthumus is led away, however, the homely philosopher has some surprising final thoughts:

> Unless a man should marry a gallows and
> beget young gibbets, I never saw one so prone. Yet,
> on my conscience, there are verier knaves desire
> to live, for all he be a Roman; and there be some of
> them too that die against their wills. So should I, if I
> were one. I would we were all of one mind, and one
> mind good. O, there were desolation of jailers and

[25]The importance of the vision of Jupiter and of the providential theme has been discussed (somewhat more appreciatively) by Wilson Knight, *Crown of Life*, pp. 168–202, and Kenneth Muir, "Theophanies in the Last Plays," in *Shakespeare's Late Plays: Essays in Honor of Charles Crow*, ed. Richard C. Tobias and Paul G. Zolbrod (Athens: University of Ohio Press, 1974), pp. 32–43.

gallowses! I speak against my present profit, but my
wish hath a preferment in 't.

(V.iv.198–206)

The common, unnamed Jailer, characterized by his reflections on
the everyday business of eating and drinking, has the last word on
Stoicism and suicide in Shakespeare's Roman vision. From his
humble perspective life is better than death, even for Romans. The
Jailer's wish that all were "of one mind" and "one mind good"
anticipates the final melting of the differences between characters
and nations in the play.

The dizzying revelations of the last scene accomplish first the
reunion of the lovers, Posthumus and Imogen. With Cymbeline's
help the disguised Imogen prompts Iachimo to reveal his treachery. He tells the whole tale of how his "Italian brain" (V.v.196)
operated in "duller Britain" (197) and cost Posthumus his wager
and his wife. Enraged, Posthumus breaks off the account and
reveals his identity. After Imogen unmasks, the lovers embrace,
and the daughter receives her father's blessing. Thus, form and
feeling are finally reconciled in Britain. What is more, Posthumus
demonstrates that he has finally learned to harmonize Roman
aggression and British compassion. After explaining that he was
the "forlorn soldier," he accepts his due honors and the King's
gratitude. Instead of claiming the life of his enemy as he first
threatened, Posthumus spares Iachimo a second time:

> Kneel not to me.
> The pow'r that I have on you is to spare you;
> The malice towards you, to forgive you. Live,
> And deal with others better.
>
> (417–20)

Pointedly revising the wager story in *The Decameron* and *Fred-
eryke of Jennen,* Shakespeare depicts the deceiver forgiven, not
exposed and cruelly punished.

Cymbeline's recovery of his daughter and his acceptance of
Posthumus as son-in-law begin the reconstitution of the royal fam-
ily. The evil Queen dies despairing off-stage, killed by her own
shameless desperation. Guiderius's account of the fight with
Cloten permanently settles the question concerning the ignoble
Prince's whereabouts. The dying of the old family, of course, is

necessary prelude to the rebirth of the new. Intuitive familial sympathy manifests itself again in Cymbeline's knighting of the princes, now "companions to our person" (21), and in his instinctive attraction to the disguised Imogen: "What wouldst thou, boy? / I love thee more and more" (108–9). Miraculously, Cymbeline regains his lost children and his identity as parent. Amazed, he exlaims: "O, what, am I / A mother to the birth of three? Ne'er mother / Rejoic'd deliverance more" (368–70). The references to himself as mother and to the process of birth suggest the intensity of the moment and the power of the love that binds.[26] Like Posthumus earlier, Imogen resides in the middle of a warm family circle, this one consisting of Cymbeline (who is father and mother), and two long-lost brothers. Fittingly, the circle widens to include Belarius, whom Cymbeline embraces as a "brother" and Imogen accepts as another "father" (399–401).

The reconciliation and reunion of the royal family in *Cymbeline* leads directly to the reconciliation and reunion of nations. Initially, it appears as though the Britons will be barbarous victors. The kinsmen of the slain demand the lives of the Roman captives so as to appease the souls of the dead "with slaughter" (72). Lucius's calm and courageous response, "Sufficeth / A Roman with a Roman's heart can suffer" (80–1), points up the primitive cruelty of the request. The scene closely parallels the opening of *Titus Andronicus,* wherein victorious Romans butcher Alarbus "*ad manes fratrum*" (I.i.98).[27] Significantly, however, the sacrifice of the Romans in *Cymbeline* never takes place. Inspired by Posthumus's forgiveness of Iachimo, Cymbeline pardons all the prisoners. The contrast between the early and late sacrifice scenes graphically illustrates the differences between Roman and British civilization, the one founded on self-assertion, revenge, and bloodshed; the other, on forgiveness and mercy.

"Although the victor" (460), Cymbeline promises of his own free will to submit to Caesar and send the tribute. Shakespeare may have found precedent for Cymbeline's actions in Heliodorus's *Aethiopica,* wherein King Hidaspes freely restores his defeated

---

[26]The difference between Cymbeline's perception here and Caesar's vision of himself as *mater patriae,* from whom "great Rome shall suck / Reviving blood" (*J.C.* II.ii.87–8), is instructive.

[27]See Kittredge, *Complete Works,* p. 1332.

enemy's lands in order to keep peace and foster "amity."[28]Like Hidaspes's, Cymbeline's donation does not cancel out the triumph, but demonstrates the victor's generosity and nobility. As Frank Kermode comments: "We are meant to conclude that the valour of the British royal family is 'gentle', and not simply a brute toughness which must set the nation against the forces of civility and religion."[29] The gift of tribute completes the comic ending, dissolving rather than resolving the differences between opposing nations.

For his earlier kindness to Imogen and his present show of courage, Lucius is included in the final comic circle. His presence there symbolizes the greater harmony now existing between nations. This harmony is familial in nature, not only because it derives from the reunion of Cymbeline's family, but because it unites both the Roman and British descendants of Priam and Aeneas.[30] The grand conclusion of *Cymbeline*, then, reconciles the warring factions of the larger, extended Trojan family and thus creates the blessed peace that descends upon all, Briton and Roman alike.

Shakespeare's increasingly critical scrutiny of Rome concludes in *Cymbeline*. British valor triumphs over Roman might, but more importantly, British flexibility and humility overcome Roman constancy and honor. The siege and invasion motif, appearing here on both the sexual and national levels, articulates no vision of impious violation. Instead, it leads to a scene of toleration and forgiveness, wherein each side accepts the other in human kindness.

[28]*An Aethiopian Historie*, trans. Thomas Underdowne (1587), fol. 131. Carol Gesner notes this and other parallels in *Shakespeare & the Greek Romance: A Study of Origins* (Lexington: University Press of Kentucky, 1970), pp. 90–115.

[29]*Shakespeare: The Final Plays* (London: Longmans, 1963), p. 21.

[30]See the British response to Caesar's demand for tribute in "Caius Iulius Caesar," in *Parts Added to "The Mirror for Magistrates" by John Higgins & Thomas Blenerhasset*, ed. Lily B. Campbell (Cambridge: Cambridge University Press, 1946), p. 293. In an appendix to Nosworthy's Arden edition, Harold F. Brooks discusses Shakespeare's indebtedness to the work of Higgins and Blenerhasset in *Cymbeline* (pp. 212–16). Holinshed emphasizes Britain's Trojan connection through Brute.

Romans may hold to "*suum cuique*" as their justice, but Britons, Shakespeare demonstrates, share their victories. The halcyon peace that closes the play results from the integration of opposites and the gathering of enemies into familial harmony. In Shakespeare's Rome *pietas* demands the honoring of family, country, and gods, that series of concentric and increasingly important values. In Shakespeare's Britain, however, the smallest circle, the family, expands outward to include the rest and to eliminate the possibility of conflict with them. Private and public obligations become one and the same.

The differences between Roman Britain in *Cymbeline* and the Romes of Shakespeare's other works come into focus upon recollection of *Titus Andronicus*, a play much in the dramatist's mind during the construction of his last Roman effort. In that early tragedy private emotion sharply conflicts with public obligation, and the resulting battle rages through scenes of ghoulish bloodletting and barbaric ritual. On stage and in language the pastoral world, symbolic of the nonurban, un-Roman, and therefore, private sphere, is repeatedly violated, its innocent life hunted and maimed, its branches lopped, its green shade turned red with blood.[31] In *Cymbeline*, however, the pastoral world withstands the Roman invasion unscathed. Indeed, the air itself subdues the enemy:

> *Iachimo:* The heaviness and guilt within my bosom
> Takes off my manhood. I have belied a lady,
> The Princess of this country; and the air on't
> Revengingly enfeebles me.
>
> (V.ii.1–4)

Noble pastoral residents conquer the would-be destroyers and proceed to take their place in a new civilization, wherein natural and Roman, private and public join in accord. The conflict between the two worlds results not in mutilation, but in magical restoration and growth.[32] The lopped branches of the stately cedar revive, become jointed to the old stock, and freshly grow.

---

[31]See Albert H. Tricomi, "The Mutilated Garden in *Titus Andronicus*," *ShakS*, 9 (1976), 89–105.

[32]The magical process remains inscrutable despite the attempts at Christian and topical explication. The Christian category includes variously Moffet, "*Cymbeline* and the Nativity"; Hunter, *Comedy of Forgiveness*; Felperin, *Shake-*

Cymbeline, no one will deny, differs considerably from Shake-speare's other Roman works. Comparatively slapdash in construction (witness the Cloten scenes in the beginning and the prophecy at the end), the play is crowded with characters and plots. The imaginative process at work does not fuse classical images and themes with stage action to create moments of high intensity and thematic significance; instead, classical elements and allusions are in most instances decorative, part of that peculiar style of language called "Neo-Arcadian" by one commentator and by another, "a Euphuism of imagination."[33] Despite such differences from other Roman works, *Cymbeline* stands as Shakespeare's valedictory to Rome, the city that long engaged his attention and inspired his art. Perhaps it is enough simply to remember the soothsayer in the play. In his as well as in Shakespeare's Roman vision, the eagle flies westward and vanishes in British sunlight.

---

spearean Romance; Richmond, "Shakespeare's Roman Trilogy"; Leggatt, "Island of Miracles"; Lawry, "'Perishing Root.'" The topical category includes Jones, "Stuart Cymbeline"; Wickham, "From Tragedy"; Yates, *Shakespeare's Last Plays;* and Bernard Harris, "'What's past is prologue': Cymbeline and Henry VIII" in *Later Shakespeare,* Stratford-upon-Avon Studies, No. 8 (London: Arnold, 1966), pp. 203–34. The two categories often overlap. For caveats against such interpretation, see Philip Edwards, "Shakespeare's Romances: 1900–57," *ShS,* 11 (1958), 1–18; Hallett Smith, *Shakespeare's Romances: A Study of Some Ways of the Imagination* (San Marino, Calif.: Huntington Library, 1972), pp. 211–15.

[33] Nosworthy, Arden edition, p. lxviii; Granville-Barker, *Prefaces,* Vol. I, p. 498. Cf. E. C. Pettet, *Shakespeare and the Romance Tradition* (London: Staples Press, 1949), pp. 180–2; Traversi, *Last Phase,* pp. 43–104, passim; Brockbank observes that the imagistic patterns and iterations are "signs of opportunities lightly taken . . . sequences meant to be glimpsed rather than grasped" ("History and Histrionics," pp. 47–8).

VIII

CONCLUSION

Like the historical city, Shakespeare's Rome rises and falls. In *The Rape of Lucrece* and *Titus Andronicus* Shakespeare depicts the city by relying heavily on stock myths and legends. Romans here, for the most part, are stereotypes, stiff figures of cardboard and paste, constructed from materials lying in the Elizabethan treasure chests of classical learning. Few have ever wept for Lucrece; fewer for Titus Andronicus. Both the narrative poem and the early play are exercise pieces: They give the artist a chance to compose Roman music, to try difficult themes, to practice his technique. Only style — artificial, overbearing, and rudimentarily conceived — holds them together.

Shakespeare's early experimentation results in two assured masterpieces, wherein imaginative vision fuses various traditions and soars to challenge and enthrall. *Julius Caesar*, Shakespeare's portrait of Rome divided, skillfully and movingly depicts the city that entangles itself with its strength. The playwright achieves this depiction by balancing audience sympathies and by creating a web of political and moral paradoxes. *Julius Caesar* is Shakespeare's Roman fugue — a contrapuntal composition in which the Caesar theme receives exposition and development by various voices. Each recurrence of the theme reveals new facets and evokes a slightly different response. *Antony and Cleopatra*, Shakespeare's study of Rome and the world, is his symphony. The play astonishes with its large scope, its sonorous majesty, its variety of mood and emotion. The contrasting Roman and Egyptian movements come to harmony and glorious resolution with the deaths of the lovers.

Descending from the heights, Shakespeare's imaginative vision of Rome concludes in *Coriolanus* and *Cymbeline*. To be sure, traces of the former power and control appear in *Coriolanus*, that intellectual and sophisticated exploration of the *urbs,* of the self in society. Yet, the performance as a whole is less satisfying because Shakespeare seems impatient or out of sympathy with his absolute and epic hero, who, it should be noted, resembles the early Titus more than Brutus, Cassius, Caesar, Antony, or Octavius. Certainly there is epic grandeur in Coriolanus's death, but precious little of that tragedy which catches the throat, swells the heart, and lifts the spirit, leaving us wise and rich in sorrow. The play is a somber concerto, a tense, compelling, and dramatic dialogue between its soloist and the city's ensemble. Shakespeare's final Roman work is a farewell suite, a series of fragmented Roman images and motifs. *Cymbeline*'s loose aggregation of miniatures combines to portray a Rome that gradually yields to Britain. The chaste Roman matron Lucrece finally gives way to Imogen, the British maiden for whom honor and reputation are idle impositions, oft lost without deserving. Comic flexibility, evident in Posthumus as well as in Imogen, succeeds tragic constancy as austere *Romanitas* dissolves into historical-pastoral romance.

Because Shakespeare's Rome does not rise and fall in isolation from the rest of his canon, this study can be only a modest beginning. Much remains to be said about the pervasive patterns of Roman allusion in Shakespeare's other works, viewed individually and collectively. Such saying will require at the outset careful definition of terms and assumptions, but it will yield, most probably, significant results. Moreover, although this study focuses on Vergil, it recognizes that he is only one of many influences on Shakespeare's eclectic imagination. As the Elizabethan background receives more systematic and open-minded attention, new and important sources, influences, and analogs will undoubtedly come to light. And as the theory and practice of *imitatio* become better understood, Shakespeare's Rome can emerge more clearly and stand beside those of other Renaissance artists, English and Continental. Finally, there is always with us the mystery of Shakespeare's creative processes. Endlessly fascinating is his habit of creative coalescence, that sudden and unpredictable joining of disparate elements into new wholes. The tracking of these elements through the fields of Shakespeare's own poetry as well as through the miscellanea of what Virginia Woolf calls "the Elizabethan lumber room" ought to occupy students of Shakespeare's Rome for some time to come. Once inside Shakespeare's Eternal City, travelers soon discover that the streets, roads, and paths facing them are as many and varied as those that lead to its gates.

INDEX